WHERE THERE IS LOVE, THERE IS GOD

Mother Teresa

WHERE THERE IS LOVE, THERE IS GOD

A PATH TO CLOSER UNION
with GOD AND GREATER LOVE FOR OTHERS

Compiled and Edited by
BRIAN KOLODIEJCHUK, M.C.

IMAGE

New York

Published in the United States by Doubleday Religion, an imprint of the Crown Publishing Group, a division of Random House, Inc., New York.
www.crownpublishing.com

IMAGE, the Image colophon, and DOUBLEDAY are registered trademarks of Random House, Inc.

Originally published in hardcover in the United States by Doubleday Religion, an imprint of the Crown Publishing Group, a division of Random House, Inc., New York, in 2010.

Nihil Obstat: Donald F. Haggerty, S.T.D., Censor Librorum
Imprimatur: + Timothy M. Dolan, D.D., Archbishop of New York
The *Nihil Obstat* and *Imprimatur* are official declarations that a book or pamphlet is free of doctrinal or moral errors. No implication is contained therein that those who have granted the *Nihil Obstat* and *Imprimatur* agree with the content, opinions, or statements expressed.

Cataloging-in-Publication Data is on file with the Library of Congress

ISBN 978-0-385-53180-1
eISBN 978-0-385-53179-5

PRINTED IN THE UNITED STATES OF AMERICA

Book design by Diane Hobbing of Snap-Haus Graphics
Cover design by Nupoor Gordon
Cover photography © Raghu Rai/Magnum Photos

10   9   8   7   6   5

First Paperback Edition

$\mathcal{T}$he most beautiful thing
in the world is to love one another
as God loves each one of us. And
it is for this purpose that we are in
this world.

Contents

Preface

BRIAN KOLODIEJCHUK, M.C.

Where There Is Love, There Is God is in some ways a sequel to *Mother Teresa: Come Be My Light*. The latter presents Mother Teresa's life from the perspective of her relationship with God and her commitment to those He called her to serve—the poorest of the poor. Sent to alleviate the sufferings of the poor, she was to be identified with them, experiencing, in the depths of her soul, their struggle and pain. She embraced these persistent and intense sufferings with heroic courage and fidelity, giving evidence of her extraordinary faith in God and surrender to His will. The encouragement that the disclosure of this hidden aspect of Mother Teresa's life has been to many led to the idea of making more of her insights available as they can teach us much in dealing with our own struggles and sufferings.

This publication is not an exhaustive anthology of Mother Teresa's teaching. *Where There Is Love, There Is God* attempts, rather, to impart succinctly what she believed and taught about some of the fundamental issues of human life, particularly relevant in our times. Given her constant interaction with people of diverse cultures and backgrounds, no life situation was foreign to her, and she had many opportunities to pronounce her views on a wide range of subjects. She unflaggingly communicated her convictions as to where true peace and happiness are to be found, inspiring her contemporaries by the sincerity of her words, and even more by the authenticity of her life.

While she is more of an example and model for us in *Mother Teresa: Come Be My Light*, here her role is primarily one of teacher and guide. Through the practical and timely advice she offers, Mother Teresa sets us on the path to closer union with God and greater love for our brothers and sisters. Selections from her wealth of insight are compiled in the pages that follow with the hope that her example of love and her words of wisdom will help us to bring more love into our world and make it a little better place in which to live.

Introduction

If Mother Teresa's entire life and message were to be summarized and described in only two words, without question those words would be *God* and *love*. In truth, God was the center of her existence, her very life, and love—for God and neighbor—her message. But if pressed to use just one word, *love* would express it all, "for love is of God, and he who loves is born of God and knows God . . . God is love" (1 John 4:7, 8). Mother Teresa's simple statement, *"Where there is Love, there is God,"* chosen for the title of this book, reflects this profound truth.

God uses human instruments for His purposes and He used Mother Teresa's hands and heart to manifest His love in today's world. By her life, words, and work, she proclaimed that God is real, that He is with us and that He "still loves the world through you and through me." Specifically called to be a Missionary of Charity—a carrier of His love to the poorest of the poor, indeed to each person she met—she did not think that this was a vocation uniquely hers. Every person, she believed, is to be "a missionary of charity," a carrier of God's love in whatever their state of life. She strove to make others aware of this fundamental call and invited them to respond generously.

Mother Teresa's zeal in assiduously carrying out her mission was striking, even in her advanced years. What was the source of her dynamism and determination? Faith in God. This is what shaped her personality and permeated every aspect of her life. She spoke of God or of the things of God in virtually every conversation, "for out of the abundance of the heart, [the] mouth speaks" (Luke 6:45) and she did so spontaneously and naturally. Hers was not an artificial piety, aimed at impressing others. Neither did she cater to human respect, fearful of expressing her faith and convictions. She expressed simply and sincerely what she believed, with the sole aim of pleasing God and doing good to souls.

Mother Teresa's upbringing and environment were conducive to growth in the Faith, and she developed an intimate relationship with God early in life. At the age of eighteen, she took the decisive step to pursue a life of total dedication to God, answering His call to become a missionary in India. After living as a Loreto nun for nearly twenty years, she received what she would term "a call within a call," while traveling by train to Darjeeling for her annual retreat. God was asking her to be a Missionary of Charity, a carrier of His love to those who felt most unloved, unwanted, uncared for, those who often find it difficult to believe in His love because of their circumstances. Though it would entail a radical change in her life, she willingly embraced this new mandate.

The inspiration Mother Teresa received on the train gave her profound insight into God's love. She understood as never before how much God desired, longed, "thirsted" to love and be loved: He thirsted for her love and for the love of each person He created, especially those most in need. Jesus' words from the Cross, "I thirst," were for her the expression of this intense love and, were always to remind her of the call she had received, a call to satiate His thirst. Satiating Jesus' thirst for love and for souls implied a willingness to strive for ever greater intimacy with Him. It also implied a readiness to be a channel, heedless of the cost to self, through which God's love could be communicated to His children. This call gave Mother Teresa a sense of responsibility and urgency toward her mission. If Divine Providence placed someone in her path, she would do all she could to help that person come to know God better and so enter into a closer relationship with Him.

Despite the obstacles she faced in responding to her new call, Mother Teresa enjoyed an abundance of consolations in the months following the inspiration. Yet, as she started her mission to the poor she was plunged into the dark reality of desolation that those whom she served experience: the feeling that God was no longer present, that He no longer loved her or cared for her. Nevertheless, she remained truly and profoundly united to God, even though her feelings suggested the opposite. She became one with Jesus in His agony and one with the poorest of the poor in their sufferings by experiencing their pain at being unloved, unwanted, uncared for. In sharing their sufferings, she was indeed taking upon herself something of the pain of those she loved.

Nearly half a century lived in spiritual aridity did not hinder Mother Teresa's ability to perceive the hand of God in the ordinary as well as the challenging circumstances of life, and to respond to Him in love. An impressive manifestation of this was her ability not to get disheartened by the daunting hardships nor overcome by the sufferings or the evil that she witnessed daily. She deeply believed that God in His love could bring about a greater good even from apparent or real evil. In the midst of her own spiritual darkness, her unfaltering commitment to her mission and the constant smile that hid her pain attested to her deep faith that God, whom she no longer felt to be close, was still "in charge." This unshakable faith carried her through life. No matter how demanding it was, she remained serene, and even joyful. In fact, the darker the darkness, the more tenacious was her faith.

While her interior suffering mounted, her mission among the poor flourished. The expansion was rapid and global: In the first 25 years of their existence, the Missionaries of Charity had 704 sisters in 87 foundations, caring for thousands of the poorest of the poor—the dying, the orphans, the leprosy suffers, the physically and mentally challenged, those who found themselves at the margins of society. In 1963 Mother Teresa had also founded a branch for brothers. In 1976, the contemplative sisters were founded and 1977 saw the establishment of a branch of contemplative brothers. A branch for priests came into existence in 1984. At the time of her death there were 3842 MC Sisters in 594 foundations in 120 counties; 363 MC brothers in 68 foundations in 19 countries, 14 MC Contemplative Brothers in 4 foundations in 3 countries and 13 MC Priests in 4 foundations in 3 countries. Her religious family also included diocesan priests and lay associates who desired to share in her mission of love.

To all the members of her religious family and to those who desired to share in some way in the MC charism, Mother Teresa frequently addressed words of instruction and encouragement and, at times, of admonition as well. These exhortations are the primary source of this collection of quotes. Other sources are her public speeches and open letters. Though addressed to a particular group, Mother Teresa's teachings are applicable to all. Human nature, being what it is, presents the same challenges regardless of vocation or occupation.

The quotes have been grouped according to five central themes, each having a broad range of sub-themes. Part I examines who God was for Mother Teresa, Part II her relationship with Jesus, and Part III gives practical examples of the many obstacles we encounter within ourselves that prevent us from loving. The two final sections contain Mother Teresa's teaching on how to put our faith into action by loving (Part IV) and how to be a cause of joy to one another by living lives of love (Part V). Each part is preceded by an overview of the themes presented in the particular section.

Where There Is Love, There Is God

I

God Is Love

In reply to the question "What or who is God?" Mother Teresa on one occasion said, "God is love and He loves you and we are precious to Him. He called us by our name. We belong to Him. He has created us in His image for greater things. God is love, God is joy, God is light, God is truth." This statement encapsulates her belief in God and her experience of Him: God exists and is the Source of all that exists; His very being is love; He has created us in his likeness with spiritual powers of intellect and free will, with the ability to know and to love; He is a Father who loves each of us uniquely, personally, and He ardently desires our happiness. No hardship or suffering, her own or that of her poor, could undermine Mother Teresa's conviction that God IS love, that all He does or permits is ultimately for some greater good and, therefore, an expression of His immense and unconditional love.

St. Augustine wrote at the beginning of his *Confessions:* "You have made us for yourself, O Lord, and our hearts are restless until they rest in you." It was Mother Teresa's conviction that all people "deep down in their heart, believe in God." There is a longing for God in each of us and though it may not be recognized or consciously expressed as such, the search for joy, for peace, for happiness and above all for love, is a manifestation of this longing. Though the desire, or "hunger" for God, as Mother Teresa expressed it, is implanted in every human heart, entering into a relationship with Him depends largely on our cooperation with His grace. The freedom to cooperate or not is yet another expression of the love and respect that God has for each of His human creatures. He does not force Himself on anyone; He leaves it to our choice. Yet, the response befitting a creature before its Creator, who is infinite love and wisdom ought to be one of love and trust, praise and adoration, recognition and thanksgiving.

Loved so greatly by God, each person is called to share that love; as Mother Teresa often affirmed: "We have been created for greater things, to love and to be loved." To love as God loves, meeting daily with Him through prayer is essential. Without it love dies. Mother Teresa stressed its importance by saying, "What blood is to the body, prayer is to the soul." But to enter into prayer, silence is necessary, for "in the silence of the heart God speaks." Her aphorism[1] expressing these truths has become well known:

---

[1] *After Mother Teresa began receiving international recognition, she started distributing a small card. On one side were the words, "God bless you," and her signature, and on the other the following saying: "the fruit of silence is prayer; the fruit of prayer is faith; the fruit of faith is love; the fruit of love is service, the fruit of service is peace." With a bit of impish humor, she referred to this card as her "business card." Unlike standard business cards, hers did not bear the name of her organization, nor her title, contact information or phone number. Yet the sequence of phrases can be taken as the formula of the "success" of her "business." Without intending to advertise her undertakings with this well-known quote, Mother Teresa indicated that her endeavors were of a spiritual nature, focused on God and directed toward her neighbor.*

The fruit of silence is prayer.
The fruit of prayer is faith.
The fruit of faith is love.
The fruit of love is service.
The fruit of service is peace.

This simple yet profound saying places silence as the
point of departure for practical love, peace, and service. As
Mother Teresa asserted: "Silence is at the root of our union
with God and with one another." Silence and recollection
are the indispensable conditions for prayer. An atmosphere
of exterior silence is certainly very helpful, but Mother
Teresa, who spent most of her life in large, overcrowded
cities, learned to be interiorly silent and recollected in the
midst of much noise and activity. She shows us that to practice silence one need not flee from the world and live as a
hermit. What is necessary is to learn to quiet the mind and
heart to dispose ourselves for prayer.

Prayer permeated Mother Teresa's day: she started, ended,
and filled each day with prayer. Her first words upon rising
were addressed to God, and throughout the day she spontaneously spoke to Him of her love and gratitude, her plans,
hopes, and desires. As soon as some need or difficulty presented itself, however small and insignificant, she turned to
God, making her requests with the trust and the expectation
of a child dependent on its father. In addition to daily Holy
Mass and the morning and evening Liturgy of the Hours
(containing psalms, Scripture reading, and intercessions), traditional prayers such as the Rosary, the Stations of the Cross,
litanies, and novenas, kept her in continual union with God.

An important time of prayer for Mother Teresa was
her daily half-hour meditation on the Sacred Scriptures.

Formed in the traditional Ignatian method of meditating on the Word of God, principally the Gospels, Mother Teresa was led to intimate conversation and communion with God. Through this prayerful reading, the Word of God took root within her, inflaming her love, influencing her words, and directing her actions. She also nourished her soul each day with an additional half-hour given over to the reading of the lives and writings of the saints or other ascetical works. To help foster recollection throughout the day, Mother Teresa was in the practice of praying "aspirations"—short prayers that raise one's mind and heart to God in the midst of daily activities. These repetitions were a great aid to keeping herself in God's presence. Through these means, she grew in deep knowledge and love of God and was able to respond to Him and to her brothers and sisters in love.

Since "love is of God" [1 Jn 4:7], human love is to be a reflection of and a sharing in divine love, which is entirely selfless and seeks only the good of the other. True love is self-giving, self-sacrificing, a "dying to self" in order to love and serve others, and this was the love that Mother Teresa exemplified. In a culture where "love" is overly identified with feelings rather than an act of the will, with pleasure rather than sacrifice, Mother Teresa's life and teaching, modeled on that of Christ's, exemplifies the Christian ideal of love.

In an interview Mother Teresa was once asked, "Can you sum up what love really is?" She promptly replied: "Love is giving. God loved the world so much that He gave His Son. Jesus loved the world so much, loved you, loved me so much that He gave His life. And He wants us to love as He loved. And so now we have also to give until it hurts. True love is a giving and giving until it hurts."

Who Is God?

God *is*.[2]

God is love.[3]

God is everywhere.[4]

God is the Author of life.[5]

God is a loving Father.[6]

God is a merciful Father.[7]

God is all powerful and He can take care of us.[8]

God is love and God loves you and loves me.[9]

God is joy.[10]

God is purity Himself.

God is with us.[11]

God is in love with us.

God is in your heart.[12]

God is faithful.[13]

God is love, God is joy, God is light,[14] God is truth.[15]

God is thoughtful.

God is so good to us.

---

[2] *Cf. Ex 3:14.*

[3] *1 Jn 4:8, 4:16.*

[4] *Cf. Ps 139:7-10.*

[5] *Cf. Jn 1:1-4; Acts 3:15.*

[6] *Cf. Mt 6:25-32.*

[7] *Cf. Tob 13:4-6; Eph 2:4.*

[8] *Cf. Wis 11:21; Mt 6:26.*

[9] *Cf. Jn 16:27; 1 Jn 4:16.*

[10] *Cf. Neh 8:10; Jn 17:13; Jn 15:11.*

[11] *Cf. Mt 1:23.*

[12] *Cf. Rom 10:8.*

[13] *Cf. Dt 7:9; 32:4; 1 Cor 1:9.*

[14] *Jn 8:12; 1 Jn 1:5.*

[15] *Cf. Jn 14:6.*

God is so generous.
God is so preoccupied with you.
God is a faithful lover.
God is a jealous lover.[16]
God is so wonderful.[17]

✦

When God created us, He created us out of love. There is no other explanation because God is love. And He has created us to love and to be loved. If we could remember that all the time, there would be no wars, no violence, no hatred in the world. So beautiful. So simple.

THERE MUST BE A GOD, SOMEWHERE!

The other day a voluntary worker with long hair . . . was talking to me and he kept on saying, "I don't believe in God." So I said to him, "Supposing, just now, as you were talking, you got a heart attack . . . can you stop it?" He got such a surprise that he didn't say that phrase any more. He was beginning to realize that, in the end, no matter how much we talk, we can't change the time of our death. A few days later I heard that, after a lot of thought, he was beginning to make the reservation that there must be a God, somewhere!

---

[16] Cf. Dt. 4:24.
[17] *This list of statements reflecting who God was for Mother Teresa has been compiled from her talks given on various occasions.*

WHERE THERE IS LOVE, THERE IS GOD

One man told me: "I am an atheist," but he spoke so beautifully about love. Mother told him: "You cannot be an atheist if you speak so beautifully about love. Where there is love, there is God. God is love."

LOVE, NOT IN WORDS

First, God proved to us that He loved us. God loved the world so much that He gave His Son Jesus.[18] And Jesus loved you, He loved me and He gave Himself on the Cross for us.[19] He was not afraid to love us and He loved us until the end.[20] He gave up everything that was beautiful and was really like us, a human being. He was like us in everything except sin.[21] But He loved us tenderly. And to make sure that we understand His love, that we don't forget that He loved us, He makes Himself the hungry one, the naked one, the homeless one. And He says, "Whatever you do to the least of my brethren, you do it to Me,"[22] and explains to us what to do and how to do it. Before He taught the people, He had pity on the multitude, and He fed them. He made a miracle. He blessed the bread, and He fed five thousand people.[23] It's because He loved the people. He had pity on them. He saw the hunger in their faces and He fed them. And only then He taught them. And so it is so wonderful to think that you and I, we can love God. But how, where? Where is God?

---

[18] *Jn 3:16.*
[19] *Cf. Gal 2:20.*
[20] *Cf. Jn 13:1.*
[21] *Cf. Heb 4:15, 2:17–18.*
[22] *Cf. Mt 25:40.*
[23] *Cf. Mt 14:13–21; Jn 6:1–14.*

We believe He is everywhere. We believe that He has made you, and made me, not just to be a number in the world, but He has made us with a purpose. There is a reason for our being here. . . . And that reason is to love. You have been made to love and to be loved. That's why it is so wrong not to love. And that's the most beautiful thing that the human being has or can give: Love. Not in words. Because we are human beings [and] we want to see, we want to touch. That's why the poor people give us much more than we give to them—because they give us an opportunity to love God in them. When I give a piece of bread to a hungry child, I believe what Jesus said, "You give it to Me." And I give it to that child.

GOD'S LOVING CARE

A few weeks ago, I had the very extraordinary experience of this tenderness of God for the little one. A man came to our house with a prescription from a doctor. He said the child was dying, his only child was dying in the slums of Calcutta and that medicine could not be got in India anywhere. It had to be brought from England. As we were talking, a man came with a basket of medicines. He had gone round to the families and gathered half-used medicines for our poor people—we have these mobile clinics all over the slums of Calcutta and all over the place, and they go round to the families and gather half-used medicines and bring them to us, and we give them to the poor people.—And there he came, and right on the top of that basket was that medicine. I just couldn't believe because if it was inside, I would not have seen it. If he had come before or after, I would not have connected. I just stood in front of that basket and kept looking at the bottle and in my mind I was saying, "Millions and millions and millions of children in the world—how could God be concerned with that little child in the slums of Calcutta. To send that medicine, to send that man just at that time, to put that medicine right on the top and to send the full amount that the doctor had prescribed." See how precious that little one was to God Himself. How concerned He was for that little one.

He Is Our Father

The tenderness of God's love—no one can love as God. He has made us in His image. He made us. He is our Father.

FATHER AND CHILD

"The Father loves me, He wants me, He needs me." That kind of attitude is our trust, our joy, our conviction. Anything may come: impatience, failures, joy, but say to yourself, "The Father loves me." God has created the whole world, but He is our Father. In prayer, create that conviction from the inside: Father and child.

NO ONE SPOILS US AS MUCH AS GOD

There is great talk going on all over the world that Mother Teresa is spoiling the people by giving them things free. In Bangalore, once at a seminar, in the name of the whole group, one nun got up and said to me, "Mother Teresa, you are spoiling the poor people by giving them things free. They are losing their human dignity. You should take at least ten naya paisa[24] for what you give them, then they will feel more their human dignity." When everyone was quiet, I said calmly, "No

---

[24] *Less than a few U.S. pennies.*

one is spoiling as much as God Himself. See the wonderful gifts He has given us freely. All of you here have no glasses, yet you all can see. Say, if God were to take money for your sight, what would happen? We are spending so much money for Shishu Bhavan[25] to buy oxygen for saving life, yet continually we are breathing and living on oxygen and we do not pay anything for it. What would happen if God were to say, 'You work four hours and you will get sunshine for two hours.' How many of us would then survive?" Then I also told them: "There are many congregations who spoil the rich, then it is good to have one congregation in the name of the poor, to spoil the poor." There was profound silence; nobody said a word after that.

GOD'S CARE

One day right in the beginning, we had no rice for dinner and then a lady came and brought rice. She said she was coming back from the office "and something in me told me to go to Mother Teresa and bring her rice." And so she brought rice. I said: "Please excuse me, I will measure first and then I will tell you." It was exactly the amount we cooked for dinner, no less, no more, not even half a cup. I told that lady what had happened and she began to cry. She was a Hindu, and she said, "To think that God used me, spoke in my heart. In the whole world, there are millions and millions of people, there are millions of people only in India, and God's concern for Mother Teresa." His tender love—you must experience that . . . even when it is hard, when there is suffering, when there is humiliation.

---

[25] *The Missionaries of Charity (MC) home for abandoned children.*

Silence

If we talk always we cannot pray. Jesus is not present within me. We must keep silence. When a person really keeps silence, she is a holy sister.

GOD SPEAKS IN SILENCE

In the silence of the heart God speaks and this is the time that He will speak to you. To be able to listen you have to be like a little child. Try to have extra devotion to the Little Flower.[26] She understood the Gospel very well. She realized that she had to become a little child. Read her life—you will find nothing really special or extraordinary, but what is striking is that fidelity in small things with great love; that fidelity to silence.

LISTENING TO THE VOICE OF GOD

Listening is the beginning of prayer, and what we listen to is the voice of God, God that cannot deceive or be deceived. Then if we keep silence, silence cannot be corrected; if we speak, if we answer back, we make mistakes.

In the silence of the heart God speaks; let God fill us, then only we speak. Often we say uncharitable words. They come from us, from our heart, not from God speaking through us, because we are not listening to God.

---

[26] *Saint Thérèse of the Child Jesus and the Holy Face, commonly known as St. Thérèse of Lisieux (1873–1897).*

✦

If you want to know how much you love Jesus there is no need to ask anybody to tell you; you are old enough. In the sincerity of your heart you will know [it] yourself, if you practice silence. . . . Try to be alone. Try to keep that really deep silence to get rid of bitterness or hatred.

FULL OF SILENCE

I think it is very important, that union with God. You must be full of silence, for in the silence of the heart God speaks. An empty heart God fills. Even Almighty God will not fill a heart that is full—full of pride, bitterness, jealousy—we must give these things up. As long as we are holding these things, God cannot fill it. Silence of the *heart*, not only of the mouth—that too is necessary—but more, that silence of the mind, silence of the eyes, silence of the touch. Then you can hear Him everywhere: in the closing of the door, in the person who needs you, in the birds that sing, in the flowers, the animals—that silence which is wonder and praise. Why? Because God is everywhere and you can see and hear Him. That crow is praising God—I can hear its sound well— that stupid crow; we can see Him and hear Him in that crow and pray, but we cannot see and hear Him if our heart is not clean.

ALONE WITH JESUS

I want you to spend your time being alone with Jesus. What does it mean to be alone with Jesus? It doesn't mean to sit alone with your own thoughts. No, but even in the midst of the work and of people, you know *His presence*. It means that you know that He is close to you, that He loves you, that you are precious to Him, that He is in love with you. He has called you and you belong to Him. If you know that, you will be all right anywhere; you will be able to face any failure, any humiliation, any suffering, if you realize Jesus' personal love for you and yours for Him. Nothing and nobody![27] Otherwise you will be so preoccupied with unimportant things that slowly you will be a broken sister. . . . It is not worth it to leave father and mother and house if we are not all for Jesus.

THE NEED FOR SILENCE

The silence of the heart—if we don't have that silence, we may say many prayers but it won't come from our heart. [We] need that inner silence, the purity . . . undivided love for Christ before we can give to the sisters. . . . People in the world also keep that silence often. We can acquire that silence only through purity of heart and sacrifice.

FORGIVENESS PRECEDES SILENCE

And there can be no real silence in my heart if there is something I don't forgive, if there is something that I don't forget. I am busy with that one—so I cannot hear. . . . How can I hear what God is saying if something is there in my heart?

A SIGN OF ONENESS WITH GOD

We must pray, we must really bring Our Lady into our life fully because she was the one who taught us how to find Jesus. And how did

---

[27] *Cf. Rom 8:35, 38.*

she find Jesus? By just being the handmaid of the Lord. She was surprised when she was called "full of grace."[28] She didn't understand, but she understood beautifully when she said, "I am the handmaid of the Lord,"[29] and she remained like that. She could have gone round [talking], but she did not even tell St. Joseph. Poor St. Joseph did not know till the end. She couldn't say anything—the handmaid, that silence. Because God speaks in the silence of our hearts. And Our Lady knew that silence and because she knew that silence, she was able to love from the fullness of her heart, and this is what the young people want to see—that silence. Silence is a sign of our oneness with Christ, of our surrender to Him, of our being His totally, and for vocations to grow, we have to teach them that silence. Because . . . we need that silence to learn to pray . . . the young people want to learn to pray. Not in noise but they want to pray in the silence of their hearts, to teach them to hear that voice, to hear God in their hearts. And so they want to see what is our silence. They have to learn this silence from seeing us, from being with us and as we know, silence cannot be corrected also. It is so beautiful. I am seeing these young people during our adoration—we have adoration every day for one hour. I've seen these people, these young sisters, these young "come and sees" completely, really one with Jesus . . . because their hearts have understood "you are precious to Me, you are Mine."

Do We Make Time?

Today God continues to call you and me—but do we listen? "I have chosen you—you have not chosen Me."[30] Have we heard His Voice in

---

[28] *Cf. Lk 1:28.*
[29] *Cf. Lk 1:38.*
[30] *Cf. Jn 15:16.*

the silence of our hearts? Do we make time to "be still and know that I am God"?[31]

For God cannot be heard in the midst of noise and the clamors of the world. Do we make time for prayer in our day? Do we love Him enough to want to listen to His call to let go of everything and follow Him in the freedom of poverty, with undivided love in chastity, through total surrender in obedience? From the Cross, Jesus cries out, "I thirst."[32] His thirst was for souls—even as He hung there—dying, alone, despised. Who will bring those souls to Him to satiate that thirst of the infinite God dying of love? Can you and I continue to stand by, a mere spectator? Or pass by and do nothing?

✦

I shall keep the silence of the heart with greater care so that in the silence of my heart I hear His words of comfort and from the fullness of my heart I comfort Jesus in the distressing disguise of the poor.

✦

Our Lady pondered His words in her heart . . . We too like Her must learn that silence which will enable us to ponder His words in our hearts and so grow in love. We cannot love nor serve unless we learn to ponder in our hearts. Knowledge of Christ and Him in His poor will lead us to personal love. This love only can become our light and joy in cheerful service of each other.

---

[31] *Psalm 46:10.*
[32] *Jn 19:28.*

Business Card

The fruit of silence is prayer.
The fruit of prayer is faith.
The fruit of faith is love.
The fruit of love is service.
The fruit of service is peace.

This is very good "business"! And it makes the people think. Some of them hold it in their hands and read it over and over again. Sometimes, they ask me to explain it. But you see, everything begins with prayer that is born in the silence of our hearts. Among yourselves, and with the Sisters and Brothers, you can share your own experience of your need to pray, and how you found prayer, and what the fruit of prayer has been in your own lives.

If you are hungry to hear the voice of God, you will hear. To hear, you have to cut out all other things.

Prayer

What is prayer? For me, prayer is that oneness with God.

A Clean Heart Sees God

We need to pray—for prayer gives a clean heart and a clean heart can see God in each person. If we see God in others, naturally, we will love one another as God loves each one of us. Love begets peace. Works of love are works of peace.

Our Foundation

If our life is without prayer, it is like a house without a foundation. The other day I saw a ten storey building, beautiful, completely finished, but they had to break it down because the foundation was only for a one storey building, and they were forced to break it down—and the whole thing was completely painted and everything—but they had to break it down. Our life of prayer . . . let it be the foundation, the beginning. But then that life of complete surrender and loving trust, these are storeys to help us climb closer, closer. And as we come, first thing: that pure heart, and that real union, that complete attachment to Christ. If that is not there, it is like building a ten storey building on a foundation made for only a one storey—and what happens? It breaks.

Be a Soul of Prayer

A Missionary of Charity has to be a soul of prayer. If we don't learn to pray in the Novitiate, all our life we will be like handicapped people. So, do this, listen to God speaking in your heart, keep silence of the tongue, of the eyes of the feet (not making noise).

The Prayer Is to Be United to God

To pray we need a pure heart. Prayer is to be united to God. Why was Mary chosen? Because her heart was clean and prayer will always give us a clean heart. Often during the day, feel the need to pray—when you are washing, studying—that union with Jesus. The more you pray, the more you will love to pray.

Prayer Is Oneness

Prayer cannot be switched on and switched off. Prayer is oneness. Fullness of attention is not possible, but fullness of intention. For whom? That act of love, it is a small thing.

Learning Through Prayer

There is no time for not learning. How do we learn? Through prayer. We talk to God, listening then speaking, this is prayer. If we have not listened, we have nothing to talk about. So we must take the trouble to listen. For this we need silence of the mind, silence of the heart, silence of the eyes, silence of the hands. . . .

It is wonderful to learn to pray, for prayer always gives us a clean heart. Unless your heart is clean you cannot speak to God. A clean heart will see God[33] and if we see God we can obey. St. Ignatius, such a big man, said, "The sound of the bell is the voice of God." He could see God saying, "Come." And he obeyed for he could see the will of God. Who was the one who best obeyed? Our Lady! She said, "I don't understand, but I obey."

Pray the Prayers

It is not enough to *say* the prayers, you have to *pray* the prayers; pray with your heart and mind. Pay attention to whom you are speaking, pay great attention to whomever you are speaking—to Jesus, to Our Lady, to God, to the guardian angel, or to the saints—because they are

---

[33] Cf. Mt 5:8.

listening to you. You can speak to any saint. They are waiting, "What is she going to say?" Immediately you get the answer if prayer is really prayer and comes from the heart, and then miracles happen. And then you are surprised for what happens—"It is a miracle!"

What is important is not to say the prayers but to pray the prayers. You pray from the heart, mind, soul—from the bottom of our hearts. Saying prayers, you are just uttering words but not in your heart. Prayer is from your heart to the heart of Jesus. If it is [to] Mary, from your heart to the heart of Mary, or to your guardian angel, it must be from the heart to the heart.

THE HOLY SPIRIT

Read something very simple on prayer . . . not a big theological explanation of prayer, but just something very simple—maybe how Mary prayed, how St. Joseph prayed, how your guardian angel prays. We all have a guardian angel and he is praying for us at all times—interceding for us. Ask your guardian angel to teach you to pray. Above all, ask the Holy Spirit to pray in you. Ask the Spirit to come in you to pray. . . . Learn to pray, love to pray, and pray often. Feel the need to pray and to want to pray.

FULL OF PRAYER

Be full of prayer. It is a beautiful gift. Pray for our poor to make use of their poverty to grow in holiness—so pray with them and for them. And pray always for yourself that you may grow in that holiness for which Our Lord has created you. It is now necessary to make it our own so that we really, really love prayer, so that we spread His love, His compassion, His presence wherever we go. Silence is a time to talk with Jesus. The more silent we are, the closer to Jesus we become and the more we are like Jesus, the more holy we become. So deepen your union with Him by your prayer life. So let us pray and ask Our Lady to pray so that we become holy. If we know how to pray, how to talk to Jesus, we are sure to become holy.

Where Are You Going?

Often, often, often we talk much about prayer; many books have been written on prayer. St. Ignatius [says, at the beginning] of prayer—[ask yourself] where are you going? Before whom are you going? Sometimes, rushing, rushing. He was the master of prayer. He has not written much about prayer—but the small things: stop for a second before taking holy water, grace before meals—all these are small things, yet some sisters have big ideas on prayer, yet these small deliberate things help silence of the heart and mind. A very big theologian, when he came to our house, saw the holy water and said, "This must be a fervent community because holy water is there." Same thing when we hear the bell in the morning and the first word we utter in the morning, the first person we address in the morning. The Hindus, they put that *tikka*[34]—they put it for beauty but it has a tremendous meaning, "God centered."

Meditation

Meditation is talking to Jesus. It is not just thinking, otherwise it is just like a philosopher, only thinking. You must make that Word of God

---

[34] *The dot or* bindi, *usually red, worn by Hindu women on their foreheads as a religious observance and traditionally a symbol of marriage.*

your own. It is a deep intimate conversation with Jesus. You must hear Him and He must hear you.

YOUR TREASURE

You may be praying and heart and mind may be very far away—and you may not be praying at all. Where does your mind and heart go to? Where your treasure is, there is your heart.[35] As soon as you get up in the morning, do your mind and your heart go first to Jesus? This is prayer—that you turn your mind and heart to God. In your times of difficulties, in sorrows, in sufferings, in temptations, and in all things, where did your mind and heart turn to first of all?

ONENESS WITH THE WORD

This is what a Brother of the Word has to be—a complete oneness with the Word of God. And that Word of God that you receive in prayer, in adoration, in contemplation, in that aloneness with God, that same Word you have to give to others. A real thing—let God become flesh during the day, during your meditation, during Holy Communion, during contemplation, during adoration, during silent work, and then that Word in you, you give to others. That's why it is necessary that the Word lives in you, that you understand the Word, that you love the Word, that you live the Word. You won't be able to give that Word unless you have it there. And to be able to have it, a continual and undivided love is necessary.

---

[35] *Cf. Mt 6:21; Lk 12:34.*

No Complications

Where can I learn to pray? Jesus taught us to pray, "Pray like this: Our Father . . . Thy will be done . . . Forgive us as we forgive."[36] It is so simple yet so beautiful. It comes throughout the day in every day of our lives. If we pray the "Our Father" and live it, we will be holy. Everything is there: God, myself, my neighbor. If I forgive, then I can be holy and I can pray. . . . All this comes from a humble heart and if we have this we will know how to love God, to love self and my neighbor. You see in this a simple love for Jesus. There are no complications and yet we complicate our lives so much, by so many additions. Just one thing counts: to be humble, to pray. The more you pray the better you pray. How do you pray? You should go to God like a little child. A child has no difficulty in expressing his little mind in simple words, but they express so much. Jesus said to Nicodemus, "Become as a little child."[37] If we pray the Gospel, we will allow Christ to grow in us.

When We Can't Pray

And when time comes and we can't pray, it is very simple: if Jesus is in my heart let Him pray, let me allow Him to pray in me, to talk to his Father in the silence of my heart. If I cannot speak, He will speak; if I cannot pray, He will pray. That's why often we should say, "Jesus in my heart, I believe in Your faithful love for me." And often we should be in that unity with Him and allow Him, and when we have nothing to give—let us give Him that nothingness. When we cannot pray—

---

[36] *Mt 6:9–15.*
[37] *Cf. Jn 3:3–8, Mt 18:3.*

let us give that inability to Him. . . . Let Him pray in us to the Father. Let us ask Him to pray in us, for no one knows the Father better than He. No one can pray better than Jesus. And if my heart is pure, if in my heart is Jesus, if my heart is a tabernacle of the living God to sanctify in grace: Jesus and I are one. He prays in me, He thinks in me, He works with me and through me, He uses my tongue to speak, He uses my brain to think, He uses my hand to touch Him in the broken body.

And for us there is the precious gift of Holy Communion every day. That contact with Christ is our prayer. That love for Christ, that joy in his presence, that surrender to His love is our prayer. For prayer is nothing but love, complete surrender, complete oneness . . .

What Jesus Taught Us

The most important thing is to learn to pray. Very strange. Jesus did not enter into long discussions—high flown language, but He said: "When you pray, pray like this: *Our Father* . . ."[38]—that intimate oneness with the Father. He was so intimately united with Him that He wanted to be like Him. Again and again that beautiful simple word: *Father*. "My Father"—even little children can say it. We are creating all kinds of difficulties in our prayer. Let us go back to what Jesus has taught us—simple and intimate prayer—"Our Father." Avoid anything that will take you away from this, so that in your teaching, in your life, you can hear Him in all that He says, and do the will of the Father. For this we need a clean heart.

---

[38] Cf. *Mt 6:9.*

THE FRUIT OF PRAYER

The fruit of prayer is a deepening of faith, and the fruit of faith is love; and the fruit of love is service, in whatever form, even in our family. Love begins at home. And how does it begin? By praying together; for the family that prays together, stays together. And if you stay together, you will love God as He loves you. You will love one another as He loves you. What a wonderful thought, that God loves me, and that I can love you, and you can love me, as He loves us. What a wonderful gift of God!

PRAY FOR FAITH

Let us remember that Jesus always praised the faith of people[39]—therefore, often during the day we will pray: "Jesus in my heart increase my faith, strengthen my faith. Let me live this faith through living, humble obedience."

Love Begins with God

Love to be true has to begin with God in prayer. If we pray, we will be able to serve and therefore today let us all promise that we will give our hands to serve the poor. That we will give our hearts to love them for they too have been created for greater things, they are the great people—the poor.

---

[39] *Cf. Mt 8:10, 15:28; Lk 5:20, 7:9; Mk 2:5.*

"IT IS GOOD FOR US TO BE HERE"

Are you really in love with Him, with that intimate love for Him, that personal attachment, like St. Peter? "It is good for us to be here."[40] Is it good for you to be with Him?

YOUR HAND IN HIS HAND

Put your hand in the hand of Jesus—walk alone with Him all the way. We try to hold something else—we are human beings; that's why people need to hold, that's why we hold the hand of Jesus.

DO WE KNOW THAT LOVE?

[Jesus] didn't complain of big sinners, He didn't complain of the people who do bad things. He complained of people like you and me, Christians, who should be known by that love for one another.[41] The Christians, you and I, the tabernacle of the Living God—you and I who receive Him maybe daily in Holy Communion. And He has very clearly said, "My own, My own." You and I are His own. Do we know that love? Have we experienced the joy of loving Christ? Have we experience of loving others as Christ loves you and me? So let us pray. Let us pray that each family becomes another Nazareth where prayer, joy, love, peace come and if there is peace, joy, love, prayer in the family, there will be holiness.

---

[40] *Mt 17:4; Mk 9:5; Lk 9:33.*
[41] *Cf. Jn 13:35.*

NOTHING WILL SEPARATE US

The Mother of Jesus, she loves us tenderly. Because she knows that we belong to her Son, that He has chosen us for Himself. Let us [recall] the words of Isaiah number 43 and where he says, "I have called you by your name, you are mine. Water will not drown you, fire will not burn you. I will give up nations for you. You are precious to me. I love you."[42] This is what God says to each one of us. We are precious to Him. He loves us. And because He has carved us in the palm of His hand,[43] nothing will separate us from the love of Christ, because we are precious to Him. He loves us.

Love Is a Giving

For God so loved the world, so much, that He gave his Son.[44] Love is a one-way street. It always moves away from self in the direction of the other. Love is the ultimate gift of our selves to others. When we stop giving we stop loving, when we stop loving we stop growing, and unless we grow we will never attain personal fulfillment; we will never open out to receive the life of God. It is through love that we encounter God.

---

[42] Cf. *Is 43: 2–4.*
[43] Cf. *Is 49:16.*
[44] Cf. *Jn 3:16.*

A GIVING

Charity is love, it's a giving: like God loved the world, He gave His Son; Jesus loved the world, He gave His life and He said, "Love one another as I have loved you,"[45] so if we really love one another, we must give until it hurts. It's a giving. It's an understanding love, understanding the human weakness, the human misery, the human joy, the human happiness and accepting it . . . very difficult to explain—it's easier to live and to share . . . That's why we need a pure heart to be able to understand it . . . you must be able to love to be able to do. And with God, it is not how much you have given, but how much love you put in the doing, and that love for God in action is the service of the poor or the service in the family. . . . This also can sanctify you if you do it with love.

"WE WANTED TO SHARE THE JOY OF LOVING"

[A young Hindu couple] came to our house and they gave me lots of money and I asked them, "Where did you get so much money?" And they said, "Two days ago we got married, but before marriage we decided we would not buy wedding clothes, we will not have wedding feast, we will give you the money." And I looked at them and I said, "But how—in our Hindu families that is not done, why did you do [this]?" And the answer they gave me, I can never forget, "Mother, we loved each other so much that we wanted to share the joy of loving with the people you serve." And for rich people like these two people were, she had an ordinary sari, cotton sari like mine. And he had ordinary clothes. The only thing that they had—they had the ring, nothing else.

---

[45] *Cf. Jn 13:34, 15:12.*

She could have had a sari of 1,000 rupees and she had a sari of 40 rupees. So you can imagine the sacrifice those young people made to share the joy of loving. That's why your vocation is so great that you can share the joy of loving continually every time you take care of the sick.

IT'S NOT THE MONEY

Yesterday a wealthy man from Holland came and said, "I have lots of money." He was shocked to hear me say, "I don't need your money." He just looked at me. He expected me to become all excited and to start listing the places where we need money for this and that. Then he said, "But I want to do something." Then of course I gave him the address of our sisters in Tanzania, where the people are starving. . . . When I gave him that address, you could see the joy in his face. First there had been surprise and then joy. We need to show the people that it's not their money that is important but the "giving."

That man who came to see me said, "I have a big house in Holland. Do you want me to give it up?" I said, "No." "Do you want me to live in that house?" I said, "Yes." "I have a big car—do you want me to give that up instead?" I said, "No. But what I want you to do is to go back and see some of the many lonely people that live in Holland. Then every now and then, I want you to bring a few of them at a time and entertain them. Bring them in that big car of yours and let them enjoy a few hours in your beautiful house. Then your big house will become a center of love—full of light, full of joy, full of life." He smiled and said that he would be so happy to bring the people to his home but that he wanted to give up something in his life. So I suggested that, "When you go to the store to buy a new suit or some clothes, or when someone goes to buy for you, instead of buying the best that would cost fifty-five dollars, buy one for fifty dollars and use that extra money to buy something for someone else, or better still, for the poor." When I finished saying this, he really looked amazed and exclaimed, "Oh, is that the way, Mother? I never thought of it." When he finally left, he looked so happy and full of joy at the thought of helping our sisters, and he was already planning to send things as soon as he reached Holland.

II

Jesus

Mother Teresa was once asked to comment on the fact
that many people today find it difficult to fully accept the
presence of Christ. Her response to the interviewer was
simple and frank: "It's because you don't know Him." This
was definitely not the case with her.

Jesus was undeniably the center of her life, as anyone
who knew her well can testify. The Incarnate Son of God
was not a concept or a remote Being or an image on the
wall, but a living reality, a Person she knew and with whom
she had a deep and intimate friendship. She loved Jesus
with "all the powers of a woman's heart," so much so
that she desired to "love Him as He has never been loved
before." The intimacy and the totality of this relationship
is best described in her own words: "To me, Jesus is my
God. Jesus is my Spouse. Jesus is my Life. Jesus is my only
Love. Jesus is my All in All. Jesus is my Everything." He
had primacy of place in her life and "nothing and nobody"
could separate her from Him.

Mother Teresa endeavored to understand, appreciate, and imitate the different characteristics of Jesus' life on earth. Thus, the hidden and simple life that the Son of God chose for Himself on becoming man never ceased to inspire her. Living in Nazareth, an obscure place, working as a humble carpenter and doing the ordinary things of everyday life for thirty years in obedience to His Father's will and in submission to His own creatures, revealed God's closeness to us and the value of the ordinary. This life of humility and simplicity, of silent and dedicated service in obedience to God's will was what she strove to imitate.

In His brief public life, Jesus "went about doing good" (Acts 10:38). Mother Teresa's apostolate as a Missionary of Charity was to follow the example of Jesus particularly in His preferential love for the poor and His merciful love toward sinners. Her works of love for the most disadvantaged were a sharing in the mission that Christ entrusted to His Church and that has been realized through different charisms[1] throughout the centuries.

Of all the mysteries of the life of Jesus, though, it was His Passion that most profoundly impressed itself on Mother Teresa's soul. She was awed by the depth and the breadth of God's love shown in Jesus' final hours on earth, from His agony in the garden to the crucifixion. The Cross was the ultimate proof of His love: "Greater love has no man than this, that a man lay down his life for his friends" (Jn 15:13). Mother Teresa often pondered the events of Jesus' Passion, spoke about them and, most important, based her response to suffering, an inevitable part of every human life, on Jesus' own example. Desiring

---

[1] *A* charism *is a particular and distinctive way of living the spiritual life and serving people.*

to be one with her Beloved who loved to the end, suffering all out of love for us, she embraced her many sufferings in union with him as a means to show "greater love" for God and to obtain grace for souls.

While frequent meditation on the mysteries of Jesus' life as revealed in the New Testament deepened her knowledge and love of Him, the Eucharist, in all its mystery and sacramental reality, was Mother Teresa's privileged way of encountering Him daily. It was indispensable to her life of union with Him. The Mass, in which the mysteries of faith that took place in the past were again made present, was the most important moment of each day. To make her life a true sacrifice of love, she united herself to Jesus' sacrifice in the celebration of the Eucharist, and offered herself with Him to be broken and given to the poorest of the poor. There at Mass, she received the graces necessary to accomplish what God desired of her that day. When opportunities to "make up in her own flesh what was lacking in the sufferings of Christ"[2] presented themselves, she accepted them as a living out of the Mass.

Daily Eucharistic adoration was an added opportunity to sit at the Lord's feet and listen to Him. It was a time to love Him and let herself be loved by Him; to tell Him of her love and of her desire to quench His thirst. She was there to console Him and in turn she was consoled by Him, not in feelings but in the reality of faith. Though silent, His presence filled her with peace, strength, and zeal to radiate His love to others, especially the poorest of the poor whom He called her to serve.

---

[2] *Col. 1:24.*

The Word Made Flesh

He had come to give us the Good News of the tenderness and love of a Father—to whom we are precious because He has created us in His own likeness for greater things—to love and to be loved.

We read in the scriptures that God loved the world so much that He uttered the Word and the Word became Flesh; and He comes and dwells within us and with us.[3]

HOW DOES JESUS LOVE US?

Jesus came from heaven, became man, became poor, died on the Cross (nowadays we see a beautiful Cross with clothes, and so on) but He came to give us the message that God loves us. I asked a big theologian in Bombay a question, "How does Jesus love us? God loved Jesus by giving Him to us and Jesus loved us by giving us to the world. That is how I understand." And the father said, "It's a mystery." We are entering that mystery and we are proclaiming that mystery—that God loves that person.

UNCONDITIONAL TRUST

Jesus' trust is *unconditional*. He accepted to become man like us in all things except sin. We do not realize what this means, "He being rich became poor."[4] He who is "God from God, Light from Light, begotten not made, one in substance with the Father, through whom all

---

[3] Cf. Jn 1:1, 14.
[4] Cf. 2 Cor 8:9.

things were made . . . born of the Virgin Mary." The Creator chose to become a creature, one with us, like us, to be dependent on others, to need food to eat, clothes to wear, drink to quench His thirst, to need rest, to be tired like us. . . . One with us in all things: Why? For love of us, with unconditional trust in the Father. He chose to be born of a woman, the Virgin Mary, to take human flesh and blood. "To live in Nazareth."[5] "Can anything good come out of Nazareth?"[6] asked Nathanael. Christ accepted to belong to that utter lowly place that had no good name, to work as a carpenter. "Is He not the Son of Mary and Joseph?"[7] You know Christ was not accepted in Nazareth because He accepted to have Mary and Joseph as His parents. His preaching was not accepted there, and they wanted to stone Him because He claimed to be the Son of God.[8] He was totally rejected. "He came among His own and His own knew Him not."[9]

JESUS' CHOICE

In heaven, the Blessed Trinity must have talked it over, "What is the best way?" God loved the world so much—that's you and me—[He chose] not the riches, not the greatness but to become so small, not in a palace, to a virgin; so small, not even [born] as a natural ordinary child, but in a manger. Mother Mary, she did not expect Him to be born this way, so strange—why? Let us stop and think, why? Poverty must be so beautiful in heaven if Jesus became so small—childlike simplicity, animals—poverty must be so beautiful in heaven. It is not that Jesus could not have it but He chose. He could have had a palace. Ask

---

[5] *Cf. Lk 1:26–35, 2:1–7.*
[6] *Jn 1:46.*
[7] *Mk 6:3.*
[8] *Jn 10:33.*
[9] *Cf. Jn 1:11.*

yourself, "Why did Jesus choose?" To make it easy we must know in reality—to be able to understand [the] poor—we must know what is poverty. Why did Jesus make Himself so poor? To be able to understand my poverty, my smallness, my weakness, my littleness.

He Came to Give the Peace of Heart

He had told us the Good News when He said, "My peace I leave with you, My peace I give unto you."[10] He came not to give the peace of the world, which is only that we don't bother each other, He came to give the peace of heart, which comes from loving, from doing good to others. And God loved the world so much that He gave His Son; it was a giving. God gave His Son to the Virgin Mary and what did she do? The same. As soon as Jesus came into Mary's life, immediately, she went in haste to give the Good News and as she came into the house of her cousin, Elizabeth, Scripture tells us that the unborn child, the child in the womb of Elizabeth,[11] leaped with joy at seeing the womb of Mary. Jesus brought peace to John the Baptist who leaped for joy in the womb of Elizabeth. And as if that were not enough that God's Son should become one of us and bring peace and joy while still in the womb of Mary, Jesus also died on the cross to show that greater love.[12] He died for you and for me and for that leper and that man dying of hunger and that naked person lying in the street not only of Calcutta, but of Africa and everywhere.

[10] *Jn 14:27.*
[11] *Lk 1:39–45.*
[12] *Jn 15:13.*

THE HUMANITY OF CHRIST

Christmas time shows us how small God is. Go to the crib and see how small God became. . . . We must realize Sisters, that God, who made everything and made you and me,[13] became so small. How He lived that total surrender to the full. We sing such beautiful hymns, but it must have been terrible for Mary and Joseph in that cold. This is why we must learn, Sisters, to be that child, in complete surrender and trust and joy. See the joy of Christmas and the joy of the Child Jesus. Never be moody Sisters, never let anything take away that joy. Christmas shows us how much heaven appreciates humility, surrender, poverty, because God Himself, who made you and me, became so small, so poor and humble.

NO JESUS, NO MARY

Last time when I went to Holland, one protestant man came with his wife and said straight to me, "You Catholics are so mad with Our Lady." I just told him that without Mary there is no Jesus. He did not tell me anything at that time, but after a few days, he sent me a big postcard and on the top of it was written in big words, *"Without Mary, no Jesus!"* See how he changed his view! It should be for us also. Remember the first miracle in Cana? Mary observed the host's embarrassment and when the wine was short, she told Jesus. After telling Jesus, she told the servants, "Do whatever He tells you." See how clever she was because she knew Jesus well, she was able to tell them, "Do whatever He tells you."[14]

---

[13] Cf. *Jn 1:1–3.*
[14] *Jn 2:1–10.*

When we read the Gospel something struck me so much. Our Lady is mentioned at the Annunciation. God did not speak to her, He sent the angel to give this important message. She answered the angel, "Be it done to me according to thy word."[15] Whose word? [The] angel's word. [The] angel is only a creature. We see [Our Lady] again in Bethlehem, near the manger with a little swaddling cloth.[16] I suppose she didn't expect that she would give birth now, so she didn't have many things but the absolutely necessary things. See the manger full of straw and nothing else. Again we see her looking for Jesus, and after three days finding Him, and she told Him: "Thy father and I were looking for Thee." His answer: "Did you not know that I should be at my Father's business?"[17] With the crowd [Our Lady] also moves towards Calvary. She meets Jesus on the way, face to face. She must have seen his body beaten, full of wounds, the head from the crowning [with thorns] bleeding, face dirty with spittle and swollen with blows, hands full of blood. What a sight! What she must have felt. She had the courage to look at her Son and suffer with Him. We don't hear her voice. She followed Jesus until the Cross—the selfless love of a mother. She stood by [Him] in His humiliations, up to the Cross.[18] She must have heard the people speaking badly about Him, the High Priest, the Pharisees and the others, cursing and saying ugly things. Her silence was great; she knew who her Son was. She didn't fall on the ground, didn't try to catch attention on herself. She stood by the Cross. She didn't judge, she didn't grumble, she didn't call them names. But surprisingly, at the Resurrection her name is not mentioned. Mary Magdalene, John, Peter and all are there, except Mary.[19] She is not at the glory.

---

[15] *Lk 1:28–36.*

[16] *Lk 2:7.*

[17] *Lk 2:49–51.*

[18] *Jn 19:25.*

[19] *Jn 20.*

The true love of the mother is shown when her children suffer. Then we see Mary's motherhood. We might take it for granted.

MEEK AND HUMBLE OF HEART

The whole life of our Lord—from first, middle, last—meekness and kindness.

I believe when Jesus passed by, the children cried, "Sweetness is passing." In the community, love as Mary loved Jesus and Jesus, Mary. Joseph, when he learnt that Our Lady was with child, he could have made it public—[but] see his meekness.[20] He did nothing special. He could have been harsh with Mary, but he was ready to risk his own life. . . . See Jesus in His Passion. He never blamed, He did not shout.[21] "Why did you strike?"[22]—only that one question. See the delicate meekness of Jesus. He knew the whole time what Judas would do.[23] Let us ask for this meekness. Keep that meekness, kindness, thoughtfulness. Jesus wanted to teach humility: He washed their feet[24]; He did not explain. "Learn of Me; I am meek and humble of heart."[25] Jesus taught simply. We need meekness, thoughtfulness. Let us pay attention to our words. One word—so much hurt. Jesus taught meekness in little things—Bethlehem, Nazareth.

---

[20] *Mt 1:18–25.*
[21] *Mt 27:11–55; Lk 23–24; Jn 18–19.*
[22] *Jn 18:22–23.*
[23] *Jn 13:21–30.*
[24] *Jn 13:2–7.*
[25] *Mt 11:29.*

WHO IS JESUS?

In the gospel we read: "Who are you?"[26] the people asked Jesus. Today they still ask the same question, "Who are you?" John's disciples also came to ask Jesus, "Are you the Messiah or shall we wait for another?"[27] The Bible tells us that Jesus answered them saying, "Go and tell John: the blind see, the lame walk, the dumb speak, the lepers are cleansed, the dead rise, and the gospel is preached to the poor." We are doing the same work. So wonderful is our vocation! By our works we also make Jesus present in our world of today. We proclaim [that] Jesus is the Christ, the Messiah, and He is in our midst. People kept on asking, "Who are you?" but Jesus did not answer them directly. He let the good work proclaim the good news and people meet God. They see God's love alive!

HE MUST HAVE RADIATED JOY

"Christ wanted to share His joy with His apostles 'That My joy may be in you and that your joy may be full.'"[28] Very clear. Somebody was saying: "I wonder if Jesus ever smiled." I never saw a picture. Have you ever seen a picture? With a big smile? But He must have radiated joy. Joy must be seen in your eyes, attitude, walk, listening. All that is included together.

Christ teaches us and He says that when we die, we are going to be judged on that one point and He says, "I was hungry, you gave me to eat; I was naked, you clothed me; I was homeless, you took me in."[29]

---

[26] *Jn 1:21–22; 8:25.*
[27] *Lk 7:18–22.*
[28] *Jn 15:11.*
[29] *Mt 25:31–40.*

Hunger is not only for bread, hunger is for love, to be loved, to be wanted. That terrible loneliness of the old and the . . . people is a terrible hunger. Nakedness is not only for a piece of cloth but nakedness is also that want of dignity, that beautiful gift of God, the loss of purity of heart, of mind, of body. Homelessness is not only for a house made of bricks, homelessness is also being rejected, being a "throw away" of society, unwanted, unloved, uncared [for]. There among these people you can put and I can put my love for God in a living action. There are many people I am sure in hospitals that have no one to visit them. Maybe just a little visit, a little smile, a little shake of the hand can bring joy in the lives of these lonely people who have no one.

TEACH US TO LOVE JESUS

Let us ask Our Lady to teach us to love Jesus as she loved Him. Nobody can love Jesus more than Mary, so she will be the best one to teach us to love Jesus. See St. Margaret Mary, when Jesus asked her to love Him as He loved her, she said: "How can I? If you give me Your Heart and You take my heart, then I can love You as You love me." Jesus is still thirsting.[30] Write it down, "Tell Mother Teresa, 'I thirst.'" Ask yourself, why is Jesus thirsting? [Is it because] I am not what I should be and for this Jesus is still thirsting?

---

[30] *Jn 19:28.*

Our Lady and the Holy Family

ANNUNCIATION

This is a tradition: The Blessed Trinity discussed how sin had penetrated man, how man had to be saved. And then the Second Person of the Blessed Trinity said, "Father, use me. I will go. I will become one of them." Mary was so spotlessly pure that she attracted the presence of God, so much that even before the time He became man. See what a gratitude we owe to Mary, that she gave her flesh. He could not be born in anybody. The Holy Spirit could not come into a sinful body. There was no other human being involved. . . . Even St. Joseph—I have great love for St. Joseph because he has such deep charity.

MARY'S FIRST COMMUNION

What Mary received, we too receive in Holy Communion. Bishop Fulton Sheen used to say, "The Annunciation was Mary's First Communion day," and we receive Jesus everyday! What a beautiful thing.

THIS IS LOVE

When [St. Joseph] saw Our Lady was pregnant—that she was going to have a baby—immediately he was hurt. But he loved Our Lady. Deep down in his heart he loved her and he knew in his mind, "If I go to the priest and tell, immediately they will stone her." He did not know that Our Lady had conceived by the power of the Spirit, but he knew that if he told she would be stoned[31]—and if he was silent *he* would be stoned. So what did he decide? "I will not tell. I will leave her and go away and people will blame me."[32] This is love.

THE FIRST MISSIONARY OF CHARITY

She "is most beautiful, for she, of all creatures, most perfectly mirrors the likeness of God." She is a creature and yet most like the Creator. Of all human beings, Mary resembles God most. Mary is the Queen of heaven and earth, the mediatrix of all graces. All graces you received, you are receiving, or will receive, come only through Mary. I think none of you have realized the most wonderful part of the mission of our Society.

The Society is dedicated to the Immaculate Heart of Mary, Cause of our Joy and Queen of the world. Again, we come to the term "world." What are we doing in the world? By our life and deeds of love, we are making the Church fully present in the world today. The Society was founded to spread the kingdom of the Immaculate Heart among the poorest of the poor. Mary is the first person in the whole of creation who received Jesus physically in her body and she is the one to carry Jesus to John. She went in haste.[33] She is the first one to nurse Him, to clothe Him, to feed Him, to look after Him, to take care of Him, to teach Him.[34] . . . That is why she is the first MC[35]—carrier of God's love—and we, like her, do what she did: receive Jesus and give Him in haste.

---

[31] *Dt 22:20–21.*
[32] *Mt 1:18–19.*
[33] *Lk 1:26–44.*
[34] *Lk 2:5–51.*
[35] *The commonly used abbreviation for Mother Teresa's order, the Missionaries of Charity.*

Just think of the purity and the attractiveness of Our Lady so as to make Jesus leave heaven and come down to be in her, with her, to receive her flesh and blood, her love and affection, her care and devotion. St. Bernard said that Our Lady's purity was so great and so attractive that, even before time, God decided to become man. There were many generations in which Christ could have been born; He could have been born later, but He could not wait because Mary was so beautiful. Even Almighty God fell in love with her.

SHE CAN TAKE YOU TO JESUS

You can never be only all for Jesus if your love for Our Lady is not a living reality. Come so close to Our Lady that she can take you to Jesus. Avoid many distractions. Be alone with Jesus and ask Our Lady over and over again, "Make me only all for Jesus." Be holy like Jesus and Mary. Think over it, pray over it.

ST. JOSEPH

Then we know what happened. At night the angel came. "No, you don't go. The child with Mary is of the Spirit and you will take care of them both." St. Joseph had decided, "Let them kill me." He did not know how and from whom Mary conceived, but that she had a baby. Now, when he is told "of the Spirit"—he accepts.[36] What would we have done?

---

[36] Cf. Mt 1:18–25.

✦

He was a just man; that means a holy man. He gave to God what belonged to Him and to the creatures what belonged to them.[37] Being "just" means to give every person their due. We must show them love because they all belong to God. God loves us and the others also. We believe that we are tabernacles of the living God; the other sisters also; the people also. . . . Saint Joseph [had] two talents—faithfulness and love—to serve Jesus. He was a common carpenter and became the foster father of Jesus and spouse of the Mother of God. In all sincerity everybody must say, "I have used what I have got." I must be *just* to others. . . . People who want to become holy must pray to St. Joseph.

THE MOST BEAUTIFUL PRESENCE

We read in the Scripture that God loved the world so much that He gave His Son Jesus,[38] and He gave Jesus to a virgin, Mary, the Mother most pure, and when He came in her life, immediately she went in haste to give the joy of the presence of Christ to her cousin Elizabeth.[39] And there it begins, the most wonderful story of the unborn child. It was the unborn child that recognized the presence of Christ in the world. We read in the Scripture that the child leaped with joy when Mary came with Jesus in her womb. This is the most beautiful presence and the most wonderful presence of God's love for the world—the child.

---

[37] *Cf. Mt 22:21; Mk 12:17; Lk 20:25.*
[38] *Cf. Jn 3:16.*
[39] *Lk 1:39–44.*

MARY AT THE FOOT OF THE CROSS

At the foot of the Cross, Jesus gave Mary to John. Jesus said, "This is your Mother, this is your son."[40] [From] then on, John took Mary into his care. Have I taken Mary into my care? What place has Mary in my life? Is she my Mother? Do I [entrust] everything to her? Take her into your care, she will teach you how to go to Jesus.

Such a Great Proof of His Love

When you make the Stations of the Cross, at the tenth station you ask Jesus to take away whatever is not He in you, whatever is pride, if you really want to be holy. Holiness is "He in you"—if we are despoiled of ourselves. And also say the very fitting prayer St. Francis [de Sales] said, "Jesus meek and humble of heart, take my heart and make it like Yours." The Stations of the Cross are nothing but one continual act of humility. Look at the sixth station—see quite possibly the cloth Veronica gave was an ordinary thing, say some handkerchief, towel or whatever it may be—she had the courage. Examine—Have you helped any sister in your community or a poor person in your city? You and I, ask for that grace to have the courage to be Veronica in our community. I can live those stations if I connect them with my life. The Stations of the Cross are wonderful prayers if you make them your own, in your work.

---

[40] *Cf. Jn 19:26–27.*

I LOOKED FOR ONE TO COMFORT ME

In the Bible it is written: "I looked for one to comfort Me and I found none."[41] Jesus spent forty days alone with His Father and He prayed.[42] During these forty days take the trouble to be that one. "I looked for one." Are you there? Can you say, "Yes I am here"? Do I really belong to Jesus as He belongs to the Father? And the will of the Father was that terrible loneliness in the Garden,[43] on the Cross[44]—He was completely alone. If we are true followers of Jesus, we too must experience the loneliness of Christ. He perspired blood.[45] It was so difficult for Him to go through the humiliation of His Passion.[46] That is why that sentence, "I looked for one to comfort Me and I found none."[47] He went to the apostles and they were fast asleep.[48] Many times Jesus comes to us in suffering. Lent is just that, sharing in the Passion of Christ. We cannot do it to Jesus like the apostles were invited to do. They were called to share in His Passion. That love, that compassion, that we would have liked to give Him then, we are called to it right here, for love begins at home.

✦

When Judas came to betray Him . . . "Friend, you betray Me with a kiss?"[49] He never said, "you traitor." Same at the washing of the feet[50]—

---

[41] *Ps 69:20.*
[42] *Cf. Mt 4:1–11; Lk 4:1–12.*
[43] *Cf. Mt 26:36–46; Mk 14:30–40; Lk 22:40–46.*
[44] *Cf. Mt 27:46; Mk 15:34.*
[45] *Cf. Lk 22:44.*
[46] *Cf. Lk 22:42.*
[47] *Ps 69:20.*
[48] *Mt 26:40.*
[49] *Cf. Mt 26:48–50; Lk 22:47–48.*
[50] *Jn 13:2–5.*

though there was agony in His heart . . . He was never harsh. Again while hanging on the Cross, looking at His Mother, looking at St. John, He thought of us.[51] Who will take care of My mother? Who will take care of John? Whenever someone corrects you, scolds you, instead of becoming bitter, think of Jesus, how He thought of others even in His agony and pain. Never allow bitterness to remain in your heart.

✦

Very often I think of Jesus—from the beginning He knew Judas would betray Him. For three years Jesus knew, and even at the end, when [Judas] came to destroy Him, Jesus didn't call him a traitor, He didn't push him away, but called him "friend."[52] Wonderful, wonderful example of Jesus' tender love.

FORGIVING PETER

How all the apostles said, "We will stand by You, never leave You,"[53] yet when the time came, they ran away.[54] Peter, who two days before really proclaimed Jesus as the Son of God, yet when the woman said, "You also are a follower," for fear of this woman said, "What are you talking about? I don't know Him!" What big words he was using. Jesus had told him, "Before the cock crows twice you will deny Me three times." Read the Passion carefully. When [Peter] looked and saw Jesus, what happened? He went out and cried, cried bitterly that he, Peter, had denied [Jesus, using] big, big words—"I have nothing to

---

[51] Cf. Jn 19:26–27.
[52] Cf. Mt 17:22, 20:18; Jn 13:11, 13:21–30; Mt 26:49–50.
[53] Cf. Mt 26:33–35; Mk 14:29–31.
[54] Cf. Mk 14:50; Mt 26:47–56.

do with Him." What did Jesus do? Jesus' eyes met with Peter's eyes.[55] What a living reality. What a tremendous hurt Peter gave to Jesus— yet what tender love was in the eyes of Jesus; and Peter saw that for- giveness in the eyes of Jesus and Peter went out and cried bitterly. I read in a book that Peter cried so much there were lines in his face. After the Resurrection, when Jesus asked Peter, "Lovest thou Me?"[56] Peter wept. This is charity. When someone hurts you, look with kind- ness, never keep bitterness in your heart—take one resolution. Jesus could have said, "Peter, what are you saying?" or He could have looked with angry eyes. We receive forgiveness from Jesus [so] that we can also give that forgiveness. Keep your heart clean. If you have done something, go to confession.

THE CROSS SHOULD HAVE BEEN ENOUGH

When we look at the Cross and we look at the tabernacle, we won- der why, after such a great proof of His love and mercy, by dying for us, Jesus left us the Eucharist. Surely, one should have been enough, but Jesus thought of us and has given us the chance to share in His crucifixion, to continue it in our lives. At the Last Supper, He knew the thorns, the spittle—He knew everything and yet He connected that suffering and crucifixion with the tabernacle, His Body with the Eucharist, so that His Body, so to say, is broken again to pieces. His sacrifice—repeated daily.[57]

---

[55] Cf. Mt 26:69–75; Mt 14:66–72; Lk 22:54–62.
[56] Cf. Jn 21:16–18.
[57] Cf. Mt 26:20–29; Mk 14:17–26; Lk 22:14–20; 1 Cor 11:23–25.

"*I Thirst,*" *Love's Word*

Mary learned near the Cross. She stood by the Cross.[58] Jesus was completely covered with blood; we cannot see on our crosses now but I believe the ground was completely wet, full of blood. Do we ever hear it, do I recognize it, can we hear it? Jesus Himself said "I thirst"[59] right on the Cross, love's word. He did not say anything else after that.

Try to deepen your knowledge of "I thirst." It is a life to be lived, not a devotion, side by side with Jesus. Just as somebody says, "I thirst," I run to satiate. Just as at Kalighat somebody says, "I thirst," [I] quickly go to bring water. This is Jesus' word, "I thirst"—for love, for souls not for water. So listen.

Let us deepen our knowledge of "I thirst." We cannot love what we do not know. What did Our Lady really do when she heard "I thirst"? She must have looked round to get a bottle or something of water. She could not do anything. What Jesus suffered in body, she suffered in soul. Let us ask her to understand really. Let Our Lady teach us: "I thirst." "I satiate" must be the aim and joy of your life. With great love and trust, stand with Our Lady near the Cross. It a gift of God; we have been chosen in the Society to satiate the thirst of Jesus.

✦

What does He thirst [for]? Naturally it was a physical thirst—He lost blood—a torturing thirst. Today in Ethiopia—torturing, in blood, terrible thirst, even their clothes, thirsting for water. Put yourself there, in front of Jesus. Besides [the] terrible [thirst] of body, the terrible thirst that came from the pain of sin. He did not sin, but no one under-

---

[58] *Jn 19:25.*
[59] *Jn 19:28.*

stood sin better than He did. He wanted to clean us from sin and the effects of sin. He was thirsting for our love, and sin spoiled our hearts.

WHEN WE GIVE BITTERNESS

"To quench the thirst of Jesus for souls," means for love—for love of me and for love of others. When Jesus was dying on the Cross, He cried, "I thirst." We have these words in every chapel of the MCs to remind us what an MC is here for: to quench the thirst of Jesus for souls, for love, for kindness, for compassion, for delicate love. When Jesus was in pain on the Cross, the soldier—out of kindness and with a very good intention to help Jesus forget His pain by letting Him go to sleep, as with a tranquilizer—prepared the bitter drink of vinegar and gave it to Jesus to drink. Jesus, not to hurt the soldier, took it but He only tasted it. He did not drink it because He did not want to forget the pain and His sufferings.[60] No—He loved me and He died for me[61]—He suffered for me. Very often, we too offer bitter drink to Jesus. This bitterness comes from the depth of our hearts and wells up in our words, our attitudes to one another. "Whatever you do to the least of My brothers, you do it to Me."[62] When we give this bitterness to one of our sisters, to one another, we give it to Jesus.

HEAR YOUR OWN NAME

Sometime back I had a letter from a priest, a holy priest. He wrote a long letter and he said that he was praying without a thought about

---

[60] *Mt 27:33–34; Jn 19:28–30.*
[61] *Gal 2:20.*
[62] *Mt 25:40.*

us, and then he heard Jesus clearly say to him: "Tell Mother Teresa: 'I Thirst,'" He didn't mean Mother Teresa only, but He meant each one of you. Try today to hear your own name and Jesus saying, "I thirst." What will be your answer? Hear Jesus saying it clearly. Be convinced that it was Jesus who said it and I am very sure it must have been Jesus. Just put yourself in front of the tabernacle. Don't let anything disturb you. Hear your own name and "I Thirst." I thirst for purity, I thirst for poverty, I thirst for obedience, I thirst for that wholehearted love, I thirst for that total surrender. Are we really living a deeply contemplative life? He thirsts for that total surrender.

It All Comes Under "I Thirst"

Grow in that intimate love, and you will understand not only "I thirst," but everything. Humanly speaking, we cannot understand "Love one another as I have loved you,"[63] "Be ye holy as I am holy."[64] But it all comes under "I thirst." The fruit of faith is the understanding of "I thirst." . . . Get rid of sin quickly so we can hear Jesus say, "I thirst for your love." The most important thing is that we must encounter the thirst of Jesus, but the encounter with Jesus' thirst is a grace.

He Is There to Love Us Now

You need Jesus more than you need anything in life. Often I wonder, what would the world be if there was no tabernacle—no Jesus.

---

[63] Cf. *Jn 13:34.*
[64] Cf. *Lev 11:44; 11:45; 19:2; 20:7; Mt 5:48.*

THE EUCHARIST

In our congregation our lives are very much woven with the Eucharist. We begin with Mass and Holy Communion, and every day we have one hour of Adoration in all our houses and we feel that our lives [need] to be woven with the Eucharist: Jesus in the Bread of Life[65] and Jesus in the distressing disguise of the poor.[66] So pray for us that we may be faithful to this love, to this unity of the Eucharist and the poorest of the poor.

✦

The Eucharist is beyond understanding—we must accept it in deep faith and love. Jesus deliberately left us the Eucharist, lest we forget all that He came to show and to do. In the Gospel there are those few little words to describe His Passion and death: He was crowned,[67] scourged,[68] spat upon[69]—those few little words which by now we could have easily forgotten. The Gospels are very short in their explanation of the Passion. They avoid great description. He was "scourged," but it doesn't say that it was forty lashes or what they used to scourge Him, just words that we would have easily forgotten. Jesus understood our human nature. He understood that far from the eyes is far from the heart also. Just imagine what our lives would be without the Eucharist. What would be there to make us love Him? What would be there to make us give up everything? I don't think any one of us would be here without the Eucharist!

---

[65] Cf. Jn 6:35, 48.
[66] Cf. Mt 25:35–40.
[67] Mt 27:29; Mk 15:17; Jn 19:2.
[68] Mt 27:26; Mk 15:15; Jn 19:1.
[69] Mt 27:30; Mk 15:19.

Today let us not read much, or meditate much even, but just allow Jesus to love you. We always want to say, "Jesus, I love you," but we don't allow Jesus to love us. Today say often, "Jesus I am here, love me."

Every human being has a longing for God. "My soul is thirsting for God."[70] Christians can go even further—they not only long for God, but they have the treasure of His presence always with them. We not only have this, but the joy of getting even closer to Him by receiving Him in Holy Communion. Jesus was not satisfied with just feeding us with [the] Bread of Life but He made Himself the Hungry One in the distressing disguise of the poor. For us MCs, we cannot say that we love Jesus in the Eucharist but that we have no time for the poor. If you really love Jesus in the Eucharist, you will naturally want to put that love into action. We cannot separate these two things—the Eucharist and the poor.

THE GREATNESS OF THIS GIFT

To realize the greatness of the gift—the first time He made Himself into bread for the apostles: "This is My Body."[71] What great faith, what great love the apostles had to receive the Body of Jesus. To make it easy for the apostles, to make it easy for us, Jesus gave the apostles this special faith and special grace to understand—deep faith and great love. We also need this special grace, deep faith, love, trust. Sometimes we go to Holy Communion without preparation, our mind here, there. Remember the first time you received Holy Communion, the longing—great longing, great faith, great love. We are tempted to go without preparation, we will find it very difficult to realize; we need great faith, love and longing before receiving Holy Communion.

---

[70] *Ps 42:2.*
[71] *Mt 26:26; Mk 14:22; Lk 22:19; 1 Cor 11:24.*

TELL JESUS TO GO WITH YOU

The most important part of the day is our Mass. When you make the sign of the Cross, make it properly; a proper cross. When going out, go to the chapel and tell Jesus to go with you. Jesus dying on the Cross was a reality. And now the Holy Mass is the reality. Day before yesterday, a protestant minister said, "How fortunate you all are because you have the living God in the chapel." He is there for us. One day if there is a persecution, we will want Him, but we won't have Him. When I see a sister distracted I know that that sister is not in the presence of God. Here [is] the King of kings who has humbled Himself to come among us . . . to make Himself the Bread of Life[72] . . . we just don't care. Early morning try to be first in the chapel and see the connection between you and the Eucharist.

RECEIVE AS MARY DID

We too receive Jesus like Mary. We must receive Him with great love, with great humility, like Our Lady. How will we know we receive Jesus like Mary? By something that happens to each other—something that makes us share our joy—that forgiveness. As that woman [who] said, "If I will touch His clothes"[73]—something outside of Him, not His flesh—and something changed in her. And we are touching His flesh! What happens to us when we speak that ugly word or hurt each other straight after Holy Communion? How? We didn't believe that He has come to us.

Elizabeth said, "How is it that the Mother of my Lord has come to

[72] *Cf. Jn 6:30–58.*
[73] *Cf. Mt 9:21; Mk 5:28.*

me . . . because the child within me leapt for joy."[74] Our preparation for the coming of Jesus: Tomorrow morning and every morning, let us receive [Him] as the handmaid of the Lord and ask Him for His strength, joy. Let us pray. Let us cling to Our Lady and ask her to teach us [how] she carried Jesus. Let us ask St. Elizabeth to get us deep faith. Let us ask St. John to leap with joy with loving Jesus and share it with all [we] meet, especially my sister. Let your eyes shine with joy. Like St. John Berchmans[75]—whenever he would meet any person he would bow to Jesus in that person. Let us share the joy of receiving by sharing with each other and our poor.

TWO THINGS

Every day at Communion I thank Him for two things: I thank Him for giving me perseverance today, and I ask Him to teach me to pray. What gave St. Paul that conviction, "Nothing can separate me from the love of Christ."[76] You must be tired of hearing me saying this but I am not going to stop—I belong to Jesus, nothing can separate me from the love of Christ. Yesterday, Father was talking of that man who asked, "Have you met God?" If I believe in the Eucharist, yes, then I have met Him. If I believe in the poor, yes, I have met Him.

DO I BELIEVE IT?

This morning I received Jesus in Holy Communion, do I think of that during the day? Do I turn to Jesus within me? It is the same Jesus that

---

[74] *Lk 1:43–45.*
[75] *Saint John Berchmans (1599–1621) was a Jesuit seminarian known for his piety and humility. He is the patron saint of altar servers.*
[76] *Cf. Rom 8:38–39.*

comes to us—that Jesus about whom we read in the Gospels. That woman just wanted to touch the fringe of his garment, and she knew she would be made well.[77] The centurion said: "I do not need to see you—speak but the word and my servant will be healed. I am not worthy to have you come to me."[78] This is the same Jesus who comes to us in Holy Communion. Do I believe it?

COMMUNITY

How can we love God and His poor—if we do not love each other with whom we live and break the Bread of Life daily together? This is my feast day greeting to each one of you: that you may know each other at the breaking of Bread, love each other in the eating of this Bread of Life, and serve each other and Him in his poor by giving your whole-hearted service. . . . At the breaking of the Bread they recognized Him.[79] Do I recognize the beauty of my sisters, the spouse of Christ, at the breaking of Bread—in the daily Mass we live together?

THE JOY OF A CHILD

What a tremendous gift God has given to the priests to be able to say, "This is my Body."[80] We have in our house a mentally and physically retarded child. But whenever we had Adoration, I used to bring the child to the chapel and each time I looked at that child, the way that child was looking at the Blessed Sacrament, I used to be taken up by the brightness, by the joy that was in that child's face because she was

---

[77] *Mt 9:21; Mk 5:28.*
[78] *Cf. Mt 8:7–9; Lk 7:1–10.*
[79] *Cf. Lk 24:30–32.*
[80] *1 Cor 11:23–25.*

looking so straight and she knew [at] whom she was looking. One day I asked Father, "Father, kindly—this child seems to know, kindly give her Holy Communion." He said, "Mother, how? [She] must prepare something." But she couldn't, she could not speak, she couldn't. So, then I said, "Father I'll give her one examination," and I took a piece of bread and I took a host, ordinary host, and I took the Cross and I put them before the child. And I asked—made a sign to the child— and the child put the finger on the bread and she put that finger in her mouth. And then she put her finger on the host and she put that finger on the Cross. Father said, "She knows," and he gave her Holy Communion. See how tremendous God's longing is to come to us. And this little one, so crippled, so disabled yet deep down in her heart, it was Jesus longing to come to her in full joy. And the priest was so grateful to God that he could give this joy to that child.

My All, My Joy

Somebody asked me, "But how is that—that you go about like that? How is that that you are always smiling?" I said, "But why did Jesus make Himself Bread of Life? He came to me this morning for that reason, to be my strength, my life, my love, my joy, and He is yours."

Let Us Love One Another

He has loved us. Let us love one another as He has loved us on the Cross, as He is loving us now in the Eucharist.

Adoration

I have seen a very great change in our Society. . . . Once a week we have a day of recollection. Every day, all of us go out, but every week, once a week—every Thursday—we stay in as a day of recollection. And, on that day, we have confession and instruction from a priest and also one hour of adoration. Then in '73, when we had the chapter—we were sixty-one of us at that chapter—and suddenly when we came together, it was one voice, "Mother, we want to have adoration [of the Blessed Sacrament] every day. One hour." I said, "No, it is not possible, we have too much work to do, we have lots of work to do, the sick, the dying, the lepers, the children." I said: "It's very difficult." And, I don't know what happened, we prayed, I prayed and prayed and prayed and then we are able to have the adoration every day without cutting the work, without depriving the poor of the work. And I can tell you from that time, there is much greater intimate love for Jesus, really everybody is trying to fall in love with Jesus and then there is a much greater understanding love between us, much greater. And what is more, it has deepened our love for the poor. We have a better understanding of their suffering, better understanding of what to be and how to give to them and still more, we have so many wonderful vocations. Just now in the novitiate, between the four novitiates, we have nearly four hundred novices from thirty-five nationalities. And it is wonderful to see the generosity, the love—I always say it is the fruit of the Eucharist, of the presence of Christ, of our adoration with Him.

✦

When I was at the last synod, Holy Father—faithfully I had to go, then I had to speak to all these big bishops and cardinals. I was not afraid of the Holy Father, but I was terrified of all the others. The first thing I asked Holy Father, "Give us holy priests and then we religious and our families will be holy." And so when I came back, I talked over with the sisters what we can do to grow in that holiness, to help the priests to be holy so that we can become holy after that and we found that it was through the Sacred Heart. Our Lord had asked St. Margaret Mary for that hour of adoration on the eve of First Friday [of the month] from 11:00 to 12:00. So, we started the [eve of First Friday] in January— that would be the fourth of January; so we had—in our Society from the very beginning, we make nine days novena before the First Friday. Every First Friday, we made that preparation of nine days.—And so, we started by doing that adoration at night and then on First Friday, we don't cook anything, we don't go to lunch, we fast and we call it an "M.C. fast" and that fast, that money that we save from not cooking anything, we use it to repair the houses of our poor people.

THE TABERNACLE

Go before the Blessed Sacrament—He is there. When we look at the Cross we know how much He loved us; when we look at the tabernacle, we know how much He loves us now. "Loved," past tense; "Loves," present tense. Not only past tense, He loves us now. He loves me tenderly.

THE SILENCE OF THE TABERNACLE

In the tabernacle Jesus is silent. I can understand the majesty of God, but I cannot understand the humility of God. A little piece of bread! Jesus created the whole world and Jesus, whose Precious Blood washed away my sins, is in the tabernacle . . . This silence in the tabernacle, this perfect silence. The only sign that He is there is the burning lamp, no greatness, no show, no nothing. That is why we have to make sure the lamp is burning. If there were no lamp, none of us would genuflect, but because there is a lamp we genuflect. It is for this [that] I don't want an electric lamp, because that burning light makes the joining real. He has made Himself the Bread of Life, Sisters, to satisfy our hunger for His love, to make the joining real. When husband and wife marry, they cleave to each other, they become one, and then comes the family. In the Bible it is written, they cleave to each other,[81] and so for us with Christ in the Eucharist. To make that oneness, Jesus gives us the Eucharist. In the silence of the tabernacle, He is right there. It is not an imagination; there is really [the] living God there.

GOD IS THERE

If you go to Government House you see the flag hoisted and flying. Flag is there if the governor is in the house. When he goes out the flag is taken down, and this says that he is not there. The lamp burning [next to] the tabernacle, a small thing, yet it expresses a big thing, the presence of God, that He is there.

THE BREAD OF LIFE

It hurt Jesus to love us. It hurt Him. To make sure we remember His great love, He made Himself the Bread of Life to satisfy our hunger for His love[82]—our hunger for God—because we have been created

---

[81] *Cf. Gen 2:24; Mt 19:5; Mk 10:7; Eph 5:31.*
[82] *Cf. Jn 6:35.*

for that love. We have been created in His image.[83] We have been created to love and be loved, and He has become man to make it possible for us to love as He loved us. He makes Himself the hungry one, the naked one, the homeless one, the sick one, the one in prison, the lonely one, the unwanted one, and He says, "You did it to Me."[84] He is hungry for our love, and this is the hunger of our poor people. This is the hunger that you and I must find. It may be in our own home.

---

[83] Cf. *Gen 1:26.*
[84] Cf. *Mt 25:35–40.*

III

What Prevents Me from Loving

Created by God and for God, who is infinitely good, we are to live in a loving relationship with Him and with one another. Not only has the Creator placed in every human heart a basic moral code to direct each person to do good and to reject evil, He has also spelt out the ways of love in the Ten Commandments. Unfortunately, we discover within ourselves many obstacles to love and struggle to overcome them. Stemming from the sin of our first parents when they abused the freedom God had given them and disobeyed His command, we have a tendency to prefer ourselves to God and to act against His will and our own good. Mother Teresa puts it bluntly: "When I choose evil, I sin. That's where my will comes in. When I seek something for myself at the cost of everything else, I deliberately choose sin. Say, for example, that I am tempted to tell a lie, and then I accept to tell the lie. Well, my mind is impure. I have burdened myself. I have put an obstacle between me and God. That lie has won. I preferred the lie to God."

To attain the happiness for which we have been created, we must constantly use our will to act against any sinful inclinations, and reject all sin, for it distances us from God and enslaves us to our inordinate desires.

Being part of the fallen human race, every person is a sinner and has a "root" sin to battle against. We are therefore to refrain from judging or condemning others for their weaknesses and sins. In this regard, Mother Teresa counseled, "We must not judge . . . we cannot say they are doing the right thing—but why they are doing it we do not know." While being ever merciful to the sinner, she did not shirk from the duty of addressing behaviors that were sinful.

She often spoke of "uncharitableness," referring mainly to the sins of the tongue: detraction and calumny, or any form of gossip. These sins pained her deeply. From her own mother, she had learned a few salutary lessons about respect for others' honor and good name, especially in speech. Refusing to focus on what is negative or allow it to interfere with her choice to love, she always found something positive to say about even the most distressing situation. One felt instinctively uneasy to criticize in her presence. If anyone did pass a negative remark or criticized someone else, especially the poor, she directed their attention to a sobering reality: "If we were in their place, we do not know how we would be or what we would do—maybe worse."

Another seemingly minor fault that occupied a prominent place in Mother Teresa's list of "significant" sins was grumbling. For her, grumbling pointed to a lack of practical faith, to the failure to see God's hand in the particular circumstances, to reluctance to surrender to His will. Grumbling or murmuring are killers of joy; they destroy the joy of giving and the joy of loving. By her own example, she showed that it is much more constructive and beneficial to all to look for a way to bring out good from a situation, however far from perfect it may be.

Mother Teresa saw bitterness as a major obstacle to love and an impediment to one's spiritual life. Unwillingness to forgive results in resentment and bitterness or a desire for revenge, and is a sturdy "link" in the chain of evil. In our interactions, it is inevitable that we will get hurt and will hurt others—usually unintentionally. Holding onto hurts and bearing grudges is detrimental to all, especially to the one who does not forgive. Sensitive by nature, Mother Teresa suffered keenly from hurts, but she was determined not to let them control or influence her choices. Instead of focusing on herself, she focused on the person who hurt her, actually feeling sorry for them because she knew that in reality they were hurting themselves more than her. By her forgiveness, she offered everyone the opportunity to start anew.

"Moodiness is sickness." With this terse statement Mother Teresa placed moodiness on the list of spiritual ailments that seriously hinder love. Moodiness, a form of passive retaliation, manifested by stubbornly and silently showing one's dissatisfaction, reveals the inner reality of many hidden sins: pride, anger, lack of forgiveness, resentment. Moodiness has a paralyzing effect on others (community or family), but even more so on the one who gives into this fault, as it cripples his or her ability to love and grow in love. If joy is contagious, so is the lack of it.

God's command to love one another allows no room for indifference, no exceptions to the obligation to love, no excuses for a lack of concern. We are required, as Mother

Teresa would say, to "have eyes that see" the needs of our brothers and sisters and do something to help them. Indifference or hardness of heart toward the pain and suffering of others is an evil that she challenged. To the message, "I couldn't care less," conveyed by some, Mother Teresa's actions declared, "I couldn't care more."

Rejecting or shunning others on account of their poverty or blaming them for it, was a great injustice in Mother Teresa's eyes. Whatever the reason for a person's problems, she was convinced that help and care were their due. Her first response when encountering someone in distress was to seek to offer immediate and effective help, and only later to find out the reasons for the difficulty. Coming to the defense of the poor if someone blamed them for their poverty, she would ask, "What would you do if you were in their place?" In fact, she made her listeners aware that perhaps they might be more responsible for others' poverty than they thought.

A frequent topic in her public speeches was respect for human life from conception to natural death. In her profound respect and love for the Giver of life, she staunchly upheld His rights by opposing any form of violence against human life, speaking out in defense of the weakest and most vulnerable human beings.

She considered abortion the greatest destroyer of peace in the world. The reason behind such a statement is logical: Once it is permissible and socially acceptable to kill one's own flesh and blood, others not bound by family ties have much less "right" to love, care, and life; much more easily can they be "disposed of" at will. If, in order to protect often unjust and selfish interests such as love of comfort and pleasure, a society turns directly against the child in

its mother's womb, it will eventually and without scruple
eliminate other defenseless beings as well. It can become a
very slippery slope.

The elderly, sick, or disabled, increasingly considered "a
burden" to society, are among the vulnerable in the world
today. Mother Teresa particularly deplored any form of
disregard or neglect shown to the elderly members of one's
family in need of care. As "love begins at home," our first
responsibility is to our own. Incapacities or sufferings do
not diminish the inherent dignity of each person. Suffering
is part of every human life and, depending on one's
attitude, can be a source of tremendous blessing, not only
for the sufferer but for those close to him or her. Through
the receiving and giving of needed love and care, both
can be drawn closer to each other and to God and to the
realization of the true purpose of one's existence: to know,
to love and to serve God and so attain eternal happiness.

Another regular theme of Mother Teresa's public dis-
courses was the sacredness of marriage and the importance
of family life, as the family constitutes the basic nucleus
of society. The well-being of society rests upon the well-
being of the family. This "domestic school of love" pro-
vides the authority, stability, and relationships that children
need in order to become mature adults, able to contribute to the building of a healthy society. Her opposition to
divorce, which was roundly criticized by some, was based
on her faith in the permanence of marriage, the sacred bond
between a man and a woman. Not unaware of the difficulties that exist, she advocated that it is possible to learn to
live together in love.

The home is (or should be) the primary and the most
natural environment in which love is given and received.

The love and unity of the family serves as the foundation for the growth of the children, providing a sense of identity, peace, trust, openness, and joy that will prepare them to take their place in society. Small acts of thoughtfulness to those closest to us make them feel welcome, accepted, worthy, and appreciated. The home offers ample opportunities for sharing joys, bearing hardships together, providing support in suffering, putting oneself at the disposal of others, seeking not to be served but rather to serve—all expressions of love. Where "tenderness, forgiveness, respect, fidelity, and disinterested service are the rule,"[1] the family, both parents and children, will grow in holiness.

Still, Mother Teresa was aware that a family is affected by each member's weakness and sinfulness, so that the home can be at times a place where deep hurt is experienced. She insisted on the need for forgiveness and reconciliation, while being under no illusion of how demanding this could be. "The family that prays together stays together," Mother Teresa never tired of repeating, quoting Fr. Patrick Peyton, CSC. Like the saints before her, she was sure that all difficulties can be overcome with prayer.

When faced with the temptation to sin—to fail in love— Mother Teresa's primary counsel was to seek help where help is always available: to turn to God in prayer. She knew that God's grace would always accompany good will and effort. In this way temptations become opportunities for growth and for (even greater!) good. Counting on divine help and opening oneself to receive it were important strategies for fighting temptation and overcoming barriers to love.

---

[1] *CCC 2223.*

To overcome temptations, a strong resolve to stay on the right path is needed. "I don't want it" was her recommended response to the lure of sin. One must not be swayed by feelings or moods or by others' opinions. She frequently quoted St. Teresa of Avila: "Satan is terribly afraid of resolute souls." For Mother Teresa, everything depended on these two words: "I will" or "I won't." Thus a "strong resolution" was essential to achieve good and to avoid evil.

A resolute soul, she affirmed, has no need to be afraid even of the devil for "nobody, not even the devil, can make you do what you don't want." Aware of the pitfalls one can encounter on the way, Mother Teresa warned against the tactics of "the father of lies" who comes disguised as "an angel of light." With a bit of humor she commented, "If I were to give a Nobel Prize for patience to anybody, I would give it to the devil, for he is very clever [in] the way he works and he has infinite patience."

"Do not hide" was another of Mother Teresa's maxims. Openness with the right person (e.g., one's superior, spiritual director, or confessor) regarding some difficulty helps to prevent one from becoming preoccupied or even obsessed with oneself and one's problems. She used to advise to "speak in time," as she knew how helpful a word from someone qualified could be in the time of struggle.

"Keep busy," Mother Teresa finally recommended when faced with impure thoughts or temptations. Doing something useful to divert one's attention from such thoughts could be very salutary. Not dwelling on the problem or not struggling with it to the point of becoming obsessed by it were further practical counsels that Mother Teresa gave to help people not to lose their equilibrium.

Mother Teresa never gave in to discouragement on encountering any failure to love in herself or others. Knowing that God's mercy is greater than any sin, she turned to Him for forgiveness and encouraged others to do likewise. The sacrament of confession—this marvelous gift of God's healing love—was the great means of being reconciled with the Lord and with all one's brothers and sisters. Recognizing herself as a sinner, she approached the sacrament of reconciliation after a careful examination of conscience, admitting to the wrong done, repenting of it, and resolving to amend her behavior. From this meeting with Jesus she emerged forgiven, healed, and strengthened. Mother Teresa often repeated, "We go to confession as a sinner with sin, and we come out as a sinner without sin."

If she had wronged anyone, Mother Teresa was prompt to acknowledge her fault and apologize. It requires courage and humility to say, "I am sorry," but it is often the only path to reconciliation and peace. She not only sought reconciliation with anyone she might have wronged, but also with those who wronged her. Faithfully practicing the principles she had taught her sisters, she would "be the first to say 'sorry,'" even if she was not the one at fault, so as to give the offender the opportunity to be reconciled and begin anew. Going a step further, she even accepted being falsely accused, seeing it as an opportunity of imitating Jesus: "When somebody blames you—if your conscience is clear, thank God. Grab the beautiful chance. That is the best way to come closer to Jesus."

Sin

Everything depends on my will. It depends upon me, whether I become a saint or a sinner.

"I WILL NOT SERVE"

Go right back to heaven, where amongst the angels, God put the question. What was the question? That God the Son would become Man and they would have to obey Him. Angels are more clever in everything than man. Lucifer, the most powerful among them [said], "I will not serve."[2] *"Non serviam,"* a Latin phrase [that] has a deep meaning. How many times we say: "I will not serve"? Hell was created [at that time]. Before that there was no hell. And once you go there, there is no coming out. The only time you can come out is as a devil to tempt people, otherwise there is no permission to leave hell. [There is] neither mercy nor washing away of sins, there is no confession in hell. So Sisters, make good use of confession.

There was a beautiful man and woman, so very beautiful. There was no Jesus at that time in the world. Now there are millions and millions of people, but there were only these two [at that time]. And there were also beautiful trees in a most beautiful garden. And God Himself talked to them. He told them a very small, small thing. God told them: "You can eat of all these trees, hundreds of other trees, plenty of trees, but don't eat the fruit of this tree."[3] And instead of sitting under that tree and that tree, she (Eve) goes and sits there under the forbidden tree. And Lucifer disguises himself. He is in the tree and she is under

---

[2] *Cf. Is 14:12–15; Rev 12:1–8.*
[3] *Cf. Gen 2:7–9, 15–17.*

the tree and he begins to talk to her. "I believe you are not allowed to eat of this tree. I know why: because if you eat of this tree you will become like God and if you eat of this tree, you will know better." And Adam was looking for her everywhere and instead of telling her to come away, she called to him and said: "See, I've eaten of this fruit. I am full of life, I know now." And to please her, Adam also ate. I don't think they ate two or three apples—just one. . . . [4]

Now Sisters, pay attention well. I want you to think deeply. If Eve was not sitting under that tree, the devil quite possibly would not have tempted her. See that carelessness. That sin of disobedience brought so much evil in the world. I want you to listen well. Where did that temptation begin? If Eve had avoided sitting under that tree, there would not be the devil to tempt them. But carelessness led them to sin.

Unable to Love

Sin [is to be] unable to love. What do those words mean to me? Our Lord was very sad when He was telling Margaret Mary—she asked why He was like that and He said, "The souls very close to me, their sins cause me the most pain." Sin is an evil not created by God but created by the fruit of disobedience. [At the] beginning of life we were created to the image of God. Every little thing, so beautiful—"only from that tree don't eat."[5] And He gave no reason—such a small thing.

---

[4] Cf. Gen 3:1–6.
[5] Cf. Gen 2:17.

IS SOMETHING DIVIDING MY LOVE FOR JESUS?

"Is my heart pure, or is there something that is dividing my love for Jesus?"

As carriers of God's love we need to spend some time on ourselves. Just say you have died: you would have to face yourself and in the clear light of God, see if there is anything between you and Him. Some theologians say that those who go to purgatory are not sent there by God but they go there themselves because they realize that they are not yet able to love God completely, that their love needs purifying. They realize that between God and themselves there is no connecting link. I believe that they are happy to go there to become spotlessly clean.

Let me prepare for that day—let me not wait for then. Examine and see what is binding me, especially see what are your attachments. Not only to a human being—it may be a small thing. St. Ignatius says that it is not necessary to be bound down by a thick chain but even a thin silken thread. How many threads am I clinging to in my life? We must be completely free to belong wholly to Jesus Christ. Can I in sincerity say: "Jesus is really living in me now?" Have I come to know Jesus in reality, not only in imagination? Externally I might be very recollected and prayerful, but this counts for nothing, Sisters, unless deep down you can see that Jesus is really there.

Condemn Sin, Not the Sinner

Jesus said very clearly, "Do not judge. If you do not judge you will not be judged."[6] But when a sister is doing something wrong you cannot

---

[6] *Cf. Mt 7:1; Lk 6:37.*

say it is right. The act is wrong but why she is doing that you do not know . . . the intention you do not know. When we judge we are judging the intention of the sister, of the poor.

✦

We must remember—we cannot help seeing the faults of our . . . people and children, but . . . we must not ever pass judgment on their intentions—the intention only Jesus knows. That is why Jesus is so very kind and full of mercy because He knows what we really mean each time.

✦

Avoid judging, just as you avoid the devil—even if that sister has made a big mistake.

✦

Maybe we don't fight with gun and knife but with our criticism and rash judgment. From passing remarks, protect yourself; we can easily fall into it. Say, for example, I told a lie to you and you know it is a lie—straight away you say that I am a liar. Maybe straight after I said it, I realize and I say sorry. You know a lie is bad, but why I said the lie, you don't know. I cannot deny the fact that [lying] is bad. Have that attitude: not to pass judgment, not in words and not even in [your] mind.

✦

One sister had a terrible tongue . . . [and] one day it flared up again. Everybody got excited. I sent for her and she showed me her book—

nineteen times she had overcome herself—only once she fell, but nobody saw these nineteen, but all saw the fall. They grumbled, it must have helped her to become more humble. We can see the fault but we never know the reason. That's why Jesus said we must not judge.[7] Nobody saw the struggle in that child's heart. Now you make sure you get rid of that thing from your heart—criticism, fault finding, judging. Open your eyes and see the good in your sisters. St. John Berchmans had great difficulty in the community, so he made a litany of the saints: Brother John, humility, pray for me. Brother Paul, beautiful voice, pray for me. . . . It saved his [vocation], made him a saint. Have the joy of living together. Share with each other. Be completely at ease, open and in love with each other. We can't tell lies to Jesus. If we don't love each other, it's not true love. . . .

✦

Do not judge—we do not know. Don't allow yourselves to get into unkind thoughts. We must be kind because we love. It is so easy to be unkind in judgment. Control your judgments.[8]

✦

There was a brother dying, and his superior was anxious about him because he was laughing instead of saying sorry to God. He said, "I have never criticized, grumbled against anybody. I know I will go straight to God." You can tell lies all your life but when you are dying you can never tell a lie . . . and there he was, with a big smile. He said, "I never judged anybody and God will never judge me."[9]

---

[7] *Mt 7:1; Lk 6:37.*
[8] *Jas 4:11–12.*
[9] *Cf. Lk 6:37.*

Uncharitableness

When I am unkind, uncharitable—it's that slap I give to Jesus; it's a humiliation to God. That was the greatest suffering for Jesus to accept—that slap.[10] Connect His Cross with the cross you wear. Today did I wipe the blood from the face of Jesus?

How Unlike Him We Are

How unlike Him we are. How little love, how little compassion, how little forgiveness, how little kindness we have that we are not worthy to be so close to Him—to enter His heart. For His heart is still open to embrace us. His head is still crowned with thorns, His hands nailed to the Cross today. Let us find out, "Are the nails mine? That sputum on His face mine? What part of His body, of His mind has suffered because of me?" Not with anxiety or fear but with a meek and humble heart, let us find out what part of His body has [suffered], [what are] the wounds inflicted by my sin. Let us not go alone, but put my hand in His. He is there to forgive seventy times seven[11]; as long as I know: my Father loves me, He has called me in a special way, given me a name; I belong to Him with all my misery, my sin, my weakness, my goodness . . . I am His.

---

[10] Cf. *Jn 18:22–24.*
[11] Cf. *Mt 18:21–22.*

EMPTY YOUR HEARTS OF UNCHARITABLENESS

How many of us really listen to God speak in the silence of the heart? From the fullness of the heart, the mouth speaks.[12] . . . I repeated that we think of violence as killing or shooting with a gun. Each time only one bullet comes. . . . I want you very especially to examine. Have you heard the voice of God? Is my heart silent? If bitter words, angry words come out of your mouth, then your heart is not full with Jesus. From the fullness of the heart the mouth speaks, and in the silence of the heart God speaks. I want you to empty your hearts of all uncharitableness, all bitterness, all untruthfulness that you see and you hear.

CUTTING YOURSELF OFF FROM JESUS

God knows us best of all. He knows our capacities—His knowledge of each one is complete. Something of His beauty is in each person. We are made to the image of God.[13] His lovableness is in each one, so let us see what there is of God in each person. For this we need pure eyes and a pure heart to be able to see that beauty. When we are unkind, proud, or harsh, let us ask ourselves, "Why am I harsh today?" I am not clean of heart. Something is cutting me off from Jesus.

SEE YOUR WORDS

Ask yourself if you are holy. If you want to know if you are really holy, examine your tongue. All the biggest sins are there: lies,

---

[12] *Cf. Lk 6:45.*
[13] *Gen 1:27, 9:6.*

grumbling.[14] . . . All the beautiful things also: the Word of God. It is through the tongue that Jesus comes into our hearts. How holy must be the tongue. "Silence of the heart of Jesus, speak to me." I don't know how you can pray—everywhere talking. . . . The tongue is very closely connected with the heart. [From the] fullness of the heart the tongue speaks.[15] . . . We are surprised how the people hurt Jesus: they slapped Him, spat on Him.[16] What we throw in the drain, we throw on Jesus. And Jesus—not a word. Each time, when we say ugly things, uncharitable words, we are doing the same thing to Jesus—"You did it to Me."[17] Terrible . . . throwing, spitting—that's where Veronica came in and wiped His face. Spitting on Our Lord—"You did it to me." When? Now. We think that what they did, we are not responsible; it is exactly what they did to Him [that] we are doing now. Today I want you to go before the Blessed Sacrament—take a direct look at Jesus. Whatever you did to that sister, to that poor person, "I am spitting on Him." . . . Make this your own and you will see how your whole attitude will change. Just this morning I was with Jesus. Instead of words of love, I give dirt—sin is dirt. Jesus gives us a word of love. If you want to know if your heart is all right, see your words. . . .

HAVE RESPECT FOR ONE ANOTHER

We *must* be able to live in peace and joy and unity. How? Have respect for each other. If God chose me, He chose you. If He loves me, He loves you. If He trusts me, He trusts you. Never use ugly words for each other. Don't try to see what is bad. Find out what is nice in each other. Pope Paul [VI] tried to find what is best in each one. Maybe I'm so jealous. She

---

[14] Cf. Jas 3:6–10.

[15] Cf. Lk 6:45.

[16] Cf. Mt 26:67, 27:30; Mk 14:65, 15:19; Jn 18:22–23.

[17] Cf. Mt 25:40.

has something I don't have. Jealousy is [a] cruel matter. It breaks community. Deep rooted pride. This is something I beg of you, have deep trust and respect for each other. First of all, that respect, respect each other. I [am] used to bowing to Jesus in the heart of the person.

CRITICISM

The first weapon—the most cruel weapon—is the tongue. Now you examine, what part has your tongue played in creating peace or violence? We can really wound a person—we can kill a person just with our tongue.

ONE BAD APPLE

A soul that is humble and sincere . . . will never stoop to criticism, which in spiritual life is called "cancer of the heart." It eats up all the love of God, all the energy we have for God's interests. It is also most infectious. Let one sister start criticizing and in a short time we shall have two, four, eight, ten, following. When we were little children my mother wanted to teach us what bad company does, so she brought a basket of apples, amongst which she intentionally put a bad apple. After a few days, she called us around the basket and we saw [that] all the apples, which had been beautiful a few days before, had gone bad. She then explained how one bad apple contaminated all the others. In the same way, bad companions can harm others. Now criticism has that effect on souls. A truly generous soul must never stoop to criticism. As a rule, people that criticize never do it openly, but go about doing it in a whisper. That is a sin. Today when you go before the Blessed Sacrament, ask Jesus to preserve you from the cancer of criticism. Criticism is not a failure, not a human weakness—it is something that touches the heart. Should we have given way to it at times, let us resolve to avoid it and beg of Christ to preserve us. To keep free of criticism, we must be humble.

Words Once Spoken . . .

Right here in Rome, St. Philip Neri was the spiritual father of a lady who had a terrible tongue. He always told her that she must control it. One day, to try to get this into her head, he took her to St. Peter's, to the top, then he told her to open the pillow she had brought there. It was a pillow full of feathers. She opened it and all the feathers went everywhere. Then he said to her, "Now take the empty pillow and gather all the feathers." She couldn't gather more than ten. He said, "These are the words that you speak with your tongue." So, it is the same for us, once words are spoken they can never be taken back. Never repeat; never say things you cannot repeat to Jesus before the Blessed Sacrament. Silence cannot be corrected.

Easy to Complain

Refuse nothing, ask for nothing, and like that you will never complain. To complain is very easy, but to be happy to be anybody's walking stick is very difficult. What a lot we lose when we grumble; what a waste of energy. How foolish we are. We must all watch out because we are all inclined to it—let not our likes and dislikes be the measure of our actions. Remember, we have come to do the will of Him who called us. Watch yourselves, Sisters. Nobody can do this work for you—you must train yourselves to be happy by always saying "yes" to God. Try to give a hearty "yes" to God in your life and you will find yourself coming closer and closer to God.

GRUMBLING

A grumbling sister can't pray. And, you can see on their faces—there is something there worrying them. When I have tried to find out, it is always because of grumbling, misunderstandings, carrying tales. If this happens when you are four or when you are six, community life will become so difficult; all right when you are a big community. Just as the Americans go for a [medical] check-up, "Have I got cancer," we need to check and see that. Grumbling and criticism are always the fruit of jealousy. Jealousy, again, is nothing but hidden pride.

PREJUDICE

Refrain from prejudice, which means to set your mind against somebody or someone, and that may happen to be my superior. It is very sad when it becomes a part of my life. For us religious, a prejudiced attitude is most unworthy. Murmuring, always dissatisfied—what an evil it is! If you don't watch yourselves, you will fall a prey to murmuring, as it is a most infectious disease.

OUR TEMPER

Our lives must be connected with the living Christ in us. If we do not live in the presence of God, we cannot go on. One thing more is lacking—silence. When there are two together, they start talking. Then, without silence, there will be no good prayers. We must also control our temper. Temper means pride. We must control our temper for the love of God. In a good, ordinary family, it does not happen that we are losing our temper and answering back. It should not happen here, either.

JEALOUSY

"Blessed are the clean of heart for they shall see God."[18] One of the things that makes our heart unclean is jealousy; I want to destroy what somebody else has—grumbling, murmuring, "Why I, why not she?" Criticizing—all these are the fruit of pride. Pride has so many branches, we never know which way it penetrates us. . . . [Jealousy is to be] sad at the goodness of others. Is there anything like that in my heart?

Sins of Omission

I want you to pray and examine your conscience [regarding] sins of omission. Have the courage to say sorry. The best way of saying sorry is to do the opposite in action. If you have been moody, be happy. . . . I want you . . . not to change your place or work but to change your heart. Death can come any time.

✦

The biggest disease today is not leprosy or tuberculosis, but rather the feeling of being unwanted, uncared for, deserted by everybody. The greatest evil is the lack of love and charity, the terrible indifference towards those who are victims of exploitation, corruption, poverty, and disease. Love has to be built on sacrifice. We have to give until it hurts.

---

[18] *Mt 5:8.*

MY BROTHER LYING THERE

The other day I went to the street here [in Japan] . . . I saw a man across the road completely lost. It is true that he was drunk, but he is my brother. My brother. It hurt me. I couldn't do anything. I felt so bad that there was not a single hand—many people passed—but there was not a single hand to lift him. Even to put him on the side of the road. I could not do it. I did not know the rules here. Because I've only been here for a few days. But I felt hurt. I felt my brother lying there, and I passed him by. That was Jesus in the distressing disguise. That was that hunger for love, and I didn't give. That was nakedness of human dignity. He is a man. He must be a father of somebody. He must be the son of somebody. He must be the brother of somebody, laying there in the middle of the street. Even the cars had to pass him by. Even the people had to pass him by. How? This is where, if you really want to love, love begins; love begins at home. Right here. We must not be afraid to love. We must not be afraid to love until it hurts because love is giving until it hurts.

I HAVE NO TIME

[Jesus] loved the world so much and . . . He made Himself the leper, that miserable mental person of the street He made Himself, so that you and I can love Him, that you and I can satisfy His hunger for our love, and that's why He says at the hour of death, you and I are going to be judged—not from what big things we have done, but what we have been to the poor: that hungry man, that man that came to our gate, that lonely person, that blind person passing through the street, that person so lonely, so unwanted, so unloved in my family right here. Maybe I have an old father, old mother, maybe I have a sick child and I have no time. I'm so busy, I've no time. I've no time to smile at others. My crippled daughter, my crippled wife, my sick husband, I have no time and that is Jesus in the distressing disguise. That is the hungry Jesus right in my family, right in my community, my sister and we have no time. We have no time today to even smile at each other, and yet Jesus loves us with an everlasting love. And Jesus said, "Love as I have loved you."[19] No, He didn't compare His love with any other love. "As the Father has loved me, I have loved you.[20] Love one another as I have loved you."[21]

WHERE ARE YOU?

Maybe you don't have people hungry for bread or for rice, whatever you eat here, but there are people hungry, lonely people, those people in the street, so many people in the street. And I went to the next place also, same thing, people in the street, unwanted, unloved, uncared, hungry people for love. They had three, four bottles near them but they drink that because there is nobody to give them something else. Where are you? Where am I? Then, nakedness is not only for a piece of cloth. Nakedness; our people have lost that dignity, that human dignity, child of God. That homelessness is not only for a room made of bricks but rejected, unwanted, unloved, uncared for, thrown away, the "throw away" of society. We have so many people like that right in New York, right in London, in these big European cities—just a piece of newspaper [for covering], lying there. Our sisters go at night from 10:00 to 1:00 in the streets of Rome and they bring sandwiches, they bring something hot to drink and . . . terrible cold and just newspaper. In London, I've seen people standing against the factory wall

---

[19] *Cf. Jn 13:34.*
[20] *Cf. Jn 15:12.*
[21] *Cf. Jn 13:34.*

to warm themselves. How? Why? Where are we? So I think it is good for us to begin to love at home. Then once we have learned to love with the love that hurts, then we will be able to give that love, our eyes will open up, we'll see, we'll see. Very often, we look but we don't see or we see and we don't want to look, and so let us begin to practice at home. That tender love for our people, the husband for the wife, for the children, for the people working in your factory.

DO WE KNOW OUR POOR?

What is happening—all these abortions, all this, "I don't want you." All this is killing of that love. That is the greatest poverty in the country. Any country that kills, that destroys love is the poorest of the poor, and you and I who have received so much, we have to face our people. Do we really know who the poor are? In our own home, in our neighborhood, in the city where we live, in the world. And if we know them, naturally, we will love them. And if we love them, it is understood that we serve them. And we cannot serve them just by giving them a few dollars or a few rupees from the abundance. We must give until it hurts. We must give our hearts to love them and our hands to serve them whoever they may be, wherever they may be.

DO WE KNOW THOSE AROUND US?

We must give until it hurts. For love to be true it has to hurt. It hurt Jesus to love us; it hurt God to love us because He had to give. He gave His Son. Today we are here together—I can give you nothing, I have nothing to give—but what I want from you is that when we look together and we see the poor in our own family, that we begin at home to love until it hurts. That we have a ready smile, that we have time for our people. If we know our people, we will know then who is our next-door neighbor. We will know them. Do we know the people around us? There are many lonely people.

The other day, I was walking down the street and a man walked up to me and said, "Are you Mother Teresa?" And I said, "Yes." "Please send some of your sisters to our house. I'm half blind and my wife is nearly mental and we are simply longing to hear a human voice. We have everything except . . ." When I sent the sisters there, they found that it was true. They had everything, but the loneliness of those two—with no one to call their own. Their sons and their daughters were quite possibly very far away from them. They are unwanted now, unusable so to say, unprofitable, and so they must die of sheer loneliness.

Shunning Others

I think it's very difficult to realize what it is to be lonely unless you face it, same thing for people who speak about hunger. Unless they experience in their life, hunger, it is very difficult for them to understand the pain of hunger. Same thing for loneliness and the feeling of being unwanted, unloved, uncared. Like for example our patients that are shunned by everybody, the lepers, we are taking care of maybe 46,000 lepers. And I think more than the disease itself, I think [of] that terrible loneliness, that everybody shuns them, everybody runs away from them. I think that's much greater than the leprosy itself.

Uncared

Leprosy is a very hard disease, true. But is not as painful as the pain of being shunned by people, by being unwanted, uncared, just left alone.

I never forget one day. We had a party for our lepers in one of our centers in Calcutta, and this gentleman covered and completely disfigured by leprosy stood up and said: "Days back, many days ago, I was at the top level of the government officials. I had everything. At every step I took, I had people following me. And then when the disease caught me, I had to withdraw, and to spare my family, to spare my daughters and sons from being unwanted, I withdrew. And I withdrew and have come to this stage. I have no one now. No one loves me. No one wants me except these Sisters who have given their life for us." And this is the pain that our people feel. Or like the one whom we picked up from the street and who said: "I have lived like an animal in the street, but I am going to die like an angel." This is what our people need. They need your hands to serve them, and they need your heart to love them.

UNWANTED

I'll never forget one night, late at night—midnight—I heard the bell in our house, and I went down and there was a little child crying and I asked why, what has happened. And he said, "I went to my father, my father didn't want me. I went to my mother, my mother did not want me, but I know you want me. I came to you." Does your child feel unwanted, unloved?

SO MANY WORRIES

Once I asked a poor woman, a very good and holy woman—"What is your first thought in the morning?" I asked because I was sure that she prayed and she said, "I think of what I will give my children to eat today." She was a good woman, but she had to face that kind of worry. We don't have to think about this kind of thing.

Injustice

To me the greatest injustice done to the poor is not so much that we have deprived them of material things but that we have deprived them of that dignity of the child of God, of the respect we owe to a person who [we] think, "They are good for nothing, they're lazy," they're this, they're that—so many adjectives we add. To me, that is the greatest injustice . . . and I always tell them "what would you do if you were in their place? If you have an empty stomach day after day and saw your children dying of hunger, cold." . . . We have not experienced that. None of us experienced. I never forget once I picked up a child six or seven years old from the street and to see the face of the child—hunger, real hunger. So I gave her bread and she started eating the bread crumb by crumb like this. And I said, "Eat the bread, you are hungry. Eat the bread." And she said, "I'm afraid that when the bread is finished, I will be hungry again." So small, she was afraid of being hungry again. She has already experienced the pain of hunger. . . . That's why it's easy for us with a full stomach to pass those adjectives. And that is the greatest injustice.

Do We Know Them by Name?

Do we know our poor people by their name? Each child, each person? Do you recognize the child who has not eaten by looking at his face? You punish them when they are restless without finding out the real reason for their restlessness. You are full—so easy for you whose stomach is full—so you do not understand them. What was striking me during the silver jubilee of Nirmal Hriday celebration—the poor people taking the whole box home in order to share with their other members who have not eaten.

The other day I received a letter. He wrote, "There is so much trouble in the country—the poor and the government are to be blamed." I wrote back, "It is very easy for you to disturb the country when your stomach is so full—so easy for you, whose stomach is full—disturbing government and creating disturbance and discontent in writing this article."

CHARITY, A DRUG FOR THE POOR?

The other day, I read in one article written by a Jesuit Father, that charity is like a drug for the poor—that when we give the people things free, it is like giving them drugs. I've decided that I will write to him and ask him: "Why did Jesus have pity on the people?" He must have drugged them also when He fed them by the multiplication of the loaves and fishes.[22] He came to give Good News to the people,[23] but when He saw that they were hungry and tired, He fed them first. One more question that I'm going to ask him, "Did you ever feel the hunger of the poor? Did you ever feel the biting cold and have no blanket to warm you at night? Have you ever had a severe headache and had no aspirin to take?" It is so easy for him and for us to talk about the poverty of the poor but how little we really know of it. Today straight after Mass, without a thought, we all sat down to breakfast. We ate our share of chapattis and drank as much tea as we wanted—but did we have to think if there would be enough for tomorrow, or how much one cup of tea costs or worry if we could afford to buy more sugar?

---

[22] Cf. Mt 14:13–21; Mk 6:25–43; Jn 6:6–14.
[23] Cf. Lk 4:18.

THE FIRST VIOLENCE

What is violence? In the first place we think of weapons, knife, killing, and so on. We never think of connecting violence with our tongues. The first violence that came into the world was "a lie." The devil told a lie to Eve—and with that one lie the whole generation of mankind became sinful. What was that lie? "If you eat of this fruit, you will become like God."[24] Just think—that one lie; untruth. We can tell a lie to outsiders, to each other—but we can't tell a lie to God. The devil makes us believe that we can tell a lie to God. Even to ourselves we cannot tell a lie because we cannot hide anything from ourselves, for we know the reality. We try to believe, but we only bluff ourselves. The devil tells one thousand lies to make us believe one lie.

A LIE

It is not enough for us to say, "I love God, but I do not love my neighbor." St. John says that you are a liar if you say you love God and you don't love your neighbor.[25] How can you love God, whom you do not see, if you do not love your neighbor whom you see, whom you touch, with whom you live? So this is very important for us to realize that love, to be true, has to hurt.

---

[24] Cf. *Gen 3:1–6.*
[25] Cf. *Jn 4:20.*

Respect for Life Is Gone

Life is the gift of God, created by God Himself, to love and to be loved and so we have no right to destroy what belongs to God Himself. By destroying life, [you] are destroying love . . . destroying the presence of God . . . destroying everything that is beautiful.

THE IMAGE OF GOD

The other day, I read something that the unborn child is not a child until it is born. I don't know, I don't know how anybody could say a thing like that. For there is life, the life of God in the child, and that child has been created for greater things, to love and to be loved. And if we have so much misery in the world today, it is because we are forgetting how to love and to be loved until it hurts.

So let us pray, all of you that have gathered together—it does not matter what you believe, what faith you have—but let us all ask God to remove from our own families, from our own hearts, anything that will destroy the beautiful image of God, to remove anything that destroys peace in our families, to make every sacrifice and to help others to come closer to God by helping them to love each other, by forgiving each other. Because if there is no forgiveness, it is very difficult to have peace, it is very difficult to have love. You know, all the works of love are works of peace. So let us thank God for this beautiful opportunity.

KILLING

In the plane coming over, I was spending my time writing some letters, and each time I looked up, all I could see was the film going on, just shooting and killing, shooting, hitting, pulling—such a heavy thing. I rested my head, I looked up: killing, revolvers, guns . . . such a strain. Afterwards, I went to the Air India [office], and gave them a nice scolding. I told them: "You are making everything so comfortable but you're disturbing the minds of the people, because they learn like that." And they told me that they had never thought about it, so I told them, "You had better start thinking about it now. Evil is spreading, people are tired and need rest; each time I looked up, I never saw anything beautiful that would raise mind and heart, but only shooting, killing, revolvers." We really have to pray much.

✦

Now in Yugoslavia, people are killing,[26] cutting each other in pieces, without any feeling. I always say, "If a mother can kill her own child, what is left for man not to do?" How many millions of abortions—of babies—killed! This is the fruit of abortions, all this killing, these wars—we have to really pray. I don't know how far all this will go. Same in India, in small places, killing—everywhere so much trouble.

CAPITAL PUNISHMENT

Some time back they phoned from the U.S.A. They were going to execute a man who had committed very serious crimes. They asked me to speak to the Governor, to try to do something for that man. God helped me; I said the first words that came to my mouth, "Do what Jesus would do if He were in your place." [The man] was not executed; he is still in the prison.

---

[26] *Referring to the war in former Yugoslavia in the 1990s.*

LIFE DELIBERATELY DESTROYED

Each one of us is here today because we have been loved by God who created us and our parents who accepted and cared enough to give us life. Life is the most beautiful gift of God. That is why it is so painful to see what is happening today in so many places around the world: life being deliberately destroyed by war, by violence, by abortion. And we have been created by God for greater things—to love and to be loved.

CHILDREN CONTINUE TO SUFFER

Every child is a gift of God, loved into being, infinitely precious to God, created for greater things: to love and to be loved. Yet so many are forgotten abandoned, abused, made to suffer the most unimaginable pain in their souls and bodies. I have looked into the eyes of children—some shining with hunger, some dull and vacant with pain. I have held countless babies in my arms—dying for lack of a little milk, some medicine. And why does all this happen? Why? These children are my brother, my sister, my child. If there is such terrible suffering for children in the world today, it is because men and women have forgotten to pray, to thank God who is the Author of Life for the precious gift of life. And children will continue to suffer, and suffer terribly, for as long as men and women accept and allow the killing of children in their own mother's wombs. It is so clear. If we allow abortion, how can we stop anyone from deliberately harming a child or torturing and killing him? It is the same child inside the mother's womb and out of it.

CONTRACEPTION

I know that couples have to plan their family and for that, there is natural family planning. The way to plan the family is natural family planning, not contraception. In destroying the power of giving life through contraception [one] is doing something to self. This is paying attention to self and so it destroys the gift of love in him or her. In loving, the husband and wife must turn their attention to each other as happens in natural family planning and not to self as happens in contraception. Once that living love is destroyed by contraception, abortion follows very easily. I also know that there are great problems in the world, that mainly spouses do not love each other enough to practice natural family planning. We cannot solve all the problems in the world, but let us never bring in the worst problem of all and that is to destroy love. And this is what happens when we tell people to practice contraception and abortion.

The poor are very great people. They can teach us so many beautiful things. Once, one of them came to thank us for teaching her natural family planning because it is nothing more than self control out of love for each other and what this poor person said is very true—poor people may have nothing to eat, maybe they have not a home to live in but we can see they are great people when they are spiritually rich.

When I pick up a person from the street hungry, I give him a plate of rice, a piece of bread; for the person who is shut out, who feels unwanted, unloved, . . . thrown out of society, that spiritual poverty is much harder to overcome. And abortion, which often follows from contraception, brings the people to be spiritually poor, and that is the worst poverty and the most difficult to overcome.

THE GREATEST POVERTY

Great poverty! There is the child—the unborn child, a little child in the womb of the mother. And she doesn't want the child. She's afraid of the child. "If I have to feed one more child, if I have to educate one more child, I cannot buy another car, I cannot have a color television; therefore I must kill the child." Abortion—a murder! By whom? By the mother. By the doctor. How terrible. That little innocent child; that unwanted child; that aborted child. Great poverty! Great poverty. Right there, in the family. Maybe nobody is going to die in your family for a piece of bread. But there that little one has to die because you don't want it.

✦

For me that is the greatest poverty, that the country, that the nation, that you and I cannot afford to feed one more child, cannot afford to educate one more child, we cannot clothe one more child—the child must die. And this is what I think has brought so much unhappiness in the world—the cry of the unborn child.

LOVE OF GOD AND NEIGHBOR

Just think, God creates human life in His own image, for the same purpose for which He exists. God exists to love us—you and I and that little unborn child have been created for the same purpose: to love and to be loved. That's why I believe that abortion is an act against God Himself because they are trying to get rid of the presence of God, of the image of God.

GOD'S MERCY

I feel that in any abortion there are two killings, two murders: The child and the conscience of the mother. So let us pray that God will give them the grace to say sorry to God, to make peace in their own soul and to understand that God's forgiveness is much greater, God's mercy is much greater than their mistake, and let us show that tenderness and love for them so that they will understand, "Yes, God loves me, God has forgiven me," as that thing is very important, that they feel that they have been forgiven and that we give them a beautiful opportunity never to do it again and that they will be able to take that tender love and care to the little unborn child.

PAIN IN THE MOTHER'S HEART

The other day I was talking to a lady who had an abortion eight years ago, and what did she tell me? "Mother I have a pain in my heart. Every time whenever I see a child of eight years old, I always say my child would be eight years old. Last year, it was seven years old—it's a pain in my heart." She's a Hindu, non-Christian, who doesn't understand maybe—but deep down, Christian or non-Christian, that mother's love, that mother's instinct is there. Right up to the end of her life she will know, "I have killed my child, I have destroyed my child."

MY MOTHER

I thank my mother for wanting me. If she did not want me, I would not be a Missionary of Charity today. So I owe my mother deep gratitude and even the poor people owe my mother deep gratitude for wanting me.

GREATEST DESTROYER OF PEACE

Our children, we want them, we love them, but what of the other millions. Many people are very, very concerned with the children of India, with the children of Africa, where quite a number die, maybe of malnutrition, of hunger and so on, but millions are dying deliberately by the will of the mother. And this is what is the greatest destroyer of peace today, because if a mother can kill her own child, what is left for me to kill you and you to kill me? There is nothing between.

GET RID OF THE GIRLS

In Bombay and Delhi, they are practicing something new. They want to get rid of the girls, because when the girls get married, the parents have to give a very heavy dowry. So now they've found an instrument. After two months they can see if the child is a boy or girl, crippled or handicapped. According to calculation, soon there will be one hundred men to every twenty women, and the conclusion will be sin. Imagine the sin that will come from this; [it is] destroying family life. We must take the trouble to pray, and to bring back prayer into the families.

PERSUADING WITH LOVE

How to persuade a woman not to have an abortion? As always, we must persuade her with love and remind ourselves that love means [being] willing to give until it hurts. Jesus gave even His life to love us so the mother who is thinking of abortion should be helped to love, that is to give until it hurts—her plans or her free time—to respect the life of her child. The father of that child, whoever he is, must also give until it hurts. By abortion, the mother does not learn to love but kills even her own child to solve her problems, and by abortion, the father does not have to take any responsibility at all for that child he has brought into the world. That father is likely to put other women into the same trouble, so abortion just leads to more abortion. Any country that accepts abortion is not teaching its people to love but to use any violence to get what they want.

ADOPTION

We are fighting abortion by adoption. By care of the mother and adoption for her baby, we have saved thousands of lives. We have sent word to the clinics, hospitals and police stations: "Please don't destroy the child, we will take care, take the child." So always have someone tell the mothers in trouble, "Come, we will take care of you. We will get a home for your child." And we have a tremendous demand from couples who cannot have a child, but I never give a child to a couple who have done something not to have a child. Jesus said, "Anyone who receives a child in My name, receives Me."[27] By adopting a child, these couples receive Jesus, but by aborting a child, a couple refuses to receive Jesus. Please don't kill the child. I want the child. Please give me the child. I am willing to accept any child who would be aborted and to give that child to a married couple who will love the child and be loved by the child. From our children's home in Calcutta alone, we have saved over 3,000 children from abortion. These children have brought such love and joy to their adopted parents and have grown up so full of love.

---

[27] *Cf. Mt 18:5; Mk 9:37; Lk 9:48.*

GOD LOVES US . . .

If we remember that God loves us and that we can love others as He loves us, then America can become a sign of peace for the world. From here, a sign of care for the weakest of the weak—the unborn child—must go out to the world to become a burning light of justice and peace in the world. Then, really, you will be true to what the founders of this country stood for. God bless you all.

Broken Families

Just as love begins at home, evil also begins at home, sin begins at home.

THE WORLD IS UPSIDE DOWN

It is you and I who can give that joy of love, of peace in the family. Today, the world is upside-down, so much hatred, so much killing, so much unhappiness because love, peace, joy in the family is broken. Families do not pray any more. And because they do not pray, they cannot stay together. And if they do not stay together, they cannot love one another. And if a mother can kill her own child, then, what is left for other people [but] to kill each other.

LOVE BEGINS AT HOME

St. John said, "How can you say that you love God whom you do not see, when you do not love your neighbor whom you do see."[28] He uses a very strong word, he says, "You are a liar if you say you love God and you don't love your neighbor."[29] I think this is something we must all understand, that love begins at home. Today we see more and more that all the suffering in the world has started from the home. Today we have not time even to look at each other, to talk to each other, to enjoy each other, and still less to be what our children expect from us, what the husband expects from the wife, what the wife expects from the husband. And so more and more we are out of [our] homes and less and less we are in touch with each other.

LOVE IN THE FAMILY

I never forget my own mother. She used to be very busy the whole day, but as soon as the evening used to come, she used to move very fast to get ready to meet my father. At that time, we didn't understand, we used to smile, we used to laugh and used to tease her, but now I remember what a tremendous delicate love she had for him. Didn't matter what happened but she was ready there with a smile to meet him. Today we have no time. The father and mother are so busy, the children come home. There's no one to love them, to smile at them.

---

[28] Cf. *1 Jn 4:20.*
[29] Cf. *1 Jn 4:20.*

So Busy

In the world today married people are having great difficulties because there is not that deepening of intimate love for each other—they are busy with so many things.

·✦·

Nowadays we see many families—we are having many more broken homes. Why? Because old mothers, old fathers must go to an institution. Father is so busy, mother is so busy, the child comes home and there's no one there to love, to joke, to talk, to smile, and so on, and the child has to take to the streets. I don't know if you have seen that, but I have seen many, many young boys and girls in the streets of London, Rome and the United States. And our sisters are all over the place now and we find that terrible poverty and so this is something that you and I must understand—that love begins at home, love begins in our own community. There we see each other very often. We can neglect each other by not even having time for each other.

The Child, Where Love and Peace Begin

I was surprised in the West to see so many young boys and girls given to drugs, and I tried to find out why. Why is it like that when those in the West have so many more things than those in the East? And the answer was because there is no one in the family to receive them. Our children depend on us for everything—their security, their coming to know and love God. For all of this, they look to us with trust, hope and expectation but often father and mother are so busy. They have no time for their children. Or, perhaps they are not even married or have given up on marriage, so the children go to the streets and get involved in drugs and other things. We are talking of love of the child, which is where love and peace must begin.

PRAYING TOGETHER

One day I picked up a woman from a dustbin. She was burning with fever. I was sure that she was really on her last but she kept on saying, "I'm hurt, my son did this to me." I took her out, took her to our house. It took me a long time to pray with her, pray, pray to forgive her son. Long time it took me. If she was hungry for bread, I could have given her bread—finished. But it took me a long time to help her to say "I forgive my son." Thank God, just before she died, she said, "I forgive my son." See this terrible suffering. We have no idea, but I've seen it again and again even in rich countries—the loneliness is terrible. So I think it is today why we are gathered here together to pray for the sick, maybe we have this kind of people in our own family. Love begins at home. Love begins in our community. Love begins at home. And how does it begin? By praying together. For a family, for a community that prays together, stays together. And if we stay together, well naturally, we will love one another as God loves us. And those works of love are works of peace. In that family, naturally we live in peace.

ABUSING GIRLS

It is sad to know how impure love is spreading with the bad business that is going on—very young girls are involved. It is a business that hurts Jesus. The girls have no jobs, so they sell their bodies to live. Take care of these girls. They are in the big hotels, and every night they go there for the men to use them. Find out a little more where these girls are and how you can protect them; maybe we could get them jobs. They are using the night as a job; they are paid for being used. It depends on who is using them and according to that they are paid, some more and some less. I remember two or three girls came to me; they were forced to go to that place and when they went there and saw what was happening there—the man coming with the naked body, they jumped through the window and came to me. Help these girls, please do something for them, have a special place to protect them to live an ordinary life, and get them a real husband. We have beautiful work to do and not only girls, but women, too, are misused or given up by their husbands. Men have to pay a great price to get women. Take these people in your prayer and make real sacrifices for them. I have saved many girls in our Shishu Bhavan, and now they are settled in life. These who are misused are beautiful girls.

Where Are Our Old People Today?

I think this is where love begins—it begins at home. Where are our old people today? They are in institutions. Where is the unborn child? Where? Dead. Why? Because we do not want him. I find it great, great poverty that in the West, here in this country,[30] a child dies because we are afraid to feed one more child, to educate one more child. The child must die before it is born. Is that not great poverty? The fear of having to feed one more old person in the family means that that person must be put away, and yet, one day we too have to meet the Master. And what will be the answer? What will we answer to Him about that little child, that old father and mother, because they are His creation,

---

[30] *The United Kingdom.*

they are children of God. God has put all His love into creating that human life, and that is why we have no right to destroy it, especially we who understand that Christ has died for that life, to save that life. Christ has died and given everything for the child and if we really are Christians then for us, too, as the Hindu man put it, "It's a giving."

SACREDNESS OF MARRIAGE

Husband and wife, to remain faithful to each other . . . they bind themselves for life with the vow of marriage. Both sides have to remain pure and holy to bring joy in the family. The Church has arranged to have marriage and with the sacredness of marriage much peace and love has come to the family. It is not breakable and so we have the opportunity for our families to remain faithful to each other. Today there is much disturbance in the world. Divorce is terrible—it breaks that union. Let us pray that the families remain faithful to each other in love—one heart in the heart of Jesus and Mary.

※

Breaking the vow of marriage—to be faithful until death—is not only against true love, but it also hurts the children in a special way.

Our children depend on us for everything—their health, education, care, values, guidance, and above all—our love. But in some cases the mother and father have no time for their children, or the unity of the parents is broken so that the children leave home and wander here and there, and the number of such young people keeps increasing from day to day.

Showing What It Means to Love

If a father and mother are not willing to give until it hurts to be faithful to each other, and to their children, they are not showing their children what it means to love. And if the parents do not show their children what love is, who else is going to show them? These children will grow up to be spiritually poor, and this kind of poverty is much more difficult to overcome than material poverty.

It is true that many families have experienced much suffering because of violence, alcoholism, and abuses, which have often led to a breakdown in the relationship.

Slapdash Work

You need especially to pray, for in our society, the work is only the fruit of prayer . . . our love in action. If you are really in love with Christ, no matter how small the work, it will be done better, it will be wholehearted. If your work is slapdash, then your love for God is slapdash. Your work must prove your love.

What People Expect of Us

He has made Himself Bread of Life to satisfy my hunger for Him.[31] And then He has made Himself the hungry one for the Word of God, that I may satisfy His love for me. So, He's a hungry one also, just as we are hungry for Him. And so this will fulfill the hunger of God for

---

[31] Cf. *Jn* 6:35.

us and our hunger for God . . . That Word [has] to become flesh in each other first; that word must be lived here, that word must become flesh amongst you in love, in unity, in peace, in joy, and then you will be able to go out . . . That man sitting there drunk in the park by himself. I remember the first time when the sisters went—they're all dressed in white just like you and praying the Rosary—so they came near this man and this man saw them and said, "Oh, I'm not ready, I'm not ready, I'm not ready." And then the sisters went closer to him. "We are sisters, Jesus loves you, Jesus loves you." He said, "I'm not ready, you have come all the way from heaven, angels from heaven to take me. I'm not ready." He thought that the angels had come to take him. That's beautiful, that shows you what people expect of us. They don't expect us to be just like that.

NOT ENOUGH FAITH

Often we do our work "slapdash" because we do not have enough faith. If we truly believe we are doing it to Jesus we will do our work well. Sisters, pray, pray much to get faith, pray after Holy Communion, at adoration, pray to Our Lady to give you more faith. She will surely say, "Do what He tells you."[32]

Temptation

One day a man brought a baby to our gate and said the mother had run away. As I knew the girl, I went in search of her and found her and

---

[32] Cf. Jn 2:5.

I asked her how did it all happen, and she said to me something that sounds very strange, yet true: "I was standing on the verandah and the man came and the first day our eyes met—that's all. The second day again our eyes only met, but that look was a special look. Third day I deliberately went out—I wanted to see him. This went on for some days. Then one day he came inside and then came the day when I ran away with him." And the whole time, she never told her husband anything; that hiding made her go completely wrong. . . .

She did not tell her husband. She was hiding and got caught. These things have to come into our life, the need to be loved, the need to be wanted, but speak in time; don't be afraid—when you feel frightened, that is the temptation of the devil—speak in time.

HIDING IS ONE BIG LIE

The first thing when we begin to be impure is to hide. Satan is the father of lies.[33] He does nothing but tell lies. When we begin to do wrong—write a letter, talk to a man alone—we feel we should not tell. Hiding is one big lie. The moment you see yourself do that, be careful.

*

We can bluff ourselves so much, we can tell ourselves, "It doesn't matter, it is all right." But the very fact that you are doing it hidingly means it is not all right. That is a sign that it is wrong. If you want to know whether it is a sin or not, ask yourself, "If I was in the presence of Mother,[34] would I do it?" Then you will know if it is right or wrong.

---

[33] *Jn 8:44.*
[34] *Mother Teresa is referring to herself while speaking to her sisters.*

Evil

You don't know him. The devil very often comes as an angel of light[35]—he tried to bluff Jesus with beautiful scripture words[36]—because the closer you try to come to Jesus, the more he is after you. You should spend more time in prayer. Jesus is not waiting for you in the tabernacle but in the slums, touching, loving the poor.

Devil has very high ideas—very clever—even to Jesus he went, quoting from Holy Scripture.[37] He did not say one bad word—most beautiful words—to deceive even Jesus. He uses most beautiful things to deceive us, and St. Ignatius has a beautiful explanation: He will not bind us with a chain but a silk cord. He is much too clever.

✸

The devil tempts us not so much to do us harm as to destroy God in us. . . . We are nothing for him. He can do evil to so many but he is very anxious that in my soul he will destroy God, to separate us, because he knows Christ has died for us and he wants us to let that precious Blood be wasted in us. A hatred for God. . . . His hatred for God—he tries to make us share in that hatred by committing sin, by doing the evil action or evil desire. . . . There is no sin until we say yes. And that is the most beautiful part. Though he is the father of lies,[38] though he feels that he has got much power and yet he cannot make us say yes, not even once in the smallest thing, unless we want. . . . This is the wonderful part of God, given to each soul, that even the devil . . . all of hell cannot break you if you don't want. So sin comes only when we will

---

[35] *Cf. 2 Cor 11:14.*
[36] *Cf. Mt 4:1–11; Lk 4:1–13.*
[37] *Ibid.*
[38] *Jn 8:44.*

it. . . . The devil is like a roaring lion [that] goes round and round and round to see whom he can eat up.[39] Sin is the evil that destroys the temple of God within us, that tries to separate the soul from God. . . . And that perseverance with patience until he gets us to say yes to a sin, that is why I would give him the Nobel Prize for his persevering patience in evil.

Even in Little Ways

If we allow ourselves to be unfaithful in little things and say, "It doesn't matter," the day will come when we want to get rid of it, and we will be so blinded that we won't know how to. Jesus tells us this in one word when He describes the devil as the father of lies. He even came to Jesus as an angel of light to tempt Him in the wilderness. First he told Him, "You are hungry and that is a very good reason to turn stones into bread!"[40] But, if Jesus had done that, He would have been placing material things above the will of God. "My food is to do the will of the one who sent Me."[41] And what did Jesus answer him? "Man does not live on bread alone, but on every word that comes from the mouth of God."[42] Even a stupid man would say that Jesus had the right to change stones into bread. He had been fasting for forty days, and nobody could possibly object or complain about it. Maybe if Jesus had given in, the devil would have tempted Him a little more. When He was hanging on the Cross and they were jeering at Him to "Come down from the Cross for you are in great pain,"[43] He might have come down if He had said "yes" the first time.

---

[39] *Cf. 1 Pt 5:8.*
[40] *Cf. Mt 4:1–11; Lk 4:1–13.*
[41] *Cf. Jn 4:34.*
[42] *Cf. Mt 4:4; Lk 4:4.*
[43] *Cf. Mt 27:40; Mk 15:30.*

THE FATHER OF LIES

We are the tabernacle of the living God. We must keep the heart pure. How does our heart become impure? By pride, by lies, selfishness, insincerity, especially want of sincerity. I have looked through the life of those who have left our Society and always the cause is only want of sincerity. The devil is the father of lies.[44] He has infinite patience. He is the most helpless creature. He says a thousand lies to make you say one lie, and he has endless patience that he keeps on waiting and waiting until you have given in. You and I will be tired but he will not give up, he will come again and again with temptation. Unless I say "yes" he cannot touch me. He can say nothing unless I say, "I want." Little Flower has explained it very beautifully—the helplessness and the miserableness of the devil. She had a dream, and she saw the devil on a barrel. He was very strong, and this little child was looking at the devil. The more she was looking at him the more he was afraid, trembling, and did not know where to hide. When she realized that he was afraid of her, she looked at him more closely. Then he disappeared, so she writes how afraid and helpless the devil was. The same story applies to us also. He can do nothing unless we want. These are stupid examples but they are very living examples. You all had temptations, no human being can pass through life without temptations. Temptations are not sins. Sin comes only when you want; that's why I taught you yesterday to say, "I don't want it."

---

[44] *Jn 8:44.*

SLY

The devil will never tell you to steal something big. He is very *chalak*.[45] He will tell, "You take only ten naya paisa from the traveling tin." Next day a little more—step by step. He will never tell you the first day to take ten rupees, but the day will come when he will tell you to take a big amount from Mother's table. Just as we do small things with great love so we do small things with great hatred in our hearts.

NO ONE CAN TOUCH YOU

The whole of hell can come near you, but no one can force you, no one can touch you. There is the story of a pilgrim who comes to a great big city. He sees one small devil there sleeping and wakes him up to ask him why he is not working. The devil replies that the people there are so wicked, there is no need for him to tempt them. Then, traveling outside the city, the pilgrim came to a small house where there were a lot of devils outside—hundreds—and all were so busy; the pilgrim asked them why. They told him that inside was one hermit whom they had been told to try to catch for a second at least, but they could not succeed because this man was fervent in prayer and pure. No devil can touch me if I don't want. There is the devil, Jesus said, and he is the father of lies.[46] He will tell you one thousand lies to make you commit one sin.

---

[45] *Bengali "cunning."*
[46] *Jn 8:44.*

Fighting Temptation

You may be saint or sinner. Both have temptations. It is also something good. We have to fight—to fight the temptation like Our Lord,[47] with confidence and humility. With Him I conquer. With Him I can do all things.[48] God will help us. Alone we cannot do anything. Pride helps the devil. The devil does not come as he did to Our Lord—with the temptation in the desert, showing mountains and all the treasures of the world.[49] For us there are small things: To say prayers beautifully, to take holy water with reverence. The devil makes us think, "What is the use of always asking?" For the religious, the devil uses a silk thread to catch them, not a rope. Ropes there are also. If you think you are on a pedestal, you are wrong. [There is a] story: a saint saw in a room all the doors closed, only one door had a little devil sitting on [it], fast asleep. When he awoke, the saint asked him whether he had nothing to do. The little devil answered, "Oh, in this beautiful house I easily can manage myself, because the people here always do bad things." . . . In my heart [there] is only one seat vacant—for God—and nobody else. Temptation is like fire in which gold is purified. So we have to go through this fire. The temptations are allowed by God. The only thing we have to do is not to give in. If I say, "I do not want it," I am safe. There will be temptations against purity, faith, against my vocation. See St. Thérèse, she made so many acts of faith. God is near us, in our hearts; our temptations are coming . . . If we love our vocation, we will be tempted. Then we grow also in sanctity. Temptations we have to fight for the love of God. . . .

---

[47] Cf. *Mt 4:1–11; Lk 4:1–13.*
[48] Cf. *Phil 4:13.*
[49] Cf. *Mt 4:1–11; Lk 4:1–13.*

MARY WILL HELP US

When temptation comes, uncharitableness comes, who will help us? Mary. "Give me your heart, so beautiful, so pure, so immaculate, so full of love and humility, that I may receive Jesus in the Bread of Life, love Him as you loved Him and serve Him in the distressing disguise of the poorest of the poor. I want to be holy as you are. I want to belong only to Jesus." Make your own prayer with conviction. It will change your life. Somebody comes to talk to you against charity, or to tempt you to impurity . . . keep yourself only all for Jesus through Mary.

USE THE ROSARY

We must use the rosary like arms, like weapons against the evils—to fight—to spread the Kingdom of God; like a good soldier—to fight right in front.

KEEP BUSY

The Chinese have a very good proverb: "The bird of sorrow has to fly about but see that it does not nestle in your head." Yes, we have to suffer and, since we have to suffer, let us suffer cheerfully. The ups and downs of life must come our way, but we must not let ourselves be affected by them in our search for sanctity. Don't be surprised at your failure. We must connect every bit of our life with Holy Communion; all our failures, our weakness, our pride and our misery. See that, in spite of being tempted, you are not conquered.

WHEN SOMEONE BLAMES YOU

Remember well, Sisters, what I am saying to you now. Whenever someone blames you or you want to blame somebody, remember just this one thing: examine yourself, "Am I innocent?" Then don't give excuses, "I was doing this or that." If I have the love of silence, then immediately if what is said to me is true, I will say, "I am sorry, Sister." If it is not true, then keep silence with a humble heart. If you know you are not lazy and somebody calls you lazy, it is a beautiful chance to be humble of heart.

Learning to Forgive

"Forgive . . . as we forgive . . ."[50] What a lie to say "forgive" when you don't forgive. When you come to that part in the Our Father, stop and ask yourself, "Is it true what I am saying?" I think Jesus suffered much more just hanging from that Cross. He said, "Learn from me for I am meek and humble of heart."[51] You cannot be meek, you cannot be humble, if you don't forgive. It is not necessary to have a big thing to destroy us. . . . If I'm not able to see God—why?

BITTERNESS IN MY HEART

During this one year, let us examine ourselves and see since when have I had this bitterness in my heart. It can be from my childhood, from my

---

[50] *Cf. Mt 6:12.*
[51] *Mt 11:29.*

Novitiate, in my professed life, let us find it out and empty our hearts completely. We can do that by a sincere general confession and all bitterness is poured out and then there will be only a pure heart remaining. Find out exactly by whom and when you were made bitter and when and how many lives did you make bitter by your lack of love and unkindness, by your words and attitudes—and again I repeat, empty your hearts of it all by a good general confession.

EVEN CHRIST WAS REJECTED

Yesterday a young man came to see me. He was deeply hurt because he was rejected by his family. He just could not forgive. Then I told him, "The grace of God is not in you as long as you do not forgive." The same is true for each one of us—the grace of God is not in us as long as we do not forgive. "But, I pray much," he said. Yes, he can pray much, but there is no grace of God in him as long as he does not forgive. Then I asked him, "Have you tried to compare yourself with Christ, who was rejected all the time by His very own people."[52] Then he put his head down and said that he never had done so. You all must go through that pattern of Christ's life and then you must compare yours with His life. How many times you have been hurt and you still have that bitterness in you? Examine yourselves and see how you were in your past lives at home and how you used to be hurt and be bitter. If you see well, you follow the same pattern of life even now; that is human nature in you. I want each one of you to see this during this time and empty your hearts of all bitterness.

---

[52] Cf. *Mt 13:53–57; Mk 6:2–4; Lk 4:28–30; Mt 27:15–26; Mk 15:6–15.*

LEARNING TO FORGIVE

One day a sister came to my room. . . . She said terrible things. I listened. I was feeling so bad for her, to have allowed herself to speak like that. We cannot hurt Jesus, but Jesus feels bad because we hurt ourselves. So I came to her to give her a chance to say she's sorry. No apology came. I waited in my room. Nobody came. Again I found an excuse to ask her to do something. No apology came. Again I went to my room, praying, "Jesus give her the grace to say she's sorry." Before the fourth time she came and apologized. You must realize that. When a sister is doing something to you, don't turn to yourself. Turn to her. She is hurting herself, hurting Jesus in herself. You must learn to forgive. You must know that we need forgiveness. She realized this afterwards. It was a terrible humiliation for her when she realized it. I could have been harsh. That word could have remained in her all her life. I love Jesus. It helped me to fall in love. Humility is a great thing. If you want to be a true MC, learn from Jesus to be meek and humble,[53] and add one more word, *pure*, meek and humble. You will see a sister with new eyes. She is hurting Jesus.

WHEN WE CAN'T FORGIVE

Sometimes we can't forgive, even once: "She has called me bad names." Jesus could destroy everything with one word. He forgave.[54] Non-forgiving can destroy you for life. We keep on thinking of that word that sister said but we need to acknowledge our sin, to be able to forgive. We must forgive—don't wait. Is there unforgiveness in my

---

[53] *Cf. Mt 11:29.*
[54] *Cf. Lk 23:34.*

heart? It's an obstacle for life. When it's too late, nothing can be done.

My brother had a little pimple here and within a short time cancer had become a big root—after just three months. The same thing happens for us with unforgiveness. Don't believe the devil. Get it out. Maybe you have a grudge against your superior, maybe against your sisters, maybe against your parents. As a novice, as a junior, the devil will come to you with very beautiful ideas. Don't allow the devil to cheat you. Father, forgive me.

One [patient] was struggling to die: he could not die! A sister asked: "Is there something troubling you, something worrying you? Is there something hurting you?"—"Yes, I cannot die until I ask pardon to my father." So the sister found out the father; his father came. The father: "My beloved child," the son: "Father, forgive me." Father and son forgiving each other, kissing and hugging one another. After two hours he died. See how wonderful. . . .

BITTERNESS AND PRIDE

There isn't that total forgiveness. Show me a bitter sister and I will show you a proud sister. A bitter sister is always a proud sister also. Bitterness and pride are twin sisters—moodiness goes with it. A humble sister will not be bitter nor moody. Examine yourselves.

DO YOU HAVE ANY BITTERNESS AGAINST SOMEONE?

There is so much suffering and unhappiness because of unforgiveness. . . . Remember, Sisters, in the Our Father we say, "Forgive us our sin as we forgive."[55] If you do not forgive, you are not forgiven.

---

[55] *Cf. Mt 6:12; Lk 11:4.*

Look deep down in your heart. Is there any bitterness against any person? Then try to find that person or write to that person—maybe a sister or a poor person or someone at home. Forgive; otherwise you are not free to love Jesus with an undivided love. Do not keep any bitterness in your heart. There are so many sisters who can't forgive. Some say, "I forgive, but I can't forget." Confession is the forgiveness—the kind of forgiveness that God gives, and we must learn that kind of forgiveness. So many years ago someone said this or did that, and so I say, "She said this, she . . . and she . . . and she . . ." In one place there was a priest who was against the bishop and priests for some reason. There was so much bitterness in his speech each time I visited him and he said to me, "I will not forgive. I won't." This time when I went, I told him, "This is your chance; ask sorry from your bishop. That is the only word the bishop wants from you." And I was praying and the sisters were all praying inside. When I finished the prayer, he said, "Mother Teresa, give me paper." So, I gave him the paper, and I was so happy. I took him to the bishop and gave the paper—otherwise he might change his mind—and I told him, "This is not enough; say, 'I forgive'"—and he did.

SURRENDERING BITTERNESS

Sometime ago, a Lutheran lady minister came to Calcutta—all the way from Sweden. I think she is a teacher of theology. We talked and she told me that from childhood she had hated her father and never spoke with him because he murdered her mother. Hatred had stayed and grown with her. I told her, there is only one thing to do—go back and say you are sorry. For a long time, she could not surrender her bitterness. Suddenly she obeyed and went straight to her father and said, "I love you . . ." Now she takes care of him. She told me she never

experienced such joy as when her father embraced her. See sisters,
God forgave her, forgave him, only when she surrendered.

ONLY WE KNOW WE NEED FORGIVENESS

Remember the prodigal son? "I will arise and go to my Father."[56] Only
when we know we need forgiveness, can we forgive. You cannot say
the Our Father truthfully—you are telling a lie; examine yourself and
see, is there something there you can't forgive? Something there still
hurting? Look for that person. A sister wrote a beautiful letter to a
sister who hurt her. If you find it difficult to see Jesus in the tabernacle, to see Jesus in the poor, to see Jesus in your superior—get it
[the resentment] out—because you cannot love Christ with undivided
love in chastity. It is a lie. . . . The other day somebody was talking of
persecution—of going to jail. And this person said, "Oh, I am ready."
And after a little while somebody said something—three words—and
this person flared up. And yet he was ready to be persecuted!

I WANT, I WILL PROTECT LIFE

I want, I will protect life because that life is created by God for greater
things: To love and to be loved. And for that little one, Jesus has died
on the Cross and He died because He loved—His Precious Blood
for this little one. And so let us bring the joy of loving from all your
heart and . . . the best way to do it is to help these young mothers, I
call them young mothers, unwed mothers, but they have something to
share with you. They give you a chance to share the joy of loving and

---

[56] *Cf. Lk 15:18.*

that all you do for them . . . and go in search of them and when you find them show tender love for them, because "Whatever you do to the least," Jesus said, "you did it to me."[57]

Love Each Other with a Clean Heart

For a young man to really love a young woman, and a young woman to love a young man, is beautiful. It is a gift of God. But, love with a clean heart. Love each other with a virgin love. Love each other by keeping a virgin and pure body and soul, so that on the day you get married, as the Scripture says: "Husband and wife will cleave to each other, and they become one."[58] So that on that day of cleaving, you can give each other a virgin heart, a virgin body, a virgin soul. This is the gift of God for you.

Purity

I was thinking about little St. Agnes[59]—she was only a child—she was executed for the love of Jesus; she is an angel of purity. Each one of us can make a prayer to her asking her to help, guide, and protect us. She led an ordinary life, nothing special, but she had a tremendous love for purity. We must make a little prayer to St. Agnes—she was only thirteen when she died; what courage she had—I wonder if we would have that courage—she allowed them to cut her head [off] to protect her purity. She did not allow anyone to touch her and misuse her purity.

---

[57] *Cf. Mt 25:40.*
[58] *Cf. Gen 2:24; Mt 19:5; Mk 10:7; Eph 5:31.*
[59] *St. Agnes of Rome (c. 291–c.304) virgin, martyr, who, according to tradition, suffered martyrdom at the age of twelve or thirteen during the reign of the Roman emperor Diocletian.*

BE THE FIRST ONE TO SAY SORRY

If you are wrong then always be the first one to say sorry. In my home my father had a hot temper; sometimes he used to say some hot words to my mother. But always after a few hours, my mother would dress up and anxiously wait for him to come back and as soon as he was back—"How are you?" and a meal was ready, and so on. That was the way she said sorry and made up. If we can do all that in the world, then why not here?

※

Today write it down on a piece of paper how you have been in your past communities, then take it to adoration and read it to Jesus and tell Jesus, "Jesus, this is all I can give and I am your spouse." Always have the courage to say sorry. It does not matter to whom—be it to a grown-up person, a sister, or a child, or to Mother—once you know you have hurt someone, be always the first one to say sorry. Only humble sisters can say sorry. We hurt Jesus by our sin, by moving away from Him. We cannot hurt Jesus in the other person; we should feel bad if they turn away from Jesus, because in that way they hurt themselves very badly. For you, my Sisters, I do not want that you do not sin because of fear of hell or purgatory, but because you love Jesus. There is a hell and there is a purgatory, there is, but that is not the reason for not sinning. Remember great St. Teresa was afraid to sin for fear of hell. She is a doctor of the Church and a saint and what are we? So today, pray at adoration about all that I have told you. Empty your hearts of all bitterness. A pure heart always sees God.[60]

---

[60] *Cf. Mt 5:8.*

If You Have Been Unkind

How have you treated the poor? Were you harsh? Unkind? Rude? Pulling? Pushing? How have you treated the poor? If you have failed, then go to confession and say sorry and try to make up to Jesus. To have this fourth vow means to have a very delicate conscience. If you have been harsh, unkind, rude or anything—then ask pardon from the poor. It may be you are like that at home with your sisters—then ask pardon. Bring all the poor you have worked with here today before the tabernacle. You cannot go to each of them to say sorry, so bring them all here before the tabernacle and say sorry to each one of them whom you may have hurt. You cannot say sorry directly so say sorry to each of them in your mind, in your heart, in your spirit—bring them here before Jesus and say sorry to each of them . . . ask pardon . . . and make a resolution not to do so again.

Otherwise Keep Silent

If I am guilty say sorry—otherwise keep silent; beautiful. Humility is learned by accepting humiliations. In Our Lady we have a most beautiful example. She knew St. Joseph was hurt.[61]

Reconciliation

Jesus said if you are going up to the altar to offer sacrifice and you remember that you have something against your brother, go back and be reconciled with him first.[62] Same thing for you—don't go to bed

---

[61] *Cf. Mt 1:18–22.*
[62] *Cf. Mt 5:23–24.*

until you have said sorry to that sister or gone to confession if it is possible. Let your life, my life, be so transparent that they can "look up and see only Jesus" and so you will grow in the likeness of Jesus.

BEFORE YOU GO TO BED

If you hurt a sister, before you go to bed say sorry. Or if a sister has hurt you, don't become moody, but go to Jesus and say, "Jesus, I love you. Go into her heart."

HOW JESUS FELT

One day a sister did something terrible. I never said a word to her, but I waited . . . thinking she will come and say sorry. But she did not come, so I went after her—but no response. I found some other reason to go to her. Still no response. I did not know how she could remain in that sinful state. I felt sorry for her, so I understood how Jesus felt when we refused Him. But He is always waiting. God's mercy is greater than our sin. God has created me for greater things because He loves me.

WHAT IS GOING TO CHANGE MY HEART?

Change of place is not going to change my heart. What is going to change my heart? My love for Jesus. From you I want only to be really only all for Jesus. Let us ask Our Lady to help us during this day to really open your heart to Jesus. By yourself you don't have the courage. Confess that. Take the root out. You will find Jesus, and when you find Jesus you will find peace, love, unity.

ASKING PARDON

Let us respond to the tremendous thirst of God by our loving trust in His love for us and total surrender to His will with joy. Let us turn to God with deep faith and love, repenting for our sins and begging for His mercy. Let us turn to each other also in love and trust, asking pardon for all the hurt we have caused others and forgiving all for the hurt we have received.

Confession

Jesus had compassion on the sinners. That sinful woman standing before Jesus—Jesus did not condemn her.[63] That is confession. I, too, need to be forgiven. Confession is nothing but standing before Jesus like that sinful woman because I have caught myself in sin.

HOW THE LORD GOES AFTER US!

How the Lord goes after us! He still wants us to be holy in spite of all our sins. To the sinner He says, "Go in peace, but do not sin anymore."[64] Peter made such a big mistake, and yet Jesus said, "Do you love Me?"[65] See Sisters, this is that love of God.

---

[63] Cf. Jn 8:1–11.
[64] Cf. Jn 8:11.
[65] Cf. Jn 21:15–18.

I WILL RISE

See, that prodigal son could go back to his father only when he said, "I will rise, I will go, I will tell. I will tell my father that I am a sinner, that I am sorry."[66] He couldn't tell his father, "I'm sorry" until he took that step, "I will go." He knew that in his home there was love, there was kindness—that his father loved him. Our Lady will help us to do that. Let us do it today. Rise and go to the Father and tell Him that we are not worthy to be here—to be His own.

DO NOT BE ASHAMED

Do not be ashamed and think, "Oh, what will father[67] think of it?" Father is there to take away your sins from you. We tell our sins to God and obtain forgiveness from God. God takes away our sins. We must be simple like a child, "I shall arise and go to my Father."[68] And what does God do? "Bring the robe, the ring, the shoes, the fatted calf"[69] . . . and see the great joy. Why? Because "My son was dead and has come back to life."[70] Same for us; but we must have that simplicity of a child and go to confession. If you have problems with your chastity, Sisters, always be faithful to your confession. In the world it is happening, even among nuns and priests, not going to confession for five or six years. And what happens? When they fall, they leave and go. So never say tomorrow for going to confession. That tomorrow will become another tomorrow and another one, and it will never

---

[66] Cf. Lk 15:11–32.
[67] Refers to the priest hearing confession.
[68] Cf. Lk 15:18.
[69] Cf. Lk 15:20.
[70] Cf. Lk 15:24.

come. Who can help you to prepare yourself for your confession well? Only Our Lady—never prepare without her; always go to Our Lady. God has been so good to us by giving her as our Mother.

WE CAN BE SINNERS WITHOUT SIN

During the Stations, when you are facing the Passion of Christ, look at the Cross. I can find my sins on the Cross. We can be sinners with sin and we can be sinners without sin. Are you really in love with Christ? Can you face the world? Are you so convinced that "Nothing can separate me from Him?"[71] "Cut me to pieces and every piece will be yours."

Our vocation is not the work; the fidelity to humble works is our means to put our love into action. Yesterday, a man living in sin shook, shook—and died. It can happen to any of us. Are we ready? Have I that conviction that as an MC, I am a carrier of God's love—a spouse of Jesus crucified?

The beginning of holiness is a good confession. We are all sinners. There is holiness without sin—for we must become sinners without sin. Our Lady did not have to say, "Pray for us sinners." I am a sinner with sin. When I make a good confession I become a sinner without sin. How do I become a sinner with sin? When I deliberately say that word something tells me, "Don't say." That is why we have confession. I hope you make good use of confession every week.

---

[71] Cf. Rom 8:38–39.

THE PASSION OF JESUS

What is the Passion of Jesus? We say we hurt Jesus through our sins. No, Jesus does not get hurt. It is we who hurt ourselves. And Jesus is hurt because we do not love. He feels for us. The hurt that we cause ourselves by sin, He has taken on Himself. Before, I also used to think that way [that we hurt Jesus through our sins], but now I can understand how Jesus feels when we sin.

DO NOT BE AFRAID

Whenever you feel that you have done something, do not be afraid. He is a loving Father. God's mercy is much greater than we can imagine. Remember, He has instituted the sacrament of confession so that our hearts [can] be pure and full of love. We go to confession a sinner with sin and we come from confession a sinner without sin. What a wonderful gift of God to us all.

STAY CLOSE TO JESUS

What is the meaning of "precious"? It means special. When somebody special is coming—your mother or father—you will prepare for a long time beforehand what you will say, what you will do, and so on. We are special to God just like that. He is waiting for you to come to Him in prayer. He wants to honor you by filling you with His presence. How can anything or anybody divide that? . . . If we are really pure, how can we allow anything to separate us from Jesus?

✦

Only sin prevents love from growing. If you commit sin, let us use confession. Only see God, speak to God, love God. A clean heart is very close to Jesus, it can love Him, serve Him. If you neglect confession, sin becomes old, and then we don't bother about it. Many priests go for daily confession. Purity of heart is the best place for Jesus. Take the trouble to have weekly confession. If we stay close to Jesus it will protect us from sin. . . . Sin is a wall that separates us. A free heart can love God, serve Him, be only all for Him. "I will, I want, with God's blessing be holy." We must avoid sin, even small ones . . . it's very dangerous. The worm doesn't need a big hole, and the hole becomes bigger and bigger and then it's all rotten, then it becomes more and more difficult. Let us always say, "I am very sorry," a good act of contrition.

BEING EMPTY

We empty ourselves of all selfishness to enable God to fill us with His love.

I say it again and again, as I have said it so often, that even Almighty God cannot fill what is already full. We must be empty if we want God to fill us with His fullness. Our Lady had to be empty before she could be full of grace. She had to declare she was the handmaid of the Lord, before God could fill her.[72] So also we must be empty of all pride, all jealousy, selfishness, and so on, before God can fill us with His love.

---

[72] *Cf. Lk 1:38.*

I NEED TO BE FORGIVEN

Look at the Cross. My sins are here. There, looking at the Cross, we know how deep our sins are. Jesus said to Saint Margaret Mary, "My love for you was not a joke but something personal." The Cross in the Motherhouse near the staircase is a wonderful examination of conscience. . . . Do you really look at the Cross?—Not in imagination—take the Cross in your hands and meditate. . . . Do I have compassion? Jesus had compassion on the sinners. That sinful woman standing before Jesus—Jesus did not condemn her.[73] That is confession. I, too, need to be forgiven. Confession is nothing but standing before Jesus like that sinful woman because I have caught myself in sin. . . .

In our Constitutions, we have "I will arise and go to my Father."[74] . . . Confession—an expression of our need for forgiveness, not discouragement. Confession was not instituted on Good Friday but on Resurrection Sunday, so it is a means of joy. It was not established as a torture, but as a means of joy. In Rome, our sisters found a man in one of those houses, terribly dirty. They cleaned his house and washed him, but he did not say a word. When they finished everything, he said, "You have brought God in my life, now bring the priest also." After sixty years he made a good confession. See, Sisters, how wonderful—that humble work brought God into his life.

We need the priest to make that connection. If the main switch is not working, the whole city is in darkness. . . . The whole city is grumbling, especially those who have air-conditioning. How pure the priest must be to pour the Precious Blood on me, to wash my sins away . . . You must never doubt that word, "I absolve you, I free you." Even if that priest is a bad priest, he has the power to forgive you, to

---

[73] *Cf. Jn 8:1–11.*
[74] *Cf. Lk 15:18.*

make you free. Maybe it might require an act of humility from us, but he is still the switch, the connection.

A REAL JOY

Confession must be a real joy. I must not neglect confession. . . . I must go to confession with love because I have an opportunity to make my soul clean, to become pure. Confession is coming face to face with God. When I die, I have to come face to face with God, but now I have the chance to go to Him with sin and come away without sin. . . .

Examine your confessions. Do you make them with a real desire, with real sincerity to say the things as they are, or do you say "half-half,"[75] hiding something or taking away something? The devil is very clever. Jesus has said, "Do not be afraid."[76] If there is something that is worrying you, say it in confession and once you have said it, do not be busy with that anymore because sometimes, after many months, the devil is after us until he breaks our love for confession. It is not meant to be a torture. . . .

Confession is not a place where you have to stay hours and hours and hours. Confession is Jesus and I, and nobody else. Remember this for life. Don't make confession a place of talk, but a place to confess my sins and receive absolution. Let us thank God and let us never miss confession.

---

[75] *Saying only half of the things.*
[76] *Cf. Jn 14:27; Mt 10:28; Lk 12:4.*

DON'T WASTE TIME

Don't waste time on what had happened before. If something is hurting you inside, preoccupying you, get it out, make a good confession. Don't be busy with this or that, even with your [novice] mistress[77]—the baby does not examine what is given. Just be busy with Jesus and use your time to be alone and stay with Jesus. It will never come again.

A SACRAMENT OF LOVE

We call it penance, but really it is a sacrament of love, a sacrament of forgiveness. That is why it should not be a place of talking for long hours about our difficulties. It is a place where I allow Jesus to take away from me everything that divides, that destroys. When there is a gap between me and Christ and my love is divided, then anything can come to fill up the gap. If you really want to understand the love of Christ for us, go to confession. Be very simple and childlike in confession: "Here I am as a child—going to my Father." If a child is not yet spoilt and has not learnt to tell lies, he will tell out everything. This is what I mean by "childlike," and this is what we must imitate in confession.

Confession is a beautiful act of great love—only to confession can we go as sinners with sin and come out as sinners without sin. We don't measure our love by mortal sin or venial sin, but when we fall, confession is there to cleanse us. Even if there is a big gap, don't be ashamed. Still go as a child.

---

[77] *The sister in charge of formation.*

THE NEED FOR CONFESSION

There is a lady who is coming to Mass here every morning. She was a drunkard until something came into her life. Then she took the next step—to come all the way from the U.S.A. Now there she is every morning, even before we are there. She puts plenty of rouge color on her nails, on her lips, on her cheeks and I asked her why she puts so much. She told me something really surprising: "Mother, it is all part of the self-discipline that I am trying to practice. I have a set time every day for doing my nails, for putting on my make-up, for getting ready to come to Mass. I have to keep myself busy all the time." Today as I was speaking to her, I said that it was very beautiful that she had started attending daily Mass, but what about going to confession? She asked me why she should go. She felt no need to go to confession. So I pointed out to her that when she goes for confession it is as a sinner with sin but when she comes out, it is as a sinner without sin. "Oh," she said, "then I want to go for confession. But I need help to prepare myself." So she is coming tonight for Adoration, and I will help prepare for tomorrow's confession. When she got up to leave, she looked so happy she had made the decision to confess her sins and already she was experiencing the freedom, the joy, of that peace. She had accepted that she was a sinner with sin, and wanted God in her life.

THANK YOU, JESUS

I read the other day, Jesus said, "Give me your sins." What for me is the greatest sin is that we do not trust Jesus, and do not believe in His Word. Let us look straight to Him and say sorry—that sorry with conviction. And after that one word, "Thank you, Jesus, for taking away my sins." After Holy Communion—"Thank you, Jesus, for taking my sins without anything remaining"—that tender love.

NOT TO THE PRIEST, BUT TO JESUS

Why do you make a general confession? Not because I am doubting but to make that connection; to realize how good the Lord God has been to me—the goodness of God. I come to the confessional as a sinner, but when I go out I am a sinner without a sin. We make our sincere and humble confession not to the priest, but to Jesus.

PENANCE

What is the meaning of penance? Reason: first, share in the Passion of Christ, it's not the number, but how much love I put. Second, to make reparation for my sins. Who will make that reparation? If I have that thirst, I'll do penance with my whole heart. I want to do. I refused Jesus something [so] I want to do reparation. Because we choose, it's a greater act of love. Now I want. One sister—her father had a wound on the head and it hurt her, she offered it to Jesus. "My sins were His pain. My sins were the cause of the crown of thorns. I will do penance with the conviction, I share the Passion of Christ."

RESTITUTION

According to seventh commandment[78]—as a Christian I cannot steal. If I steal from a poor person it is mortal sin, also according to knowledge

---

[78] *Dt 5:19; Ex 20:15.*

and intention. When I go to confession I must not only say the sin but make restitution—either in whole or by part or at least by promise—and we are bound by that promise, otherwise Father cannot give absolution.

Humility

The way to learn from Our Lord to be meek and humble—be meek with each other. With courtesy, approach each other. We need that courtesy because we are human beings. When we have learned meekness and humility, then the other [courtesy] will come. "Love one another as I have loved you."[79] How did Jesus love others? How did He give? How will we love by giving? Best way to show thanks to God is to promise: We are going to learn to be meek. Then God will say, "This is my beloved."

How Do You Learn Humility?

The whole Gospel—if we read it carefully, prayerfully—tells us to learn this one lesson from the heart of Jesus: to be meek and humble. How will you learn humility? Not by reading plenty of books, or by listening to many words, but by accepting humiliations. In everybody's life there are continually throughout the day many of these beautiful gifts—chances to show our love for Jesus in those little things, these little humiliations. And if we are humble, we are pure in heart, then we will see the face of God in prayer and so be able to see

---

[79] *Cf. Jn 13:34.*

God in one another. It is a full circle . . . Everything is connected. The fruit of our prayer is that love for Jesus—proved by accepting little humiliations with joy.

HUMILITY IS TRUTH, NOT HIDING

Humility is not hiding talents—"I cannot do that, I cannot do this"— but humility is truth. The only thing Our Lord asked us to learn was to be meek and humble of heart[80]; not that He asked us to learn to be poor or obedient and so on, but to be meek and humble. Meekness first, because meekness is with each other. In some languages meekness is translated as sweetness, kindness. See how beautiful and meaningful is meekness. Humility is what Jesus came to teach us: the humility of the Heart of God. Humility cannot be learned from books. Humility is learned from humiliations accepted.

IN HER HUMILITY, SHE KEPT SILENT

At the Annunciation the angel is saying, "You'll be the Mother of God," and she is saying that she is the handmaid, the servant of the Lord.[81] Then she, who has been chosen as the Queen of heaven and earth, she doesn't go off to search for a palace and for glory, or even to tell St. Joseph—the first thing she does, as the Mother of God, is, [to go] in haste to serve Elizabeth. Then after three months when she returns to Nazareth,[82] she sees the distress and doubt of St. Joseph, but she waits for God to show the way. All that St. Joseph can say is,

---

[80] Cf. Mt 11:29.
[81] Cf. Lk 1:26–38.
[82] Cf. Lk 1:39–52.

"That is not my child." He doesn't try to judge her or expose her to the people, but decided to quietly break off from her.[83] Heaven had to intervene and tell him whose child it was. Our Lady never tried to excuse herself or to impress St. Joseph with the story of the angel. In her humility, she kept silent. So we must never tell a lie, but very often we cannot reveal the whole truth—then it is better to keep silent, since silence can never be corrected. This can be very difficult, but see Our Lady—she did it because she trusted the Lord.

If [you] are humble, not even the whole of hell can touch you. Humility is the destroyer of pride. Humility is the destroyer of the devil.

JESUS UNWANTED

No one has been more unwanted than Jesus Himself. We will never experience what Jesus experienced. We read on the first page of St. John's Gospel: "And the Word came into the world, among His own and His own did not receive Him."[84] Read carefully: all the four Gospels speak of Jesus being unwanted by His own people. I think in all the crowd of people, only Our Lady understood Jesus, wanted Jesus. And if we are the spouses of Jesus Crucified, we must share that. We must become more and more like Him by accepting humiliations and accepting them with joy. Today I have an opportunity. Sisters, it is wonderful if we get into the habit: when humiliations come, grab the chance. Say you are blamed for something you have not done. Naturally the words come right up, and you answer back. Instead, wait a second; if it is true what Sister says, if your heart is clean, if there is no sin in your heart, immediately you have the answer. If the answer is

---

[83] Cf. Mt 1:19.
[84] Cf. Jn 1:11.

yes, say: "Sorry Sister, I will not do it again." If it is not true, grab the chance, Sisters. It is a wonderful humiliation, and that humiliation will make you a humble sister. Mother can sit here all day and all night and talk about humility—and you will probably feel tired and will sleep—and you can read all the books about humility, but still you will not be humble. But when those little humiliations come, grab them. You must experience the joy of being a humble sister. Be humble like Mary.

ZACCHEUS

Zaccheus[85] was a man, a rich man, a tax collector and he was a [well-] known man. He was very anxious to see Jesus. He could not see Him, and one day he realized, "I am small," and he did something that a small child would do, and that act of humility obtained for him the grace. Jesus came right near the tree. That's why you and I, too, must realize that we are small to desire to do small things with great love. When Little Flower died and she was going to be canonized, everybody asked for what will Holy Father canonize her . . . and Holy Father wrote one sentence—"I will canonize her because she did ordinary things with extraordinary love." Small things with great love. So, we have a chance to be canonized also to do only small things because we as religious are souls totally consecrated to Jesus, to cling to that little-ness, to that emptiness, to that smallness. Jesus, to prove His Father's love for the world, He became so small, so helpless.

---

[85] *Cf. Lk 19:1–9.*

LEARNING FROM GOD

One virtue that the devil fears most is humility. He is not even terrified of deep faith but of humility. Humility is the one thing that makes us like Jesus. He has asked us to learn from Him. "Learn of me for I am meek and humble of heart."[86] To learn from God Himself, not from books. If we try to learn from books, we become confused and it seems so difficult to imitate the "way of humility." . . . In the Gospel, Jesus gives us the example of that woman who continued to beg Jesus for what she wanted until, in the end, she got it.[87] So for us, we too must beg Him for this gift of humility until He gets tired of our prayer and gives it to us. . . . Since the fruit of humility is meekness, if you are humble you will have no trouble with charity. Proud people cannot be filled with love. The fruit of pride is hatred, bitterness. The fruit of pride is jealousy. So it is easy to tell if you are humble or not.

LET IT GO

Mother has said again and again, when the people praise you, let it be for the glory of God. When the people despise [you], don't let it hurt you. [When they praise you,] don't let it make you proud. Let it go in through one ear and out through the other. Never let it go into your heart. God has given [me] one grace—when the people tell me something, before I leave the place I have forgotten already. God knows what would happen to me otherwise. Never hold to yourself, God has given to give; people will always say many different things.

---

[86] Cf. *Mt 11:29.*
[87] Cf. *Mt 15:21–28.*

Humiliations—Beautiful Chances

We must become holy at any cost. Mother receives many humiliations—more than you—but I think they are beautiful chances. A man
in Puna,[88] Rajashree, wrote in the paper many ugly things. He called me
a hypocrite, a religious politician making others Catholic, and about
the Nobel Peace Prize and many other bigger adjectives. I wrote back
to him that I felt sorry for him. I really feel sorry for him because he
hurt himself much more than he hurt me and I believe that many people
wrote to him ugly letters because of what he has said. It was written in
the newspapers: Rajashree calls Mother Teresa "Hypocrite." I wrote
back to him that I forgive him because of God's love and I invited him
to come and see Shishu Bhavan. When he got that letter he got more
angry and began to write many more things. He called me "Mister" so
I was thinking of calling him also "Miss." It was again written in the
newspaper: "It is not that she is not sincere, she is very sincere, but
she is leading the people the wrong way. She is still a hypocrite." You
see, Sisters, we must accept. That man got very angry because I said,
"God bless you, I forgive you." So, when you are scolded, forgive—
and you will be all right anywhere. If I had used other words, I would
have lost the chance of giving God's love, God's joy. That is public; we have many other chances every day. Remember those words:
"To accept whatever He gives and to give whatever He takes with
a big smile"; that is holiness. If they praise you, accept it . . . whatever He gives . . . praise all right, blame all right; no blame or failure
or praise will separate me from Him. If you would only understand
that "belonging." Don't say, "I'm not worthy" and so on. The more
you say, the more attention you draw to yourself, and the more proud
you become. The same people who praise you today will say "crucify"

---

[88] *The eighth largest city in India.*

tomorrow. In the *Jan Sangh* paper in Delhi something ugly was written. A Jesuit Father wrote to me and said, "I have written, but I want you to answer also. Mother, you must reply." But I wrote to that priest that we must forgive—that for Jesus they said, "Crucify Him,"[89] and also a few days before, "Hosanna."[90]

Learn from Me

We have the most beautiful way of coming close to Jesus, if only we have a clean heart, a humble heart. For this Jesus said "Learn from me for I am meek and humble of heart."[91] Not from books, not from people, but from Him. He said it in all sincerity. For our Society humility is the most necessary virtue. The work given to us is something holy, something real. To do His work we need humility. Our Lord has entrusted to us the most beautiful work. One priest wrote, "I want to satiate His thirst." He said he is suffering, longing to satiate the thirst of Jesus. "I thirst" is continually in his mind, heart, body. But we have this in our Society, this work, a vow, a vow with God, not a devotion, a vow with God, like poverty and obedience.

We need a clean and humble heart. "Learn from me!"[92] Jesus said, directly from Him. He did not tell us to take trouble to do this or that.

---

[89] Cf. *Mt 27:22–23; Mk 15:13–14.*
[90] Cf. *Mt 21:9, 15; Mk 11:9–10; Jn 12:43.*
[91] Cf. *Mt 11:29.*
[92] *Ibid.*

IV

Faith in Action Is Love

Our work, to be fruitful and to be all for God, and
beautiful, has to be built on faith—faith in Christ
who has said, "I was hungry, I was naked, I was sick,
and I was homeless and you did that to Me." On
these words of His all our work is based. . . . Faith
to be true has to be a giving love. Love and faith go
together. They complete each other.

With these words, Mother Teresa makes clear that her
work for the poor was but the practical expression of
her faith. In almost every talk she gave, she referred to
Chapter 25 of the Gospel of Matthew whereby Jesus
declares that whatever is done or not done to the least of
His brothers and sisters is or is not done to Him.[1] This
passage was the basis for her conviction that Jesus is present
in the poor; with absolute faith in His words, she regarded

---

[1] Cf. Mt. 25:40.

her apostolate as a service done to Jesus Himself. Her faith in His presence in the "least of His brethren"[2] was so real that every encounter with the poor meant a mystical encounter with Jesus Himself: "We are contemplatives in action right in the heart of the world, seeing and loving and serving Jesus twenty-four hours in the distressing disguise of the poorest of the poor."

Mother Teresa's faith in the presence of Jesus in the Eucharist was based on Jesus' words in the gospel: "This is my Body . . . This is my Blood."[3] To "see" Jesus in the Eucharist and in the poor requires a humble faith: "Externally you see just bread, but it is Jesus. Externally you see just the poor person, but it is Jesus. Difficult to explain, it's a mystery of love. It is one of those things the human mind cannot reach but we have to bend [and accept]."

When asked where she found the energy to accomplish her extensive and demanding activities, Mother Teresa would regularly point to the tabernacle. It was from the Eucharist that she drew strength for her work among the poor. Her day revolved around the celebration of the Mass in the morning and the hour of Eucharistic adoration in the afternoon. Nourished by the Eucharist, she went out to seek and serve Him in the poor, giving expression to her love: "Jesus made Himself Bread of Life to satisfy our hunger for love for God and then He made Himself the hungry one so that we can satisfy His hunger for our love. So the Eucharist and the poor—we are fed by Him and then we feed Him in the poor."

---

[2] *Mt. 25.40.*

[3] *Mt 26, 26–28 and its parallel passages; Mk 14, 22–24; Lk 22, 19–20; 1 Cor. 11, 24–25.*

"The Eucharist commits us to the poor. To receive in truth the Body and the Blood of Christ given up for us, we must recognize Christ in the poorest, His brethren."[4] This exhortation given by the Church was particularly evident in Mother Teresa's life. She often referred to Jesus' identification with the poor and connected it with His presence in the Eucharist. "Never separate Jesus in the Eucharist and Jesus in the poor." Jesus is present, truly and substantially, in the Eucharist under the appearance of bread and wine and He is present in the "distressing disguise" of the poorest of the poor. These two forms of presence, both "disguises," gave her the opportunity to put her faith and love into action and she often encouraged her sisters to "keep the joy of loving Jesus in the poor and in the Eucharist and share this joy with all you meet."

Though the manner is not the same, her faith in the reality of Jesus' presence in both the Eucharist and His presence in the poor was so vivid, that when exhorting her sisters to greater love and dedication in the service of the poor she used the same expressions as she did when exhorting priests to celebrate Mass:

The other day I was talking to a group of priests and I said to them, "How clean your mouth must be to be able to say, 'This is my Body.' How clean your hands must be to touch the bread that will become the Body of Christ." How clean your hands must be to touch the Bread—and how clean my hand must be to touch the broken Body of Christ.

---

[4] *CCC 1397.*

And to her sisters she said:

> At Nirmal Hriday—the living tabernacle of the
> suffering Christ—how clean your hands must be to
> touch the broken bodies—how clean your tongue
> must be to speak the words of comfort, faith and
> love, since for many of them, it is the first contact
> with love, and it may be their last. How much you
> must be alive to His presence, if you really believe
> what Jesus had said: "*You did it to Me.*"[5]

"Jesus in the distressing disguise of the poorest of
the poor," an expression Mother Teresa coined, not only
reveals her firm belief in Jesus' presence, but also her
convictions about that presence. First, Jesus' presence in
the poor was not obvious. He was there, but in disguise:
it required the eyes of faith to recognize Him. Second,
it was distressing to her; it caused her pain to see Jesus'
continued passion in the poor and the suffering person
before her. This pain impelled her to do all she could to
lessen the suffering she beheld. Always practical, Mother
Teresa translated her distress into "living action" by
loving and serving the poor; it was a means of showing
her genuine love for them and of expressing concretely her
heart's desire to relieve the suffering of Jesus.

Our Lady was the first "carrier" of God's love to the
world, for on receiving the Word of God, Jesus, she went
in haste to bring Him to others. It was to her that Mother
Teresa turned, entreating her help to fulfill her own call to
bring the light of God's love to the poorest of the poor.

---

[5] "*You did it to Me*" was for Mother Teresa the gospel on five fingers.

The prayer she composed well expresses her sentiments: "Mary, my dearest Mother, give me your heart so beautiful, so pure, so immaculate, your heart so full of love and humility, that I may be able to receive Jesus in the Bread of Life, love Him as you loved Him and serve Him in the distressing disguise of the poorest of the poor."

There is an inseparable connection between her work for the poor and her call to satiate Jesus' thirst: By the faithful living of her consecrated life of service to the poor, she was satiating His thirst and thus fulfilling the aim of her congregation. The words, "I thirst," sum up Mother Teresa's call, while the words, "I satiate," sum up her wholehearted response. "You did it to Me" became, as it were, the watchword for all her activity, a constant reminder of the reality of Jesus' presence in the poor.

Directing her love to the most vulnerable members of society, Mother Teresa saw in each one a child of God capable of receiving and giving love. By meeting the needs of the poor, and even more by giving them the opportunity to receive and to give love, she restored to them their innate human dignity. Furthermore, she freely chose to identify with the poor, living a lifestyle that would resemble theirs as closely as possible. By embracing voluntary poverty in union with the poor, she was able "to go down [to their level] and lift them up."

"Our people are great people," Mother Teresa often said, speaking of those she claimed as "our poor." "They are such wonderful people . . . You will gain much to know them; they will give you much more than you give them. I can say that I have received much more from the poor than I have given to the poor." They were her "heroes," whose goodness she set as an example for others to imitate. She was particularly touched at how they were able to show joy in spite of their suffering, at how generous and concerned they were for others in the midst of their own want, or how they forgave and refused to be bitter or resentful even in the face of deep hurt. "This is the greatness of people who are spiritually rich even when they are materially poor."

Although the term "poor" is usually taken to refer to those lacking material resources, Mother Teresa had a broader understanding of the word. The "people who have forgotten what is love, what is human love because they have no one to love them," were also the poorest of the poor. However difficult and burdensome material poverty may be, the poverty of being "unloved, unwanted, uncared for" was more painful. Mother Teresa found this kind of poverty everywhere, in affluent countries as well as in developing countries, and realized that it was much more difficult to remedy than material want.

With the firm conviction that each person she met was unique and precious and that in each she was meeting and loving Jesus, Mother Teresa gave her undivided attention and love to the individual before her, "one-one," as she liked to say. Even in the midst of a crowd, she would spot and reach out to the individual most in need. This "purity of vision" and single-mindedness were the fruit of both grace and her own effort.

Mother Teresa readily recognized and encouraged the good in others. Her openness, warmth, respect, and lack of prejudice made each person feel accepted in their uniqueness. She allowed the time and opportunity needed for growth, thereby exemplifying that patience which

St. Paul lists as one of the qualities of love.[6] It was this
love that helped her to tolerate others' weaknesses and
limitations, however challenging they could be for her
strong character.

Aiming at bringing out the best in each person,
Mother Teresa could be firm and demanding. Not a
"people pleaser," she was uncompromising in her ideals
and convictions, opposing with undaunted courage all that
was harmful or destructive to the individual or to society,
even if this caused displeasure in some. Yet she was not
inflexible, and remained consistently understanding and
merciful when meeting the weaknesses of others.

"Love to be true must hurt," Mother Teresa's oft-
repeated maxim, indicated her realization that there was
a price to be paid in placing the loved one and his or her
concerns before oneself. That price is often a death to self-
love and self-interest and this is what hurts. The more one
is willing to suffer for the other's sake, the greater is one's
love. Jesus, perfect model of self-giving love, "loved to the
end," willingly taking upon Himself all our sufferings; each
one of us can say with St. Paul, "He loved me and He died
for me." As His followers, we are in turn called to "love
until it hurts" in imitation of Him.

Mother Teresa's own life was filled with opportunities
to love until it hurts, perhaps the most obvious being her
painful interior trial. The thick wall of darkness, obscuring
the One she loved more than life itself, could be pierced
only by a radical and pure faith. The more she wanted
God, the further He seemed to be. Her longing for Him

---

[6] Cf. *1 Cor 13: 4–7.*

sharpened all the more the loneliness that His apparent absence left in her soul. She truly loved God until it hurt, seeking Him continually in spite of the pain she felt.

In her love for the poor, she wanted to be one with them, willing even to suffer in their place. In a mystical but very real way her desire was fulfilled: "The physical situation of my poor left in the streets unwanted, unloved, unclaimed— are the true picture of my own spiritual life, of my love for Jesus, and yet this terrible pain has never made me desire to have it different." Embracing this agony was a heroic way of loving the poor until it truly hurt.

Though the acceptance of her inner darkness may have been the most painful and remarkable proof of her love for God and the poor, it was not the most recognized one during her lifetime. Instead, her loving service to the most abandoned and the most neglected of human society had placed her in the limelight for almost half a century.

"Love in action is service," Mother Teresa claimed. Service presupposed a willingness to give of oneself, of one's time, effort, and material means. It expressed the love of the giver and met a need of the receiver. It was the normal way of letting the other know that he or she is loved, wanted, and cared for.

Mother Teresa responded generously to God's call to be "His light" and to carry His love to the "dark holes" of the poor. A Missionary of Charity in name and in fact, she carried out her mission to those most in need as one identified with them, both interiorly and exteriorly. She was "translating" into concrete language the mystical call to be a carrier of God's love, an extension of God's "hand" and "heart" in the world today. In her ministry she wanted to remain "right on the ground," relying on the power of God while using the simplest means to meet the needs of the poorest of the poor. Yet, through her humble service, she was making love a reality in their lives.

Radiating love, joy, hope, peace, and enthusiasm, and with her habitual concern for the individual sufferer, she would make one feel loved and special even in one short meeting. The reason for this extraordinary effect on people was not because of any special qualities or talents she had. Rather, it was to be found in the radiance of her personal holiness, of the power and attraction of a soul totally given to God. She was so united with God, that through contact with her, people felt that God was listening to them, helping them, caring for them, loving them. The prayer, "Radiating Christ," which she prayed daily with her sisters after Mass, had become a reality in her own life. She asked in this prayer: "Let them look up and see no longer me, but only Jesus," and, indeed, it was Jesus and the light of His love that she radiated to others.

Mother Teresa reached an eminent degree of holiness through her unwavering "yes" to God and His loving will, despite the hardships it involved. Thus she would often remind her listeners of a simple albeit demanding truth: "True holiness consists in doing God's holy will with a smile." God calls everyone, with no exceptions, to strive for the perfection of love—for holiness—in accordance with his or her state of life. Echoing the teaching of the Church, she insisted that by faithfully living one's vocation as a lay or consecrated person or as a priest, one could become holy. This is not an option but a duty placed on us by God, for besides the benefit that results for oneself, a person's holiness contributes to the good of the Christian community and society as a whole.

With her own sisters, Mother Teresa was particularly firm about the obligation to strive after holiness: "With you, my sisters, I will not be satisfied by being just good religious. I want to be able to offer God a perfect sacrifice. Only holiness perfects the gift." Mother Teresa considered holiness, reached through the faithful living of the religious vows of chastity, poverty, and obedience, and wholehearted and free service to the poorest of the poor the very reason for their existence.

Why profess vows? Is love not sufficient? In Mother Teresa's mind, binding oneself with a vow was an expression of love. A vow ensures that we remain faithful to our commitment, despite fluctuating feelings that may make our initial fervor wane. Further, religious vows are a way "to love until it hurts," as Mother Teresa would say. Our fallen human nature tends to seek inordinate pleasures (lust), superfluous possessions (greed), and power and control (self-will and pride)—tendencies opposed to the complete gift of self in love. We convince ourselves or let others convince us that these are real and legitimate needs, but in reality they impede our ability to love, to give, to share. The traditional remedies for these ills[7] as found in the gospels are the three evangelical counsels of chastity, poverty, and obedience. For those called to it by Christ, the profession of vows in the consecrated life is intended to guide a person to follow Christ more closely and to give themselves to God, loving Him above all. It is "one way of experiencing a 'more intimate' consecration, rooted in Baptism and dedicated totally to God."[8]

---

[7] These are called "concupiscences" in spiritual literature.
[8] CCC 916.

"Jesus offers us His lifelong, faithful, personal friendship. To make that friendship complete, He espouses us to Himself in tenderness and love. And then to complete even this, He gives us the Eucharist." With these words Mother Teresa summarized the essence of the vow of chastity, upon which the other three vows are built. This vow sealed her exclusive and unique relationship with Jesus, her complete belonging to Him in spousal love. It was not just a renunciation of marriage; it was a way of living her intimate relationship with Jesus and expressing the fundamental need of the human heart to love and be loved. Chastity must be rooted in love and manifested in the love freely given to all God's children. "Freedom of the heart, undivided love, no one—nothing, but only Jesus. We cleave to Jesus—I can love all people, but the ONE I love is Jesus."

The fruit of Mother Teresa's fidelity to her vow of chastity was spiritual motherhood. Being attuned to the needs and sufferings of the poor, she responded to her own call to spiritually nurture all those whom God in His providence had entrusted to her care. As a true mother, she was there to love, care, exhort, praise, encourage, support, and guide, but also to correct or reprimand, and at times to simply suffer in silence with or even because of her children. These qualities of motherhood, abundantly found in her, were highlighted by the late Holy Father, John Paul II:

It seems that we still see her travelling the world in search of the poorest of the poor, ever ready to open new areas of charity, welcoming to everyone like a *true mother*. . . . It is not unusual to call a religious "mother." But this name had special intensity for

Mother Teresa. A mother is recognized by her ability
to give herself. Seeing Mother Teresa's manner,
attitudes, way of being, helps us understand what it
meant to her, beyond the purely physical dimension,
to be a mother; it helped her to go to the spiritual root
of motherhood.

"Poverty is love before it is renunciation," Mother
Teresa often stated, revealing the reason behind the
radically poor lifestyle she chose. This poor and simple
lifestyle encouraged sobriety in the use of created things so
as to remain focused on more important and lasting goods.
She advocated detachment and freedom in the use of things,
insisting that "the less we have the more we can give."

The life of privation that Mother Teresa lived—the
"poverty of the Cross"—and the constant contact with
the hard reality of the destitution of the poor she served
increased her love and compassion for them. She was
adverse to superfluities, which she saw as a hindrance to the
spiritual life and to charity for others. Burdened with riches
and luxuries, the human heart tends to close itself to the
reality of suffering and become blind to others' needs. When
she knew that the poor did not have, how could she justify
waste or keep a surplus? She did not hoard things for fear of
want, but shared what she had with complete trust that God
would provide what was needed when it was needed.

As the vow of chastity was the expression of Mother
Teresa's "undivided love" for Christ, so the vow of obedience was the means to put that "love in action" through the
submission of her will to God's will manifested through her
superiors. "Submission for someone who is in love is more
than a duty—it is blessedness," was Mother Teresa's sum-

mary of religious obedience. She obeyed simply, constantly, cheerfully, promptly, using the gifts of nature and grace to execute commands intelligently and responsibly out of love for her Divine Spouse. Her manner of obeying shows great humility, wisdom, and maturity. Mother Teresa trusted that those in positions of authority, despite their shortcomings, were invested with God's power to exercise the authority entrusted to them. She believed that through prayer, discernment, and dialogue with her superiors, God's will would always become manifest.

Besides obeying God's will as expressed through her superiors, Mother Teresa submitted to whatever she perceived to be a manifestation of His will through people, events, or circumstances. This desire for absolute oneness with God's will called her to remain constantly lifted up with Christ on the Cross, accepting all that He asked of her "with total surrender, loving trust and a big smile," as a chance for showing greater love. Here again, Christ was her model: "For Jesus also—who had come to do the will of His Father found obedience—surrender—acceptance of the will of His Father so difficult, that He perspired blood in Gethsemane.—That is why He prayed the longer to be able to obey the will of His Father. . . ." In imitation of Him, Mother Teresa was ready to embrace the "obedience of the Cross."

In response to the call of Christ to dedicate her life to the poor, Mother Teresa professed a special vow of "wholehearted and free service to the poorest of the poor" and made it a requirement for her religious family. By this vow Mother Teresa and the members of her religious community bound themselves to be constantly at the disposal of the poor, laboring wholeheartedly for their

"salvation and sanctification" without counting the cost.
The vow demanded giving to the poor not only hands to
serve but also hearts to love, without seeking any reward or
even gratitude, freely giving what has been freely received.
Expressing her love and compassion in such manner,
Mother Teresa likewise wanted to make reparation for the
sins of hatred, coldness, and lack of concern and love for
the poor in the world today.

Wholeheartedness was a distinctive feature of her personality, the hallmark of her words and deeds. Full attention, single-minded dedication, and joyful eagerness in
accomplishing even the simplest task were the qualities
of her service to the poor. Opposed to wholeheartedness
is carelessness, or "slapdash work," as she called it,
accomplishing one's task without interest, attention, and/
or love. In her opinion, anything worth doing was to be
done with love, and if it was not done with love it was not
worth doing at all.

Mother Teresa had a very special love and respect for
priestly vocations. She saw each priest as an *alter Christus*,
"another Christ," "a man who holds the place of God,"
to use the words of St. John Mary Vianney. Called to be
an instrument of God's love and mercy, every priest plays
an important role in the formation of the People of God,
helping them develop a loving relationship with Him.
Only by living in close intimacy with the Lord would a
priest be able to live a life of complete self-abnegation
and dedication to God and His Church. Mother Teresa
insisted on the need of personal holiness in the life of
each priest. She appreciated their efforts and the example
of their devout, zealous, and self-sacrificing lives, often

spent in silent service of God's people. At the same time, aware of the high demands of the priestly vocation and the fragility of human nature, she helped and supported them in hardship and difficulty, always ready with a word of encouragement and appreciation.

Lay people, as noted previously, are not exempt from the obligation to strive for holiness either. "Love begins at home," Mother Teresa was fond of repeating. A cradle of love, the home is also to be a cradle of holiness. The lay faithful are to fulfill the mission entrusted to them by God so "that by exercising their proper function and led by the spirit of the Gospel they may work for the sanctification of the world."[9] Precisely for this reason, Mother Teresa held that holiness is a simple duty for everyone, regardless of their state of life or profession.

We Are Contemplative in Action

When we speak of contemplation, we think of the Contemplatives, but in our Constitutions it is beautifully put, "We must be 'deeply' contemplative." It means that deep oneness with Him, to have that clear vision so that He can use us as He wants!"

---

[9] *Lumen Gentium, 31.*

PRAY THE WORK

We are real contemplatives in the heart of the world. If we learn to pray the work, we will do it with Jesus, we will do it for Jesus, and we do it to Jesus—it is not difficult. And this is what we try to learn and to teach our sisters—and we are teaching also the laypeople, families, to do the same thing—to bring Christ into the family life especially through the consecration to the Sacred Heart.

✦

There is always the danger that we may become only social workers or just do the work for the sake of the work. It is a danger if we forget to whom we are doing it. Our works are only an expression of our love for Christ. Our hearts need to be full of love for Him, and since we have to express that love in action, naturally then, the poorest of the poor are the means of expressing our love for God.

CONTEMPLATIVE IN THE HEART OF THE WORLD

My vocation is to belong to Jesus, to cleave to Jesus. The work is the fruit of my love and my love is expressed in my work; that's why I say we are contemplatives in the heart of the world. Prayer in action is love in action. Holiness is not special for us—it is a simple duty. Nothing special for us to be holy, we are consecrated, Jesus and I are one. When I talk to ordinary people I tell them, "Be holy"; how much more for us who are consecrated. We are not sinless, but we must be sinners without sin. What we need is a deep life of prayer; we have to be fervent, holy.

WE DO IT FOR SOMEBODY

Sometime back I had to meet the Minister of Social Welfare, a Hindu man, and he said to me, "Mother Teresa, there is a great difference between you and me. We both do social work but we do it for something, namely—money, glory, ambition, family—nothing wrong but the difference comes because you do it for someone." He must have thought about it—Who is that somebody? God Himself, and it makes all the difference. You can kill yourself with work, but if you lose that grip on Somebody, Jesus, you lose everything.

"MY GOD, I LOVE YOU!"

Let us live the life of union with God. All my little actions may be offered through the Precious Blood—through Jesus. We have to learn that. Let us never be satisfied. Jesus wanted to give all—not only some drops of blood. Let us also do the same and give all. . . . We must take the trouble and say often, "My God, I love you!" In our work, we can show this love for God. We have, this month, the means in our hands: the Precious Blood of Jesus, so we must work beautifully. St. Ignatius said, "I must do my work as if everything depends on me—and the result I leave to God." The people in the world take so much trouble—we also must do the same. They sit hours to make their hair to attract people. We must make ourselves attractive to God, like Our Lady. God came to her and she conceived and she brought forth the Child—Jesus. How beautiful.

THE DISTRESSING DISGUISE

Dear Lord, help me to understand now what wholehearted service means . . . the meaning of distressing disguise. How can we see Jesus in the poor leper, the broken body? Charity for the poor must be a burning flame in the Society.

There was a queen who was a holy person, but her husband was rather cruel. Yet, she treated him as she would treat Christ. She had a mother-in-law who was jealous of the love her son bore his wife. One day Queen Elizabeth offered hospitality to a leper man and even gave him her husband's bed to lie on. The mother-in-law, seeing this, seized the opportunity to set her son against his wife. The husband dashed angrily into the room, but to his surprise he saw the figure of Christ on the bed. Elizabeth could have acted thus only because she was convinced she was doing it to Christ Himself. We must therefore be proud of our vocation, which gives us the opportunity to serve Christ in His poorest. It is in the slums that we must seek to go and serve Christ. We must be happy supernaturally to go to Kalighat, to go to Shishu Bhavan, to go to the leper work; to see them, to touch them. We must go to them as the priest goes to the altar—full of joy. That happiness must make us do efficient work.

At the altar, how gently and tenderly the priest touches the consecrated host, with what love he looks at it. The priest believes that the host is the disguise of Jesus. Now in the slums, Jesus chooses as His disguise the miseries and poverty of our people in the slums. You cannot have the vow of charity if you have not got the faith to see Jesus in the people we contact. Otherwise our work is no more than social work . . . "We do it for Somebody." What about if you feel a disgust and run away? Feelings don't count. Run away but come back and don't delay in going back.

FINDING JESUS

I will never forget, a girl came from France, from the University of Paris. When she came, she was preparing to do her final Ph.D. She told her parents: "Before I do the final examination, I would like to spend two weeks with Mother Teresa in Calcutta." And when she came, she seemed preoccupied, and then after a few days she came to see me and put her [arms] around me and said, "I found Jesus." I said, "Where did you find Jesus?" And she said she found Him in Kalighat. And I said, "What did you do with Jesus when you found Him?" She said, "I went for Confession and Holy Communion after fifteen years." . . . And Sisters, I can't tell you what radiant joy was in her face because she found Jesus in her heart—to be able to receive Jesus with real radiant joy. Then I said, "What else did you do when you found Jesus?" She said, "I sent a telegram to my parents to tell them I found Jesus." See Sisters, she found Jesus in the humble work. . . . There are so many young people who are going to confession and coming for adoration because they found Jesus in the humble work, and touched Jesus in the distressing disguise.

"WHY DO YOU DO THIS?"

One day they brought a man from the street and half of his body was all eaten up. Worms were crawling all over his body and nobody could stand near him—the odor was so great. So I went to clean him. And he looked at me, and then he asked, "Why do you do this? Everybody has thrown me away, why do you do this? Why do you come near me?" "I love you," I said. "I love you, you are Jesus in the distressing disguise. Jesus is sharing His Passion with you." And then he looked up, and he said, "But you, you, too, by doing what you are doing, you, too, are sharing." I said, "No, I am sharing the joy of loving with you by loving Jesus in you." And this Hindu gentleman, so full of suffering, what did he say? "Glory be to Jesus Christ." There was no complaint of those big worms eating into his body, there was no crying, no calling, he realized that he was somebody, that he was somebody, that he was loved. This is the hunger for love, or hunger for holiness or hunger for compassion—whatever word you want to use is the same meaning, hunger for holiness. And these people, our people, understand, they understand, and we try to make good use of their suffering. We ask them, we teach them how to offer all for peace in the world. And I can tell you, again I say the same thing, we have received much more from them because they have given us an opportunity to be twenty-four hours with Jesus, for whatever we do to them, to the little ones, we do it to Jesus. He has said so, it must be so.

Co-Workers of Christ

We will say a prayer for our poor people throughout the world. *Make us worthy Lord to serve our fellow men throughout the world who live and die in poverty and hunger. Give them through our hands this day their daily bread and by our understanding love, give peace and joy.* I am grateful to God to have given me this opportunity to be with you and to share with you the gift of God, the privilege of being with the poor, the privilege of being twenty-four hours in touch with Christ, for Jesus has said, and He cannot deceive us, "You did it to me. I was hungry and you gave me to eat; and I was thirsty, and you gave me to drink, and I was sick and in prison and you visited me and I was homeless and you gave me a home. You took me in."[10] We are trying to do, you and I together, to bring that joy of touching Christ in the distressing

---

[10] *Cf. Mt 25:35–40.*

disguise. Our sisters, to be able to do this, take a special vow of giving wholehearted free service to the poorest of the poor, to Christ in the distressing disguise. We have the sisters and the brothers who do so, but we have another group of people, men and women, old and young, who make some kind of a promise to do the same thing first of all in their own homes and to the neighbor, then on the street where they live, in the town they live, in the world they live. And we call them the co-workers, for we are all co-workers of Christ today.

You Did It to Me

We all want to love God because we have been created for greater things—to love and to be loved. How do we love God? Where is God? Jesus has answered: "Whatever you do to the least of My brethren, you do it to Me"[11]; and when we are dead, when we go home to God, God is going to judge us on what we have been to the poor. And He says, "I was hungry and you gave Me to eat, I was naked and you clothed Me, I was sick and you took care of Me, I was homeless and you took Me in, I was lonely and you smiled at Me. . . . Whatever you do to the least of My brethren, you have done it to Me."[12] And this is what Jesus again and again told us: to love one another as He has loved us.

GOSPEL ON FIVE FINGERS

Our work for the poor is so real, so beautiful, because if our heart is pure we can see, we can touch Jesus twenty-four hours, because He

[11] Cf. Mt 25:40.
[12] Cf. Mt 25:31–46.

has made it so clear: "Whatever you do to the least of My brethren—You—did—it—to—Me:[13] the Gospel in our five fingers. That is why we need that deep life of prayer that will help us to grow in that intimate and personal love for Jesus and complete attachment to Him—so that our sisters and our poor can see Jesus in us, His love, His compassion.

✶

One day a Jesuit priest visiting Calcutta from Rome, a big professor, came to join our adoration. Beforehand we had a long talk together and I spent the time teaching him the five finger [gospel]: "You did it to Me." Afterwards he told me that he spent adoration only meditating on these words, and later, on returning to Rome, he wrote to me. He said that he always used these words in his lectures, and that they had a real effect on him and on the students; it had changed his whole approach to theology.

He Is Hungry for Our Love

It hurt Jesus to love us. It hurt Him. To make sure we remember His great love, He made Himself the Bread of Life to satisfy our hunger for His love[14]—our hunger for God—because we have been created for that love. We have been created in His image. We have been created to love and be loved, and He has become man to make it possible for us to love as He loved us. He makes Himself the hungry one, the naked one, the homeless one, the sick one, the one in prison, the lonely one, the unwanted one, and He says, "You did it to Me." He is hungry

---

[13] *Cf. Mt 25:40.*
[14] *Cf. Jn 6:35.*

for our love, and this is the hunger of our poor people. This is the hunger that you and I must find. It may be in our own home.

HUMBLE WORKS OF LOVE

In thanksgiving to God for having chosen us to be His Missionaries of Charity in His Church and for His Church, I cannot think of a better way than to turn to Our Lady, for it was at her pleading that the Society was born, and to beg her, one in mind and heart, to teach us to listen deeply in fervent prayer to the cry of her Son Jesus on the Cross, "I Thirst,"[15] so that with her and like her we learn to stand by the distressing disguise of Jesus in the world today, especially in the lives of the poorest of the poor, both materially and spiritually, and thus satiate His thirst to love and to be loved. Our humble works of love to the poorest of the poor are not just social works, but they are the wonderful means . . . to prove our love for Jesus—to satiate His thirst for love and for souls. "Whatever you did to the least of Mine, you did it to Me,"[16] Jesus said.

"WHY ARE YOU PERSECUTING ME?"

Right at the very beginning, St. Paul—he was the very first one to persecute the Church—and he was going to Damascus . . . St. Paul had the letter to go there and destroy all the Christians who were baptized by St. Peter. And he, a healthy man, fell down from the horse, and he heard the words: "Saul, Saul why are you persecuting me?" He had never heard nor seen Jesus but he knew where he was going and what

---

[15] *Cf. Jn 19:28.*
[16] *Cf. Mt 25:40.*

he had to do. And then St. Paul asked: "Who are you?" And again he heard the voice: "I am Jesus Christ whom you are persecuting."[17] And these words for us, it is very important to know. The words: "Whatever you do to the least of My brothers you did it to Me."

NOT ONLY FOR FOOD

It is always the same Christ who says:

> I was hungry—not only for food but for peace that comes from a pure heart.
> I was thirsty—not for water but for peace that satiates the passionate thirst of passion for war.
> I was naked—not for clothes, but for that beautiful dignity of men and women for their bodies.
> I was homeless—not for a shelter made of bricks but for a heart that understands, that covers, that loves.

YOU TOOK CARE OF ME

Jesus said again and again, "If you give a glass of water in My name, you give it to Me.[18] If you receive a little child in My name, you receive Me."[19] And to make it more clear, Jesus, again, again, many times He said, "I was hungry and you gave Me to eat."[20] You don't know what is hunger, but there are many children today in the world, in Africa, in Ethiopia, in India that are really hungry. There are some children

---

[17] Cf. *Acts 9:5–7, 22:1–8, 26:12–15.*
[18] Cf. *Mt. 10:42; Mk 9:41.*
[19] Cf. *Mt 18:5; Mk 9:37; Lk 9:48.*
[20] Cf. *Mt 25:35.*

today in Ethiopia that are dying of hunger. The other day our sister phoned me and said: "Mother, please send us food, send us food. Our children, our people are dying of hunger." See, we don't know. And another terrible example, one day I picked up a small child six years old in the street. And I could see from the face that that child was very, very hungry. So I gave her a piece of bread and the little one took the bread and started eating it crumb by crumb, so I said to the child, "Eat the bread, you are hungry, eat the bread." And she looked at me and said, "I am afraid when the bread will be finished, I will be hungry again." So she thought by eating it slowly, slowly, she will feel less hungry. The pain of hunger is terrible and that is where you and I must come and give until it hurts. I don't want you to give like that but I want you to give until it hurts. And this giving is love of God in action.

There are many, many people—old people, crippled people, mental people, people who have no one, nobody to love them—they are hungry for love. And maybe that kind of hunger is in your own home, your own family. Maybe there is an old person in your family, maybe there is a sick person in your family. Have you ever thought that your love for God you can show by maybe giving a smile, maybe just giving a glass of water, maybe just sitting there and talking for a little while. There are many, many in rich countries like Japan. There are many. Sisters have found quite a lot of people who have forgotten what is love, what is human love because they have no one to love them. And so begin to give the joy of loving, first in your family and next door neighbor and maybe in your classroom. The girl that is sitting beside you, maybe she's feeling very lonely, you give her a smile. Maybe there is a child there beside you who cannot study as well as you. Do you help? This is the hunger and this is a beautiful way of showing your love, that you really love God, that you really love your neighbor by making that sharing. And, nakedness: Jesus says, "I was naked and you clothed Me." There are many people in very, very cold countries—poor people who have nothing, who have died frozen because they had no clothes. But there is much greater nakedness—that loss of human dignity, that loss of that beautiful virtue, purity, and this is a great nakedness. And there you can share with them, to pray for them, make sacrifices, and you protect your own purity so that you will always remain covered with the joy of purity.

PRAYING THE WORK

Because Jesus said so, we believe that it is Jesus, just as two and two make four. And we do not doubt that, we know that it is four. Same, Jesus said, "I was hungry, I was naked. I was sick. You did it to Me.[21] If you receive a child in My name, you receive Me.[22] If you give a glass of water to someone, you give it to me.[23] Whatever you do to the least of My brethren, you do it to Me." These are all living proofs of the reality of Christ. . . . And it is for sure that it is to Jesus [that we are doing it]. That is why we have to learn to pray the work to do it with Jesus, for Jesus to Jesus—then we are twenty-four hours with Him, and that makes us contemplative in the heart of the world.

JESUS CHRIST HAS ONCE MORE COME DOWN

This reminds me that when I met the secretary of the Ramakrishna Mission—I met him in Burdwan. People there had gathered money for leprosy patients. They wanted me to go there so I went—when the secretary of the Ramakrishna Mission heard that I am going there, he also went. After the people had given me the donation, I said, "According

---

[21] Cf. Mt 25:35–46.
[22] Cf. Mt 18:5; Lk 9:48; Mk 9:37.
[23] Cf. Mk 9:41.

to our religion, Jesus said, when you give to the hungry you are giving to God. Through me, you are giving to the poor. You are not giving to me but to the poor." When I finished, the secretary got up and said, "I want to speak." He was not asked to speak but he offered himself to speak and he said: "When I look at the MCs walking down the streets of Calcutta, I believe Jesus Christ has once more come down, walking in and through the sisters going about doing good." All the Hindus were surprised and they asked me, "Has he become a Christian?" We have to examine, are we really that image to the people in Calcutta? To the world?

TOUCHING THE BODY OF CHRIST

[Our sisters] had to go to the home for the dying. And before they went, I said to them, "See, you are going there; during Mass"—we always have Mass and Holy Communion in the morning before we go—and I said, "You saw during Holy Mass with what tenderness, with what love, father was touching the Body of Christ. Make sure, it is the same body in the poor that you will be touching. Give that same love, that same tenderness." They went. After three hours they returned, and one of them came up to my room and said, "Mother, I've been touching the Body of Christ for three hours." Her face was shining with joy. I said, "What did you do, Sister?" "Well, just as we arrived, they brought a man covered with maggots. He had been picked up from a drain. And for three hours I have been touching the body of Christ. I knew it was He." There was this young sister who had understood that Jesus cannot deceive. He had said so, "I was sick and you took care of me."[24]

---

[24] *Cf. Mt 25:36.*

WHEN WE DIE

"Whatever you do—you did it to Me.[25] Whenever you are serving in My name water"—think of this, so many cups of water.[26] [The] most important thing—when we die [we will be asked], "When were you loving? You did it to Me." This is for every Christian, every human being, and we Christians have greater responsibility because we know, we have been taught. Others don't know as clear as we know.

GIVEN EVEN A SMALL SMILE

Whatever, even if you give a small smile, you did it to Jesus, God Himself. And at the hour of death when you and I die and go home to God, Jesus gave the same question that you can ask: "I was hungry and you gave Me to eat, not only hungry for bread, but hungry for love; feeling lonely, unwanted, hungry for love; not only naked for a piece of cloth, but naked for that loss of dignity, human dignity, that beautiful virtue of purity, that loss, that nakedness. Homelessness not only for a home made of bricks but a feeling of being unwanted, unloved, rejected, a throw-away of society. This is what Jesus, God, will judge us when we come before Him—"I was hungry, you gave Me to eat; I was naked, you clothed Me; I was homeless, you took Me in. Come, come blessed of my Father and enter the Kingdom He has prepared for you from all eternity.[27] And for all eternity you will be full of joy, full of peace, full of love because you fed the poor people and served them with dignity and respect, you treated the poor with respect, you gave tender love and care

---

[25] Cf. Mt 25:40.
[26] Cf. Mk 9:41.
[27] Mt 25:34–40.

to your children, to your families, you never allowed abortion to enter your families—come, for all eternity you will be happy and full of joy, peace and love." And this is what Jesus came to teach us—how to love.

DIFFICULTIES AS GIFTS

I never call difficulties "problems." I always say, "gift of God," because it is always much easier to take a gift than to take a problem.

JESUS MADE IT SO EASY FOR US
TO LOVE ONE ANOTHER

Jesus made it so easy for us to love one another. If we only remember, whatever we do, we do it to Him.

The fruit of Prayer is Faith
The fruit of Faith is Love
The fruit of Love is Service

Everything begins with prayer. Bring the rosary into your family. Where there is prayer, there is unity, there is peace, there is love. I have seen that with our poor. The joy of loving is the joy of sharing.

I would be very happy if you pray to Our Lady to share the joy of loving in your own home. For where there is love, there will always be prayer.

✦

We cannot give anything outside what we don't have inside.

I Satiate

When we talk about Jesus' thirst we mean for love of souls.

HIS THIRST

In all our chapels we see the Cross and the words, "I thirst." It is connected with the Cross and the aim of the Society—not just a decoration, not a word. It is the very reason of our existence, to satiate that thirst. On the Cross they tried to give Jesus a bitter drink, like a drug, but he didn't drink. He just accepted a little to show His gratitude for their kindness.[28] Why? Because His thirst was for souls, for you, for me. How do we satiate? By working for the salvation and sanctification of the poorest of the poor in the slums. See. What have I done here—in the community, in kindness, thoughtfulness, sharing? Every hour. In the Motherhouse is a big crucifix. Do we pass and re-pass without even turning our eyes to Jesus? Do I know that "I thirst"? Do I work for the salvation and sanctification of the poor in the slums? Works are a means to get at the salvation and sanctification of the people, bringing God, touching Christ, satiating the thirst for God in that soul. Be very strict with the humble works. If we lose that touch, that satiating His thirst, we'll be just one more Society. I thirst, I quench.

---

[28] Cf. Mt 27:34.

SHOWING OUR LOVE FOR JESUS

Remember, what we do for each other satiates the thirst of Jesus. Where is Jesus? We know He is there in the tabernacle, but we can't embrace Him there, we can't kiss Him there. How do we show our love for Jesus? By what we do for our sisters and the poor! It is clear. We don't need many books. Look at the Cross. Look at the tabernacle.

"IF YOU ARE THIRSTY COME TO ME"

Our work is not a profession but a vocation—chosen to satiate the thirst of Jesus by total surrender: complete, without counting the cost. We know it is like that. Today, let us try to go over those words "I thirst." Whenever you drink water, remember that you are satiating. This is one of the reasons why He made Himself the hungry one, the naked one, so that I can really satiate the thirst—the reason for our existence. What do those words mean? A priest got a shock when he saw those words, he heard the words. We are so used [to them], we do not connect. Today, if Jesus came here as He came two thousand years ago, would we recognize [Him]? He sent John the Baptist to prepare the way.[29] He, by Himself, could not be recognized. At 54A,[30] do we recognize Him in our sisters? We make a mistake—How did the people not recognize Him? Would something beat faster if He came here? Can Jesus say, "I can go to 54A"—and can He say He is loved, known there? Our aim is not to work only in Shishu Bhavan; it is only a means. Our aim is to satiate. If you are thirsty, come to Me,[31] He said. Tell Jesus that we are

---

[29] Cf. Jn 1:6, 23.
[30] 54A Lower Circular Road is the address in Calcutta of the Missionaries of Charity Motherhouse.
[31] Cf. Jn 7:37.

thirsty, [to] give us some drink. When you were hurt, where did your thought turn first? Each one of us has our own way of understanding this thirst of Jesus. When we sing, "Like the woman at the well,"[32] do we sing it with meaning? Let us pray to Our Lady. Ask her to give you a heart like hers—so pure, so beautiful.

Missionaries of Charity

Jesus wants to use us to be His mercy, His compassion. That is a Missionary of Charity. Carry His love, His peace.

DO PEOPLE RECOGNIZE ME AS A MISSIONARY OF CHARITY?

Most of the time we speak and think of Our Lady—and the one thing we must learn [from her]—the joy of loving Jesus in our hearts and the ones we live with. And we must share this love—Jesus said, "By this they will know [that you are my disciples, if you love one another]."[33] There were many martyrs in the early Church—because the people saw how they loved; by that they knew that they were Christians—that was the mark. Today you and I—if we did not have these clothes, would they know we are Christians? They know we are Missionaries of Charity by these clothes; everybody knows the blue par.[34] If we did not wear this, would they recognize us from the way we serve the poor, give out medicine, answer the bell, speak to people at the gate, as Christians?

---

[32] *A reference to Richard Blanchard's hymn "Fill My Cup Lord," which also contains the line "Come and quench this thirsting of my soul."*

[33] *Cf. Jn 13:35.*

[34] *The three blue stripes on the border of the MC's sari.*

Do people recognize me as a Missionary of Charity by my habit and sari? When I am at Kalighat[35]—[working with the sick]—do the people recognize me? Is that sister full of Jesus? The way we talk, walk.

DON'T DO "ANYTHING, ANYHOW"

What is the reason for our existence? We are here to satiate the thirst of Jesus . . . to proclaim the love of Christ, the thirst of Jesus for souls . . . by the holiness of our lives. You are not just a number, like in a school register. . . . The Church needs missionaries of charity. We are here to satiate the thirst of Jesus. When you came, you did not know you wanted to give souls. . . . We are here to satiate the thirst; that is why we must be holy. Unless you eat the Bread of Life,[36] you cannot be a true Missionary of Charity. Don't waste your time. Don't do "anything, anyhow."

OUR CHARITY MUST BE TRUE

We want to do something for Almighty God, and since we cannot reach God and do it directly to Him, we serve Him in the poor people of India. We are here purely for the love of God. Our charity must be true. We must feel in our very bones that we are doing it—we should be living fires of love. Every Missionary of Charity must be like a burning bush.[37] Love to be true must hurt. It must be something I want to give, cost what it may. Look at Jesus through His passion.[38]

---

[35] *Kalighat, a neighborhood in Kolkata, refers to a hospice Mother Teresa founded in 1952, which is now officially called The Home of the Pure Heart (Nirmal Hriday).*

[36] *Jn 6:53.*

[37] *Cf. Ex 3:2.*

[38] *Cf. Mt 26–27; Jn 17–19.*

EVERYONE MUST PARTICIPATE

You must pray for us that we may be able to be that good news. We cannot do that without you: You have to do that here in your country. You must come to know the poor. Maybe our people here have material things, everything, but I think that if we all look into our own homes, how difficult we find it sometimes to smile at each other, and that smile is the beginning of love.

The Poor, Who They Are

I have accepted to come here to represent the poor of the world, the unwanted, the unloved, the uncared, the crippled, the blind, the lepers, the alcoholics, the people thrown away by society, people who have forgotten what human love is, or the human touch.

✦

You see deep distress, deep feelings of being unwanted, unloved, uncared for—all these terrible broken homes, and all the terrible feelings of distress.

✦

Now, through the work, many people have come into close contact with the dying, with the lepers, with the sick, with the poor, with the unwanted.

✦

Some weeks back one of the shut-ins died in her room and when they broke open the door, they found this woman dead and the cats were already eating her body. So we tried to find out who she was and no one even the next room person knew her name, they knew her by the number of her room. This is why I asked, "Do we really know our poor, do we know our own?" Maybe our own children in the family feel lonely, feel unwanted; maybe my wife, my husband, my own father and mother, maybe they feel unwanted uncared in my own family. May be in my own community some sister feels unwanted, unloved— that is great poverty, do I know that?

✦

He makes Himself the hungry one, the naked one, the homeless one, the sick one, the one in prison, the lonely one, the unwanted one, and He says, "You did it to Me."[39] He is hungry for our love, and this is the hunger of our poor people. This is the hunger that you and I must find. It may be in our own home.

✦

For today, besides the poverty, material poverty . . . that makes the people die of hunger, die of cold, die in the streets—there is that great poverty of being unwanted, unloved, uncared for, having no one to call your own, having no one to smile at and sometimes it happens to our old people whom we call shut ins; like the sisters—they are working in the areas of Harlem—they [the poorest] are nobody, they are just

---

[39] *Cf. Mt 25:40.*

there, they're unknown, they are known by the number of their room, but they are not known to be loved and to be served.

✦

Maybe right here in this wonderful, big university,[40] maybe your companion is feeling lonely, feeling sick, feeling unwanted, feeling unloved, do you know that?

✦

That's where a wonderful gift of God that has been given to our sisters, to be twenty-four hours with the sick and the dying and the crippled and the unwanted and the hungry and the naked and the homeless: [Jesus] in the rejected, in the lepers, in the alcoholics, in the drug addicts—that presence.

✦

The sisters are now in 352 houses taking care of the poorest of the poor, the unwanted, unloved, the mental, the cripple, the lonely, all over the world. And in the countries, well-to-do countries, [there is] still that terrible loneliness, that left alone, it is a great suffering.

Unwanted, Unloved, Terrified

When I pick up a person from the street, hungry, I give him a plate of rice, a piece of bread. I have satisfied. I have removed that hunger. But a person that is shut out, that feels unwanted, unloved, terrified,

---

[40] *A seminary in Lebanon.*

the person that has been thrown out from society—that poverty is so hurtful and so much, and I find that very difficult.

Nobody to Love Them

There are many, many people—old people, crippled people, mental people, people who have no one, nobody to love them—they are hungry for love. And maybe that kind of hunger is in your own home, your own family, maybe there is an old person in your family, maybe there is a sick person in your family. Have you ever thought that your love for God you can show by maybe giving a smile, maybe just giving a glass of water, maybe just sitting there and talking for a little while. There are many, many in rich countries. There are many.

Give the Joy of Loving

Sisters have found quite a lot of people who have forgotten what is love, what is human love because they have no one to love them. And so begin to give the joy of loving, first in your family and next door neighbor and maybe in your classroom—the girl that is sitting beside you, maybe she's feeling very lonely, you give her a smile. Maybe there is a child there beside you who cannot study as well as you. Do you help? This is the hunger and this is what is a beautiful way of showing your love, that you really love God, that you really love your neighbor by making that sharing.

HOMELESSNESS IS NOT ONLY WANT OF A HOUSE

Homelessness is not only want of a house made of bricks. There are many people—the drunkards, the drug addicts, the people who feel unwanted, unloved, a throw away of society—"Oh, that one is a mental case," out; "That one is very stupid," out. This, this is homelessness and this is where you have to see, to look and do something. You see a person, a blind person crossing the road, that is homelessness. Trying to walk—you can take the hand, walk with that person. This mental case—we are inclined to laugh at the mental case, but don't laugh. Go, hold, help, be kind, be compassionate. . . . Jesus will say to you, "I was homeless and you took Me in. You befriended Me. You loved Me. You took care of Me."[41] This is love in action.

CREATED FOR GREAT THINGS

It is very strange that God used an unborn child to proclaim the coming of Christ, and today we see and we know how much that unborn child is suffering, unwanted, unloved, a throw away of society. And yet, that little child has been born for greater things: to love and to be loved. God has created that little unborn child for great things. He has created the little unborn child in His own image to love and to be loved.

THE POOR ARE YOUR MASTERS

Are you one of those who judge the poor? I want you to realize that though we do not take money, we are not living in the air. We have [a] house, clothes to wear, four meals and all the comfort necessary. When

---

[41] Cf. Mt 25:31–40.

I get up, I don't even think, "What am I going to eat today?" We have the security and this is our payment. Let us calculate our one day's expense and multiply it by thirty and see how much it comes up to. We are well paid for what we do.

St. Vincent de Paul said, "Remember the poor are your masters, your lords." Who are the poor that have leisure?

THE POVERTY OF THE WEST

I find the poverty of the West, much, much, much greater, much more difficult to remove because a piece of bread will not satisfy the hunger of the heart. And our people, the "shut-ins," as we call them, they are the hungry people. The fear, the bitterness, the hurt, the loneliness, the feeling of being unwanted, unloved, uncared for . . . I think it is a tremendous disease, much greater than leprosy and tuberculosis.

GREAT HOPE

[There is] hope, great hope. . . . Because Jesus is there, no? That's the cross. He is still—He's alive and He loves us and He wants us— that's why Jesus made Himself Bread of Life—to satisfy our hunger for love[42] and then He makes Himself the hungry one so that we can satisfy His hunger for human love, but we cannot see Him, we cannot touch Him, therefore, He makes Himself [poor]—I was hungry, I was naked, I was homeless—so that you and I can touch Him, can feed Him, to love Him in the poor. And that's how the poor become the hope of salvation to mankind.

---

[42] *Cf. Jn 6:53–56.*

People Who Have No One

Yesterday I was talking to our sisters in the place where they are. They visit a place where they have all these old people, people who have no one, people that are wanted by no one. They are just there. And they look forward and they count the time when Sunday will come, that the sisters may come and do simple things for them. Maybe just smile at them, maybe just straighten the sheet a little bit, maybe just lift them up a little bit, brush their hair, cut their nails—small things, so small that we have no time for them and yet these people, these are our people, our brothers and sisters, they look forward to that little touch. And sister told me of an incident that there was a man there who was looking forward to sisters coming because for the whole week, he has no chance to wash his mouth. Do we know that we have our poor like that? Do we know that he is our brother, our own brother—belonging to the same family of God? Created by the same loving hand of the Father? And there he was. Next week, when they went, he was already dead—died alone quite possibly.

Poorest of the Poor

And the poorest of the poor are people who have no one, who have nothing, maybe spiritually, maybe physically. In the rich countries, we have more hunger for love, there are many more people who are lonely, who feel unwanted, frightened, bitter, and that's spiritual poverty. Abortion—spiritual poverty and physical. And we have people who are dying for a piece of bread, who are cold, who have no home, have to sleep in the street. But we must know both sides. Are the people my brother, my sister? That's where you and I must be able to put our love for God in a living action. Because we all want to love God. I'm sure deep down in your heart you have that desire to love God and how will we love God? By putting that love into a living action first in your own home. Love begins at home and then after [with the] next door neighbor. And that neighbor may be a very poor person. It's a very beautiful thing.

HOPE

The people are asking for spiritual help, for consolation. They are so afraid, discouraged, in despair, so many commit suicide. That's why we must concentrate on being God's love, God's presence—not by words, but by service, concrete love, listening.

TURNING BACK TO GOD

Recently one great Brazilian man, who had a high position, wrote to me that he had lost total faith in God and in man, and he gave up all— his position and everything, even watching television—and he only wanted to commit suicide. One day, as he was passing by a shop, his eyes suddenly fell on the television and there was the scene of Nirmal Hriday, the sisters looking after the sick and dying. And he wrote to me that after seeing that scene, for the first time after many years, he knelt and prayed. Now he has decided to turn back to God and have faith in humanity because he saw *God still loves the world*—he saw this on the television.

OUR TREMENDOUS RESPONSIBILITY

Little Sunil, now twenty-one years old, was one-and-a-half years old when his father died. In despair the mother drank something and the little one sat near her, until she died. I took him to Shishu Bhavan, and he did not want to eat; I suppose he wanted to die like his mother. I told [a sister], "Try to do something for him." She must have looked like his mother . . . because he began to eat and recovered. The other day he came to me and said, "I want to do to the poor children what you have done to me." What a tremendous responsibility we have: to choose to go [to serve the poor] as late as possible or as early as possible; to do as little as possible or as much as possible.

The Poor Are Great People

We must know them, there are very loveable people, they are great people, they are Jesus in the distressing disguise.

✦

The poor people are very great people. They can teach us so many beautiful things. The other day, one of them came to thank us and said, "You people who have vowed chastity, you are the best people to teach us family planning because it is nothing more than self-control out of love for each other." I think they said a beautiful sentence. And these are people who maybe have nothing to eat, maybe they have not a home where to live, but they are great people.

A MOTHER'S SACRIFICE

We take care of 158,000 lepers but they are loved, they're somebody, there's life in them. They're terribly disfigured, but there is love between them. I never forget—government has given us land to rehabilitate them. And so in every place we have a children's home. So as soon as the baby is born, we take the baby before the mother has kissed the baby—of both father and mother, a leper. And last time I had to take that baby before the mother could kiss the baby—because the child is completely clean, born of both parents lepers, and the mother was looking with tears rolling down her face, looking and looking as I was walking. And I was holding the baby so that she could see the child like that. But I was thinking millions of children are killed and there is this poor leper woman so badly disfigured, what tenderness in her heart for her little child. What a big sacrifice she makes not to kiss her child so that the child will remain healthy. See, this is something unbelievable. And this is what we have to create—you and I.

BEAUTIFUL PEOPLE

The poor are very beautiful people. One evening we went out and we picked up four people from the street. And one of them was in a most terrible condition. And I told the sisters, "You take care of the other three, I will take care of this one that looks worse." So I did for her all that my love can do. I put her in bed and there was such a beautiful smile on her face. She took hold of my hand, as she said these words only, "Thank you"—and she died. I could not help but examine my conscience before her. And I asked, "What would I say if I was in her place?" And my answer was very simple. I would have tried to draw a little attention to myself. I would have said, "I am hungry, I am dying, I am cold, I am in pain," or something. But she gave me much more—she gave me her grateful love. She died with a smile on her face . . . this is the greatness of our people. And that is why we believe what Jesus has said, "I was hungry, I was naked, I was homeless, I was unwanted, unloved, uncared for—and you did it to Me."[43]

SHARING IN THE PASSION

I feel always that these people of ours, our poor people, who suffer so much, so much—really our homes for the sick and dying are treasure houses of the diocese, there were living Christs there going through the Passion. . . . This is what we have to help our people, suffering, to accept and to offer; not just to help them to bear with patience, no, bearing is not enough. It's acceptance, to accept what God has given them, and to give what God will take from them, with that joy, with a smile. Why? Because they are the chosen ones.

JESUS IN THE DISTRESSING DISGUISE

We have the home for the dying in many places, and I remember one day I picked up a woman from the street and I knew she was dying of hunger and I gave her a plate of rice, and she kept on looking at the rice. I tried to coax her to eat, and then she said just very, very clear, in a very ordinary way, "I cannot believe it is rice. For a long time I have not eaten." She didn't blame anybody. She didn't blame the rich, she didn't blame anybody. She just couldn't believe it was rice. They are

---

[43] *Cf. Mt 25:31–40.*

great people. We must love them not by feeling pity for them. We must love them because it is Jesus in the distressing disguise of the poor. They are our brothers and sisters. They are—all people, those lepers, those dying, those hungry, those naked—they are Jesus.

DO WE KNOW OUR NEIGHBOR NEEDS OUR LOVE?

Our sisters are very much engaged with the poorest of the poor, with the crippled, with the blind, with the mental. We have homes for the sick and dying. This year we are celebrating the Silver Jubilee of our first home for the dying in Calcutta. In these twenty-five years, we have picked up over 36,000 people from the streets and over 16,000 have died with us. I thought it would be [a] very appropriate way of celebrating the Silver Jubilee by keeping it on the first November, All Saints Day. I am very sure that all those people who have died with us [are] in heaven, they are really saints; they are in the presence of God. It may be that they were not wanted on this earth, but they are very beloved children of God. And so, I would like you to pray and to thank God for all the beautiful things our sisters have done in the Home for the Dying. Though it is part of the Kali Temple, the goddess of fear, yet there beside it is to be found the joy of helping people to die in peace with God. You would be surprised how beautifully they die. . . . Do we really know our poor? Do we know that our neighbor needs our love? Do we know that our neighbor needs our care? Do we know? This is the greatness of our people.

A WORK OF LOVE

We travel by second-class tram, and I was in the tram and this gentleman walked up to me and said, "Are you Mother Teresa?" and I said, "Yes." He said, "I have been longing to share in your work but I am very, very poor. Will you allow me to pay your ticket for you?" If I refused him, it would hurt him, and if I accept him maybe he will give everything he has, but it is better to take what he has than to hurt him, so I said, "Yes." Then he took out a dirty piece of cloth and there inside—the fare is only ten naya paisa, I don't know in American money how much it is, I don't think it is one cent even—he took this and he opened it and there was this ten naya paisa and he gave it to the conductor and he paid the ticket for me. He was supremely happy and he said, "At last, I have been able to share." Well, then he may have had to go without food or maybe he would have had to walk a long distance, but there was the joy of this wonderful man who wanted to share and he did share in this work of love.

✦

And the street people what do they give us? I have received much more from our people than I have given to them. I have received that longing, they have taught me how to love God; they have taught me how to love Jesus in sharing His passion.

LOVE IN ACTION

I have seen deep holiness amongst our people, amongst our poor people, so content. I never forget the man I picked up from an open drain—except for his face . . . worms were crawling on his body.

There were holes in his body everywhere—he was eaten up alive. He must have fainted and fallen into an open drain and people must have passed and passed, but the dirt had covered him up and I saw something moving and I saw it was a human being. I took him out, took him to our house, and he was still—I had not yet begun cleaning him—but the only words he said: "I have lived like an animal in the street, but I am going to die like an angel, loved and cared for." Two hours after, by the time we finished cleaning him, he died. But there was such a radiating joy in his face, I've never seen that kind of joy—real—the joy that Jesus came to give us. That complete content, complete surrender.

One with the Poor

Poverty is necessary [for us] because we are working with the poor. When they complain about bulgur, we can say: "We eat the same." It was so hot last night, we could not sleep. We can say, "We also felt very hot." The poor have to [do the] washing themselves, go barefooted—we also. We have to go down and lift them up. It would be very difficult to go from Loreto house to the slum. Those sisters have no experience [of poverty] in their own lives. But what opens the heart of the poor is that we can say we live in that same way. They have sometimes only one bucket of water. We also. The poor have to line up; we too sometimes. Food, clothing, everything, must be like that of the poor.

I AM ALSO A BRAHMIN

Our sisters have just started in Katmandu in Nepal. So we went to the temple. Near the temple, there are all kinds of very sick and dying people waiting for their goddess to take them. . . . They lie there on a kind of veranda and sometimes they get a little food. I went with the sisters to clean and found a woman lying on a mat. Under her was a hole full of dirt and worms. Her whole back was a big wound. I went to clean her to take off the worms but she told me, "Don't touch me. I'm a Brahmin."

For the Hindus, a Brahmin is a holy person because they are consecrated to God. I told her, "I can touch you because I am also a Brahmin, because I am consecrated to God." Then she let me touch her. I could say I am a Brahmin because I really belong to God. Sisters, see that woman's courage, even in such great pain and with the smell and dirt she still remembered, "I belong to God. I am a Brahmin." And if someone not a Brahmin will touch her, she will become unclean. . . . Each day that woman asked: "When is she coming back, the Brahmin?" You must also be able to say, "I am a Brahmin. I am all for God." Every day, the sisters go down to the Ganges to wash the dirty clothes of the people. In Katmandu, the Ganges is just at its source. The smell in that place is terrible because that is where they burn the dead bodies. The people respect the sisters so much because they do the humble works. I was walking behind the sisters and I saw the people bowing to the sisters, because they love the people and for them they will do that dirty washing. Sisters, you must radiate that contentment, that joy of belonging only to Him. There is such a connection with our vow of chastity and our fourth vow.[44] My fourth vow puts that belonging to Jesus into a living action. I pour my love for Jesus onto the people.

---

[44] *Wholehearted free service to the poorest of the poor.*

AM I ONE WITH THEM?

Once there came to Shishu Bhavan a man who was once rich but had become poor, so poor that he had to come to take the kitcheree.[45] He was so bitter and so angry when he spoke to me, because he had to eat that kitcheree. And then, thank God, I did not try to palaver[46] him or preach to him, but I could look him straight in the eyes and I could tell him: "Every day I eat the same food—kitcheree." As soon as he heard that, he seemed to feel a great consolation, and he went away at peace. I thank God that at least one person was saved from despair because I share the food of the poor. Sisters, we should be able to look at them with real sincerity and be able to say that we are one [with them].

✦

I remember a story of a young boy, fifteen or sixteen years old. One day he came crying and begged me to give him some soap. I knew the family of that boy was rich and had become poor, so I asked him what he will do with the soap. So he told me, "My sister goes to a high school and every day she is sent back because her sari is not washed and we do not have soap to wash it. Please, give me some soap so that we can wash her sari and she can go to school and finish her education." Now we see what a humiliation that family had to suffer because they became poor! And we . . . God forbid that we will not have soap for a week . . . but if it so happened, what will be our reaction? Will I grumble and say so many things unworthy of a religious? . . . Am I poor and careful about putting off [light] when not needed? . . . Do we treat

---

[45] *A common Indian food that is high in protein and easily digestible, necessary if someone is malnourished.*
[46] *To flatter.*

the poor as our dustbins to give whatever we cannot use or eat? I cannot eat this food so give it to the poor. I cannot use this thing or cloth so I give it to the poor, etc. Am I then sharing the poverty of the poor? Do I identify myself with the poor I serve? Am I one with them? Do I share with them as Jesus shared with me?

One to One

I do not agree with the big way of doing things. To us, what matters is an individual. To get to love the person, we must come in close contact with Him. If we wait till we get the numbers, then we will be lost in the numbers, and we will never be able to show that love and respect for the person. I believe in person to person. Every person is Christ for me, and since there is only one Jesus, there is only one person in the world for me at that moment.

WE DON'T EVEN LOOK

We talk much about the poor but very little to the poor. There is so much talk about the hunger and all that, that we'll have food after ten years, so much food—in the meantime, somebody's dying for a piece of bread and we don't even look at that person. When they were having a very, very big conference in Bombay and they were calculating in fifteen years' time, how much more food they'll have and right in front of the house, there was a man about twenty-five, twenty-six years old actually dying of hunger. So I took him, put him in the car with me. By the time I reached our house, he died and he died purely of hunger. This opened my eyes—they are calculating for tomorrow and the meantime, today, many people are dying for a piece of bread. I have never experienced saying to the people, "I don't have, I can't give you." There's never been a time when we didn't have one more plate of rice, one more bed, one more [dose of] medicine.

WE JUST HAVE TODAY

We are for today; when tomorrow will come we shall see what we can do. Somebody is thirsty for water for today, hungry for food for today. Tomorrow we will not have them if we don't feed them today. So be concerned with what you can do today.

✦

The future is so much in the hands of God, I find it much more beautiful and much more easy to accept today because yesterday is gone and tomorrow has not come and I have only today. So very often if I have to be busy with tomorrow, I may neglect my people today. And so, since we have just that one day, I prefer to put all my love and care and energy to that individual . . . because I believe in loving just that one person that is with me at that time. And, tomorrow may never come; that's in the hands of God, no? And that is the wonderful gift of God that He has not given us—that is His great love for us that He has not given us to know the future.

We fear the future because we are wasting the today.

Bring Out the Best in People

Each time anyone comes in contact with us, they must become different and better people because of having met us. We must radiate God's love.

FIND WHAT IS BEST IN EACH OTHER

Have deep respect for each other; that respect will lead to love, love to service. Jesus' love brought Him to serve. The apostles were shocked when Jesus started to wash the disciples' feet.[47] We don't have to do that. . . . But let us wash the feet of our sisters with compassion and love. Let us give each other all that we have received from Jesus—that tenderness. Jesus offers His tender, faithful love, to make us one in our community. Do I know what are the good qualities of my sisters? Spend your time in prayer. Pray that you may be that joy and compassion to your sisters.

"I CAME HERE FULL OF HATRED"

One day in our home for the dying, a man walked straight to the place—we have men's ward, we have women's ward—and he walked straight to the men's ward. And just at that time it happened that they brought a case from the street with terrible wounds and dirt and maggots and so on. The sister didn't realize that this man was standing behind. She washed the person, cleaned him. The way she was touching the patient, the way she was taking care of the patient, this man was looking and

---

[47] Cf. Jn 13:1–11.

looking and then he came out. And as I happened to be there—I don't even know who he was—and he talked to me and said, "I came here godless, I came here full of hatred, I came here empty of everything that is beautiful, but I go out of this place full of God's love. I have understood that God's love was coming down to that patient through the hands of that sister, through the eyes of that sister. The way she was touching, the way she was loving, I believe that she believes that, because God is there." He walked away. Who he was, what he was, I do not know, but just to show you that it is not how much we do but how much [love] we put in the action that matters to Almighty God; and that is love for God—that God keeps on loving the world through each one of us, through the work that has been entrusted to you.

Demanding Love

To approach the poorest among the poor one must become like unto them. To enable me to do this kind of work, a life of prayer and self-sacrifice is necessary; to approach the poorest among the poor, one must become like unto them. To attract the poor of Christ, complete poverty is essential.

THE GRACE TO SEE

"I looked for one to comfort Me."[48] Look for that one in your group, in your community. "And I found none." How terrible it is, if [as] an MC, carrier of God's love, consecrated fully to give wholehearted free

---

[48] Cf. Ps 69:20.

service, if that sister comes to me with a sorrow, that sister today looking so lonely, so unwanted, so unloved [and I am not there for her]. Jesus
in her, not that sister, is looking for love. Let's ask Our Lady to give us
the grace to see. "I looked for one and I found my sister." She didn't say
anything, but I understood. In a way, love begins here—right at home.
We are all women, and God has given us something special—[that abil-
ity] to love and be loved. What a terrible thing if we don't allow our sisters to love us. If we are so proud, so ugly, so preoccupied, no time to
allow sisters to love us. Let us make this one resolution for Lent: I'll be
there for my sister, my [novice] mistress, my superior—not in words, not
that *tamasha*[49]—but by my sharing and my sacrificing, by my prayer—
maybe just a beautiful smile instead of that ugly look, maybe just a beautiful word instead of an angry word. Would Jesus say, "I went through
Lower Circular Road"—three hundred sisters there "and I looked for
one and I found none."[50] How terrible if Jesus would say that about an
MC, who are sent to be His love and compassion. How terrible!

NOT SELF-SEEKING LOVE

Love—let us not misuse the word. The meaning it has in the world
today is a selfish, self-seeking love. Love is charity and we who are
called "Missionaries of Charity" need to examine our love. So many
things will be cleared up in our community and in our lives if we learn
to love and really keep that first commandment. St. John says that
"If you say that you love God and hate your brother, you are a
liar."[51] . . . During these days deepen your personal love for Jesus by
loving your sisters.

---

[49] *Literally, show, spectacle, i.e., not for show.*
[50] *Cf. Ps 69:20.*
[51] *Cf. 1 Jn 4:20.*

THE MOTHER OF LOVE

And, again, we know what happened to Our Lady—the wonderful compassionate Mother full of love. She was not ashamed to claim Jesus as her Son. Everybody left Him, she was alone with Him. She was not ashamed that Jesus was scourged, was spat upon, that He had become like a leper, unwanted, unloved, hated by all, that He was her Son, Jesus. There, too, that deep compassion of her heart. Do we stand by our own people when they suffer? When they are humiliated? When the husband loses his job? What am I to him then? Am I full of compassion to him? Do I understand his pain? And [if] the children are led away and misled—do I have that deep compassion to search for them, to find them, to stand by them, to welcome them home, to love them with a deep loving heart? Am I like Mary to my sisters in my community? Do I recognize their pain, their suffering? If I'm a priest, the priest has the heart of Mary, that compassion to be the forgiveness, to bring that forgiveness of God to the suffering sinner in front of him, that deep compassion of Mary. She was not ashamed. She claimed Jesus as her own Son.

At the crucifixion, we see her standing—the Mother of God standing.[52] What tremendous faith she must have had because of her living love for her Son—to stand there, see Him disowned by everybody, unloved by everybody, unwanted by everybody, one of the worst, and she stood. And she owned Him as her Son. She owned Him as one who belonged to her and to whom she belonged. She was not afraid to own Him. Do we own our people when they suffer, when they are thrown out, our people, our own people, our own family, do we know them, that they suffer? Do we recognize their hunger for Jesus? This is the hunger of understanding love. This is why Our Lady is so great

---

[52] *Cf. Jn 19:25.*

because she had an understanding love and you and I, being women, we have that tremendous thing in us, that understanding love. I see that so beautifully in our people, in our poor women who day after day and every day meet suffering, accept suffering for the sake of their children. I have seen parent—mother—going without so many things, so many things, even begging so that the child may have. I have seen parent holding to the handicapped child because that child is her child, she had an understanding love for the suffering of her child.

No Fear

We are not afraid to tell that that person dying in the street is Jesus; that the hungry one, the naked one, the homeless one. . . . We are not afraid to carry Jesus, not afraid to pray the rosary in the street.

It Is Not Enough to Say, "I Love You"

Do you know your next door neighbor? Do you know there is a blind person there? That there is somebody sick, that there is a lonely old person there that has no one—do you know? And if you know, have you done anything? There is the chance to give love, to come tomorrow to do something. See, look and do something and you will see the joy, the love and the peace that will come from the heart because you have done something for somebody. You have given your love for God in a living action. It is not enough to say, "I love you." Not enough; do something. And that something should be something that hurts you. Because true love hurts. When you look at the Cross, you know how Jesus loved us. He died on the Cross because He loved you and He loved me. And He wants us to love like that.

GIVE WHAT YOU RECEIVED

What you have received from Jesus give generously. He loves me. He took all the trouble to come from heaven to give us such a good news, to love one another. We must be able to love [our] sisters. Like St. Maximilian, he was not the one to be chosen. That man said, "Oh my wife, oh my children . . . " and he [St. Maximilian] said, "Take my life." And we know what happened. They put him in jail to die of starvation. We don't know what is the pain of hunger, we don't know. I've seen people die, real hunger, [for] days. So, he did not die. So they gave injection. Why did that man do that? Greater love. Would I do that for my sister?

MONEY OR GOD?

I remember when we were children at home, not so small anymore, and we were three of us, sitting together talking against one of the teachers at the school. My mother was resting and heard us and got up. And she came and said, "I can't spend money for you to commit sin," and she turned off the main switch—not just the switch in that room, but the switch for the whole house. Then for the next hour, we had to do everything—cleaning our shoes, preparing our things—in complete darkness. It taught us a real lesson. And another time—we were older—and my sister had begun accepting work as a seamstress, to earn money for the family. My mother had placed a big sign in the room, which said, "In this house no one must speak against anybody." A rich lady came one day to give work to my sister and started to speak uncharitably about someone. My mother came out and said to her, "Don't you see what is written there?" The lady was so angry, that she got up and walked away. My sister looked at my mother and complained that we had lost some good business—and the money was greatly needed at the time. My mother answered her, "What is more important? Money or God? I will work twice as hard for the money, but I will not allow such things to be said in this house." See . . . she was just an ordinary woman, and yet she knew what was right and what was wrong. I never heard her speak an ugly word.

Love to Be True Must Hurt

Jesus says, "Amen, I say to you, unless the grain of wheat falling into the ground die, itself remaineth alone. But if it die it bringeth forth much fruit."[53] The missionary must die daily, if she wants to bring souls to God. She must be ready to pay the price He paid for souls, to walk in the way He walked in search for souls.

✦

I want to be humble—then I must be ready to pay the price for that humility. When Mary accepted to be the mother of Jesus, she must have realized how difficult it would be when Joseph would begin to notice that she was pregnant.

✦

If your superior is impatient—forgive, forget! For you it is a gift of God. If she is using words that are hurting you, offer it to Jesus, offer it for that superior, pay the price for her.

---

[53] Cf. Jn 12:24.

BREAKING THROUGH THE DARKNESS

I long for God—I want to love Him—to love Him much—to live only for love of Him—to love only—and yet there is but pain—longing and no love.

Before I could spend hours before Our Lord—loving Him—talking to Him—and now—not even meditation goes properly—nothing but "My God"—even that sometimes does not come.—Yet deep down somewhere in my heart that longing for God keeps breaking through the darkness. When outside—in the work—or meeting people—there is a presence—of somebody living very close—in me. I don't know what this is—but very often, even every day—that love in me for God grows more real.—I find myself telling Jesus unconsciously most strange tokens of love.

Father, I have opened my heart to you.—Teach me to love God— teach me to love Him much. I am not learned—I don't know many things about the things of God.—I want to love God as and what He is to me—"My Father." . . . I loved God with all the powers of a child's heart. He was the center of everything I did and said.

My heart and soul and body belong only to God.

THE KISS OF JESUS

All the suffering and humiliations and the pain is but the kiss of Jesus— a sign that you have come so close to Jesus on the Cross that He can kiss you. So my child, do not be afraid. His love to be true has to hurt and therefore you being in love with Jesus—His love in you must hurt.

TELL JESUS TO STOP KISSING ME

I want [you] to become really holy, otherwise God will not be able to use you to receive suffering and pain. Once I went to a person suffering from cancer, in [such] great pain that I thought she will break the bed. I told her, "This is a sign that you have come so close to Jesus that He can kiss you" and she told me, "Tell Jesus to stop kissing me."

ACCEPT IT AND OFFER IT

Of course there will be temptations and sufferings in our life. We all have to go through it. Because the greater the love we have for Christ, the more we have to pay for it. The payment is sometimes big humiliations. For Mother it is enough to have all these people praising me— that is enough humiliation. When that humiliation comes, accept it and offer it, never hold on to it. Accept it and offer it.

SHARE HIS PASSION

Lent is coming so close to us . . . Take in the Passion, the prayer, the humiliations of being slapped—the only place He wanted to know "Why did you strike Me?"[54] He could not bear that slap in public. He bore all the external painful things—when they crowned Him with thorns, He did not say anything, crucifixion, and so on—but when they slapped Him, He asked "why without any reason"—and He accepted.

When a sister scolds you or corrects you, you feel very hurt. When the sisters come to see me and say, "She said this to me and she did

---

[54] Cf. Jn 18:23.

that to me, and so on," I ask them one question, "What was your first thought? Was it Christ or was it on yourselves?" If you aren't spiritual enough, you will resent it and give back. If you don't give back, you will go around and tell—or go bitter inside. The other day a priest in St. Lawrence died of cancer. He was not very young, but when it was found out he was already dead. This bitterness is like cancer: it grows and it will eat us up.

. . . [What] we forget is that you and I are spouses of Jesus crucified. If I am the spouse of Jesus crucified, then I must have some resemblance to Him—some sharing of identity with Him to show that I belong to Him. St. Margaret Mary has a beautiful example. She had some boils that were very painful. She had some on the face that could be seen by everyone and some on her body that were not visible. She explained that the ones on her face were big and very painful but she had less pain because everybody saw them. She, who was in such great love with Christ, in simplicity said, "The ones in the back are more painful because nobody sees them."

This is the time to share His Passion, and whether I am to become a good religious, a happy religious, a holy religious will depend on the acceptance of these pinpricks, which can destroy fidelity to that pure love.

Take the Bitter Too

One sister told me, "I want to make a sacrifice not to take sweets." I said, "No, it is better to take sweets like everybody else and tomorrow if somebody gives you something bitter, take that too."

The Saints Have the Same Difficulties

Remember the story of the Little Flower? There was one sister in her community who used to really annoy her, and she used to avoid her whenever she could. Then she made a resolution to go out of her way to be kind and loving towards that same sister. Whenever she met her, she would give her a warm smile. Then one day that sister called her aside and asked St. Thérèse, "What is it in me that you love so much?" Nobody knew how much she had been controlling herself in her heart. You see, Sisters, the saints have the same difficulties and troubles as us but the difference is that they made strong resolutions and kept them at any cost. We should be ready to accept joyfully whatever He gives us—praise or blame.

Overcome Anything with a Radiating Smile

See that fellow in Puna, how he wrote so many adjectives after my name and it was published in many of the big newspapers; so I wrote to him thanking him for the adjectives. Even for Jesus they said, "Hosanna, hosanna" and then the next day they were screaming for His crucifixion. We must try to overcome anything that hurts us or upsets us with a radiating smile. Remember that you are praying everyday: "Help me to spread your fragrance everywhere I go."

Where the Joy Comes

"To offer Him our free will, our reason, our whole life in pure faith, so that He may think His thoughts in our minds, do His work through our hands, and love with our hearts." Last year I was traveling. For ten days I was going from house to house. In the morning, "Where am I?" It was a big sacrifice. But that's that total surrender. But that's where the joy comes.

Sacrifice

Love has to be built on sacrifice, and we must be able to give until it hurts.

"AM I THE ONLY ONE IN THE HOUSE?"

"Am I the only one in the house? Again I clean the toilet!" It can happen. In spite of your feelings it happens. You must not kill your feelings, but you must offer. This is the sacrifice. This is the Cross we have to take.

HAVE YOU EVER SHARED?

Sacrifice is necessary in our life if we want to realize the tenderness of God's love. If I stay here the whole day and the whole night tomorrow and tomorrow and tell you all these beautiful things of that presence of tenderness and love of our people, men, women, children, you would be surprised that this is love, God's love in action. And that's why God sent Jesus to teach us this love, and you find out in your own life. Have you ever experienced the joy of loving? Have you ever shared? It's not to give from the abundance. Have you shared with the sick, the lonely something and together make something beautiful for God. This is something that has to come from within us, that's why Jesus made Himself Bread of Life, to create that thing in our heart and if it is not there, I think it's good to examine our hearts. Is our heart clean? Because Jesus said "Blessed are the clean of heart, for they shall see God."[55] Unless we see God in each other, we cannot love each other. And so, it is important for us to have a clean heart, and a clean heart will be able to be only all for Jesus and to give Jesus to others. That's why Jesus made Himself the Bread of Life, that's why He's there twenty-four hours, that's why He's longing for you and for me to share the joy of loving. And He says, "Love as I have loved you."[56] We have to love one another as "I have loved you."

"WHY DO YOU LOVE SO MUCH?"

Little Flower couldn't bear a sister. But she never showed it. She always gave a beautiful smile. She [that sister] asked one day, "Why do you love so much?" In her smile she saw her love. "Yes, I love Jesus." When she washed her clothes and all the dirty water went in her face. . . If I was in her place, maybe I would not say, but I would have given a good look at her. One sister made a noise with her rosary. Maybe nicely we would say, "Can't you stop." No—"Jesus, what a beautiful rosary." She knew, if she stood there she would say [it]. So she ran away. She became a saint. She was canonized because she loved God. That noise of the rosary, what a stupid thing. She could have said, "Please, stop that, I have a very bad headache." No, she offered.

---

[55] Cf. Mt 5:8.
[56] Cf. Jn 13:34, 15:12.

THE TRUE BRANCH

It is at that time when we find it difficult that we show that we are the true branch, if at that time we can smile at each other, if at that time we can see Christ in the distressing disguise of our child, of our own family, of our own Sisters, or our own Priests, Brothers . . . that is the time. It is very, very necessary that we live this life of love. . . . I don't want us to be co-workers just for the sake of the name, that we are just doing some work, that we are helping the poor, and so on and so on. This is not the aim of the co-workers. The aim of the co-workers is to spread love and compassion, and everywhere we go that love and compassion. That is the aim of the co-workers, to satiate that thirst of Jesus for love, in a very simple way and in a very small way.

A BEAUTIFUL SACRIFICE

The other day I received $15.00 from a man who has been on his back for twenty years and the only part that he can move is his right hand. And the only companion that he enjoys is smoking. And he said to me, "I do not smoke for one week, and I send you this money." It must have been a terrible sacrifice for him but see how beautiful, how he shared. And with that money, I brought bread and I gave to those who are hungry with a joy on both sides. He was giving, and the poor were receiving.

   This is something that you and I can do—it is a gift of God to us to be able to share our love with others. And let it be as it was for Jesus. Let us love one another as He loved us. Let us love Him with undivided love.

A Child's Example

I was very touched the other day, a little child from the United States wrote and said (her father wrote actually and sent me money). This little one was making her First Communion and before her Communion, she told her parents, "Please don't buy my First Communion clothes, don't buy anything nor have a party in our house for me (because she was the only child in the family) but give me that money. I will give it to Mother Teresa for her child and I will make my First Communion in my uniform." See the courage, and all the other children beautifully dressed and this little one, out of love for God's poor, for the little ones of Calcutta, she went in her uniform. And this touched the father very much, it touched the mother very much, so she gave up smoking and he gave up drinking . . . This is that beautiful love, that tenderness of God's love—it touched that little child and through that child, it touched the parents, brought peace and unity and love in the family through that little act.

Consecrated

I have seen terrible bodily suffering, terrible, and to see those people in Ethiopia. When you open the gate in the morning, they're just in front of our gate, just gasping for a glass of water, they have not touched food, they come all the way just to get a little bit tender love and care and some food. And this time when I was there with the sisters, the minister, foreign minister, who is a strong communist, he came to see me. And then just at that time, the time for the sisters to open the gate and there were about twenty-five people lying there in front of our gate, right in the road. And, [the] sisters started lifting them, carrying them, taking care of them and the man turned and said "Only a con-secrated and dedicated life can do what your sisters are doing—only a consecrated." And this consecrated means the heart in love, so let us bring that joy of loving in our own hearts first and share it with others. Do not be afraid to love until it hurts, until it hurts because to give like that is easy, to give from the abundance is easy.

Sugar

I'll just give you one little beautiful instance of a little child who loved with great love. . . . Sometime ago there was a very great shortage of sugar in Calcutta and a little child, a Hindu child, about four years old told his parents: "Mother Teresa has no sugar for her children. I'm not going to eat sugar for three days, and that sugar I'll give to Mother." And then the parents who have never been to our house before, and I don't know the child at all, they brought their child, and the child brought me enough sugar. He could scarcely speak and he said, "Mother, I did not eat sugar for three days. Give this to your children" and I think that child loved with great love.

The Small Gifts

Accepting with joy all the little sacrifices that come daily. Do not by-pass the small gifts for they are very precious.

The Fruit of Love Is Service

Faith in action is love. Love in action is service.

How Can We Love Jesus Today?

How can we love Jesus in the world today? By loving Him in my husband, my wife, my children, my brothers and sisters, my parents, my neighbors, the poor.

✦

I belong to Jesus; I have been chosen, with a purpose to satiate His thirst for love by loving Him, by putting this love for Him in action. We have to work at the salvation and sanctification of the poorest of the poor.

See What You Do

We can see how we love Him by the work we do—and the work is the fruit of prayer. If you want to see how much you love Him, see what you do. I love Jesus and I put my love of Jesus into action. My prayer for you is that you really, fully, grow into that joy and if it is not there, why? What is the obstacle? It is not pride to know that you love Jesus—let the people see your good works and glorify the Father[57]— all our good works come from Him.

---

[57] Cf. Mt 5:16.

Love Is . . .

Love is not talking, love is living. I can talk about love the whole day and love not once—looking everywhere, except looking down when there is a man dying on the street.

Not in Words Alone

I cannot love God in words only: my heart has to express it, my hands have to express it, my feet have to express it. It's not enough to just say, "I want to love the poor." Our service is to be "wholehearted"—this is an important word for MCs. . . . It is to be wholehearted not half-hearted, the proof of our love for God in action. In the Scripture it says that we must love God with our whole heart and your neighbor. This is the meaning of our fourth vow, to love the poor with our whole heart, our whole soul and our whole strength—"wholeheartedly." For us it is not sufficient to say, "Oh, I love Jesus tenderly." We have to show we love Him by our wholehearted service.

It's Not How Much We Do

It is not how much we do but how much love we put in the action that matters to Almighty God and that is love for God—that God keeps on loving the world through each one of us, through the work that has been entrusted to you. The work that you are doing in the office is sacred work. Never do it slap dash . . . it is Jesus there. Your hands are feeding the hungry Christ, your hands are clothing the naked Christ, your hands are giving home to the homeless Christ in some part of the work. So, do your work well, and do it with great love. Otherwise it is not worth doing it. It is not worth doing it half-half. That is the means for you to become holy because Jesus our God is there.

YOU ARE GOD'S LOVE IN ACTION

"Our Society makes the Church fully present in the world of today." Examine yourself and see, "Am I making the Church present?" In Ethiopia, the apostolic delegate told us during the homily at Mass, "I thank you, in the name of the Holy Father, because by your presence you are making the church fully present here." We make the Church present by proclaiming the good news. What is the good news? The good news is that God still loves the world through each one of you. You are God's good news; you are God's love in action. Through you God is still loving the world. So if you are a lazy MC, you will give a wrong picture of God's love in action. People are watching us constantly at all times and they are meeting God's love in action by our touch of compassion and love to the poor in Nirmal Hriday, in Shishu Bhavan, to the leprosy patients, anywhere.

JESUS LIVING IN ME

Jesus cannot walk in the street of Calcutta and in the streets of the world now—so what [does] He do?—Through me He walks and touches the poor and shows the world His Father's love and purity. Today God loves the world so much by sending us. He sent you through Mother wherever you have to go. To do what?—To radiate the purity of God's love.

THE MARK OF THE CHRISTIAN

Jesus said that "by this they will know that you are my disciples."[58] The early Christians were taken to the prison because they loved. When St. Lawrence was taken to the prison, the prefect asked him to bring all the riches of the Church. St. Lawrence said, "Yes, I shall bring them tomorrow morning." Next morning, he gathered hundreds of poor people in front of the presbytery and when the prefect saw them he was more angry.

Humble Deeds of Love

Fidelity to humble works is our means to put our love into action.

TAKE THE CHANCE

Take the chance to do the humble works. You must long to go to that place . . . to wash and clean, to show your love for Jesus in a real living action. . . . One Jesuit father asked me what I will do when I am no longer Mother General. I told him that I am first class at cleaning drains and toilets. Before I used to go to Kalighat every Sunday, and my special job there was to clean the toilet rooms. Those of you who have been there know that every morning the whole room is covered with dirt. A man came to me—I thought it was a brother, I didn't look very well—he said he wanted to help me. I said, "Then come with me," and I went to the bathroom. I began to sweep and pour water but

---

[58] Cf. Jn 13:35.

the brother didn't seem to know what to do. I told him to pour water for me. He did that well enough. I was thinking, "They are not teaching the brothers what to do" and grumbling inside. Then after finishing he told me, "Thank you, Mother. I don't know how to thank you." No brother ever thanked me like that, and so I looked more closely. I saw that it was not a brother but a very well-dressed gentleman. He told me he is the general manager of a big company.

PREACH GOD'S LOVE

Humility always radiates the greatness and glory of God. Let us not be afraid to be humble, small, helpless to prove our love for God. The cup of water you give to the sick, the way you lift a dying man, the way you give medicine to a leper, the way you feed a baby, the way in which you teach an ignorant child, the joy with which you smile at your own at home—all this is God's love in the world today. I want this to be imprinted in your minds: God still loves the world through you and through me *today*. We must not be afraid to radiate God's love everywhere. Once someone asked me: "Why do you go abroad? Don't you have enough poor in India?" I answered: "I think Jesus told us to go and preach to all the nations.[59] That is why we go all over the world to preach God's love and compassion by our humble deeds of love."

THE GIVER IS ENRICHED

Because people in the world have been so deeply touched by our humble works of love in action that bring God's tender love and concern

---

[59] Cf. *Mk 13:10, 16:15; Mt 28:19.*

to the unloved, the uncared for, the destitute, this has created in the hearts of so many the deep desire to share; some do so out of their abundance, but many, and maybe the greater number, by depriving themselves of something they would have liked to give themselves, so as to be able to share with their less-privileged brothers and sisters. It is so beautiful to see the spirit of sacrifice finding its way into many lives, for this not only benefits the poor who receive, but the giver is also being enriched with the love of God. This is something for which we must constantly praise and thank God.

JUST A DROP

We ourselves feel that what we are doing is just a drop in the ocean. But if that drop was not in the ocean, I think the ocean will be less because of that missing drop.

WE ARE NOT SOCIAL WORKERS

We spend ourselves and, unless we keep on with that refilling and closer oneness with Christ we will soon become social workers—and I insist on saying that we are not social workers. We are really contemplatives in the heart of the world. So, to be able to keep to that faithfully, we need this continual refilling. That's why every week we stay one day in and do deepening, reading, praying, and that day we have confession and instruction from the confessor who comes for the Sisters.

We may be doing social work in the eyes of the people, but we are really contemplatives in the heart of the world. For we are touching the body of Christ twenty-four hours! We have twenty-four hours in His presence, you and I. You too must try to bring that presence of God into your family, for the family that prays together stays together.

✴

We are twenty-four hours with Jesus in the hungry, in the naked, in the homeless, in the lonely. And they are such wonderful people, I have never yet heard them say something bad, discontent or curse. You will gain much to know them, they will give you much more than you give them.

MY BROTHER

The work is God's work and not our work, that is why we must do it well. How often we spoil God's work and try to get the glory for ourselves. My brother is in Palermo, Italy, for twenty years, but nobody knows of his existence until our sisters opened a house in that city. The people and the priests and the bishop all started asking him, "But you never told us you are Mother Teresa's brother and you are here for so many years." He would not tell anyone and when they asked him, he said, "For you, she is your sister and Mother Teresa also; for me she is my sister—let it be for me just so." And he just would not take any glory for himself. Now see Sisters, this is about people in the world; What about us religious?

GOD'S WORK

And you pray for us that we may not spoil God's work, that it remains His work. And also that we may be able to give only Jesus to our people, no matter who they are. Whether they are Christians or non-Christians, they are all children of God created to love and to be loved.

Bring Jesus

When I went to Addis Ababa with the intention of bringing the Sisters there, and everybody told me you must be either mental or you must be somebody extraordinary, because it is out of the question for you to be accepted in Addis Ababa, especially not Catholic Missionaries like that. And I said, "Nothing is impossible with Jesus ... "[60] I wanted to see the Emperor and then through somebody we saw his daughter, and his daughter, God knows what she said to him, anyway it was arranged that we went and we saw the Emperor....How tall he stood, very beautifully and standing before a missionary like that, anyway I felt much smaller than I am. He stood there like a statue and then when we all sat down, he asked: "What qualifications have the Sisters got, what are they going to do?" I said: "Our sisters will give the love and compassion of Jesus to your people, and this people will become our people." He looked at me and said, "That is so Christlike, this is what Jesus did. Come, they will be most welcome." Then I had the [miraculous] medal in my hand, and I gave it to him. I forgot that he was Emperor, and I thought he was just an ordinary man for me at the time. I gave him a medal of Our Lady. He took Our Lady's medal and he looked at Our Lady, and he said, "Mother Mary is the hope of mankind." Then he turned to the Prime Minister and said, "Let the sisters come and do all that is possible, whatever is necessary for them to have the visas as soon as possible." And within a fortnight, the Sisters received their residential visas at the airport. So we are there now, and when the Sisters came there, immediately, he gave them a place to have a Home for the Dying, and so on.

This is the thing: It struck him that the Sisters were not going to do something, social work or something. We are not social workers.

---

[60] *Cf. Lk 1:37.*

We come to give Jesus there, in haste to give Jesus. And that was the greatest miracle, that that man was so positive and everybody else was so against it.

BRING THE WORD OF GOD

I think one of the most helpful things is to bring the Word of God into their lives [lonely people] and then also our presence to them. Our sisters radiate joy, radiate compassion, and I think when they come into the homes of the shut-ins and our people that are unwanted, unloved, I think they experience that God does love them through those sisters who are the living reality of God's love for them.

✦

Lately, at the invitation of the President of Mexico, we opened a house in Mexico, and our sisters, as it is the custom in our Society, they go round and round and round and look for everybody, see everybody and they walk and walk till both their legs ache properly to see which is the worst place, where is the need greatest to begin from. But in Mexico, the poverty of the people around was very great, wherever they visited, it was in the outskirts of [Tijuana] . . . it was really very, very great poverty. But to the sisters' surprise, nobody asked neither for clothes, neither for medicine, neither for food, nothing except "Teach us the Word of God." It struck me so much, these people are hungry for God—"Teach us the Word of God."

AFTER 800 YEARS . . .

In Yemen, . . . after 800 years, Catholic sisters were asked to come there and I remember when the Prime Minister asked, I said that I was willing to give the sisters on condition that he allows the priest to come because without Jesus we don't go. And they wanted the sisters, so they allowed the priest to come. And, it was most extraordinary, after 800 years—because there were no priests, there was no tabernacle, there was no altar, no Jesus, and the moment we came there, there was Jesus, there was tabernacle, there was everything, and in building our convent for the sisters, they gave us a big place, they have a very big home for the dying there, and the governor himself told Sister: "Sister, show me how to build a Catholic church." And first Sister had asked him to build a nice chapel—special room for Jesus; and so Sister said to him, "Oh, it is very difficult to build a Catholic church, but you build a chapel for us where we can keep Jesus with us." But this man wrote to Msgr. H. and said [that] the presence of the sisters has lit a new light in the life of our people. And this is something, we are not afraid to say, that that person dying in the street, it is Jesus. That the hungry one, the naked one, the homeless one: we are not afraid to carry Jesus, not afraid to pray the rosary in the street. They look at us.

WE ARE WITNESS

A Hindu gentleman once asked me, a very big, high official: "Aren't you anxious to convert us all?" And I said, "Naturally, the treasure I have, Jesus, naturally I want to share it with you, but conversion has to come from Him. Mine is to help you do works of love, and then through these works of love naturally you come face to face with God and it is between you that that treasure, His love, is exchanged. And then you are either converted, you accept God in your life, or you don't." This is what our life must be. We, as co-workers, we are not meant just to raise money, that is the last part, or to gather things, but we are to witness that presence of Christ within us, that witnessing of His love and compassion.

Radiating Christ

Let us radiate the peace of God [and] so light His Light and extinguish in the world and in the hearts of all men all hatred and love for power.

✦

We are all capable of good and evil. We are not born bad. Everybody has something good inside. Some hide it, some neglect it, but it is there. God created us to love and to be loved. God is not separate from the Church as He is everywhere and in everything and we are all His children—Hindu, Muslim or Christian. When you know how much God is in love with you, then you can only live your life radiating that love. Keep the joy of being loved by God in your heart as your strength and share this joy with others. I will keep you in my prayers.

SHED THE RADIANCE

We must *shed the radiance of the gospel message on the whole world*. We must begin first in our small world—in our community, whether it may be among three or four, it does not matter how many sisters. Each one of us has come from different places and different backgrounds. By our living together, we proclaim that unity in the Church as well as by working with all people, serving all people, of any religion or race.

Life of Total Consecration to God

It is a privilege for us to have been chosen. He has called you by your name, each one of you have been called by your name. You belong to Him in a special way. You are precious to Him because He loves you and He has poured love into your heart to be able for you to give that love to others.

WHAT IS OUR VOCATION?

What do we call vocation? Our vocation is Jesus; we have it in the Scripture very clearly: "I have called you by name you are precious to me. . ."[61] "I have called you my friend,"[62] "Water will not drown you," water [is] the temptations, "Fire—temptation of the devil—will not burn you,"[63] "I will give nations for you, you are precious."[64] "How could a mother forget her child? Or a woman the child within her womb? But even if mother could forget, I will never forget you, you are precious

---

[61] *Cf. Is 43:1, 4.*
[62] *Cf. Jn 15:15.*
[63] *Cf. Is 43:2.*
[64] *Cf. Is 43:4.*

to me; You are carved in the palm of my hand."[65] . . . Why are we here? We must have heard [our] name; Jesus has called us by name.

EVERYBODY HAS SOMETHING

God called me first to be a religious and then to preach Christ. The greatest missionary was Christ. So we must do the same. Everyone has to say, "Yes, this is the most beautiful vocation God has given me. I am unworthy." I must feel this. Then, out of this conviction, comes my gratitude to live as a true MC—the way I talk and look at the people, touch them, speak to them. First to the sisters—I have to respect the other sister. She is part of my life, she is also a co-worker of Christ. No hurtful word—I would not hurt any part of my body, so, also I must not hurt my sister. We have to love each other—the clever, the *boka*,[66] the holy, the unholy. "Love one another as I have loved you."[67] If you study, let it be for life, —not for one week, for one day. Today I must love my sister whose face, whose voice, I cannot bear. It is like that in the community: no two noses are the same. How different must be our souls. Some have five, some two, some only one talent. Everybody has something. Do not be a coward and say, "I am good for nothing." I must not be lazy, I must try. God will make it possible for me.

JESUS IS SUFFICIENT FOR ME

Our vows are also connected with joy because I know God takes care of me today and every day. In obedience I am full of joy because I

---

[65] Cf. Is 49:16.
[66] *dim-witted*
[67] Cf. Jn 13:34.

recognize the Person of Christ in my superior. In chastity, I imitate Mary, the Cause of our Joy, the Virgin most pure. Sisters, if you want your chastity to be chaste, your virginity to be virgin, your purity to be pure, then be like Mary—the Cause of our Joy—who is all pure. If you want to be a cause of joy to God, to the Society, to the Sacred Heart, to Our Lady, to Mother, to your community, to your sisters and to the poor, then guard your vow of chastity. Chastity implies truthfulness, sincerity. To die, yes, but not to sin. If you examine yourselves all temptations against chastity come to you when you are sad and moody. A moody sister is like a ball in the devil's hands; he can do what he likes with her. It is then you will go out to look for others to satisfy your hunger for love. If you want your chastity to be chaste then cultivate this joy, this virtue of joy. "That my joy may be in you,"[68] the presence of God, union with God. Nothing can separate me from Christ.[69] I belong to Him only. Jesus is sufficient for me.

THE VOCATION OF FAMILY

That's a very happy family and that was the family—together, you pray together, that was most important part, I think. We received much from our parents because the parents loved one another and so we were able to learn from them how to love. I think very simple, nothing special. We learned from home how to love others because we saw our parents how they loved the poor and I think we learned from them how to love others. And, naturally, a life of prayer in the family, very faithful life of prayer and fidelity to the Church and the teachings of Christ. And I think that kept the family together and God's calling and then there is a sacrifice always to be made.

---

[68] *Cf. Jn 15:11.*
[69] *Cf. Rom 8:35–36, 39.*

Only to Love Jesus

St. Ignatius did not want to write a Constitution—only to love Jesus. But he did not realize that they were not all able to live it. So he wrote the Constitutions with many details: "The sound of the bell is the voice of God." For us, the Constitutions are the written will of God. It is a living thing. It is the expression of chastity, the expression of poverty, the expression of prayer life. And then the observance comes— I know what I have to do in community life, in chastity, in poverty, in obedience, in charity.

Write "Undivided Love" Everywhere

Write these words, "Undivided love," everywhere—in your mind, in your heart, on every part of your being, on every finger of your hand, everywhere—so that you will never forget that you have become completely and forever His. You are precious to God—maybe not to man. Do not be afraid, "I have called you by your name—you are mine. Waters may cover you, but you will not drown. Do not be afraid."[70] Remember that Jesus said, "Take up your cross and follow Me."[71] Once I saw a sister with a long face going out for apostolate, so I called her to my room, and I asked her, "What did Jesus say, to carry the cross in front of Him or to follow Him?" With a big smile she looked at me and said, "To follow Him." So I asked her, "Why are you trying to go ahead of Him?" She left my room smiling. She had understood the meaning of following Jesus.

---

[70] *Cf. Is 43:1–4.*
[71] *Cf. Mt 16:24.*

There is a story they tell in the Slavic countries of a rich king who became a saint, St. Wenceslaus. Each night he used to go out with clothing and food for the poor with his servant. One night there was heavy snow on the streets, and the servant was struggling to walk as he was sinking into the snow. So King Wenceslaus said to him, "Mark my footsteps." The servant started following in the footsteps of the king, in the snow. As he placed his feet in the footprints of the king, he felt deep warmth spread through his body and walking was no longer difficult. So let us too follow in the footsteps of Jesus and we will never stumble.

Nothing and Nobody

"Nothing and nobody" is the best expression we can give [of] undivided love. In the marriage contract it is the same thing—the moment something or somebody comes, that moment love is divided and that emptiness has to be filled. Jesus said to one of the saints, "My love for you has not been a joke." What do we declare before the whole world? "I have chosen to love God with undivided love." That "nothing and nobody" makes my heart pure, my heart virgin, my heart free to love Christ. In marriage that "nothing and nobody" brings forth fruits of that cleaving, which is the child, and for us our cleaving to Christ is our fourth vow. Sisters, it is something sacred, holy, something which I just cannot break like that.

Nothing Will Separate Me from Him

That vow, that love for Christ, is put into living action by my service to the poor, the dying, the lepers. I belong to Jesus and nothing will separate me from Him. Sisters, again I am saying that all the four vows[72] are so complete together that you cannot break one and keep the others. If you break one, you break the others. So today, examine yourself. What has been your attachment to Christ? Your oneness with Christ? Are your eyes so pure that you can see Christ face to face? Pride, harshness blurs the eyes; my harshness, my impatience—that is impurity.

BELONGING TO JESUS

What am I binding myself to? What am I giving my vow to God about? . . . It's a binding—I bind myself to God with undivided love. I tell Almighty God, "I can love all, but the only one I will love in particular is you, only.

To be able to love Jesus with an undivided love, I *want* to be free. I want to have nothing that will take me away from Him. Our vow of poverty gives us that freedom. Jesus could love us like that: He, being rich, became poor for love of us. We also—same. We also were rich—maybe not rich in money, but we had the love of our family, maybe our own room, the clothes I liked to wear.

If I really belong to Jesus—if I really love Jesus with undivided love, obedience will come naturally, "He went down and was subject to them."[73] He accepted the scourging, the spitting. If I am not obeying, I have to examine my heart. Do I really love Him with undivided love? And because I love Jesus, I don't go around saying, "I love Jesus, I love Jesus"—this is madness; but, I see a poor man, I take him to Kalighat. I pour my love on the poor—fourth vow. The vows are all

---

[72] *Poverty, chastity, obedience, and to give wholehearted and free service to the poorest of the poor.*
[73] *Cf. Lk 2:51.*

connected to the vow of charity. I can practice my fourth vow on my sister. Because I love Jesus I pour my love on my sister.

Signs of Consecration

The giving of a name is a sign of an internal self-effacement—that she does not exist anymore. Like St. Paul said, "I live now no longer I, but now Christ lives in me."[74] Paul also changed his name. He was Saul but now he became Paul. Peter also changed his name.

✦

Cutting of the hair is another sign of separation from the world, that we are consecrated. The people in the world do not cut their hair. The longer it is, the more shining is their beauty. It's a creation of God for a woman.

The White Sari

In Bengal we have that custom . . . , when the husband dies, the woman shaves her hair off and puts on a white sari. When I was beginning the Society, I wanted the white sari for our sisters. The people outside were talking among themselves, "I hope she will not wear a white sari, for the people will think that she is a widow." We, marrying Jesus, are very much alive, and He to us.

---

[74] *Gal 2:20.*

WHY DID HE CALL ME?

In Rome, in our novitiate house, we have a very big beautiful vine . . . [It] is spread out and it is covering the whole place. I told the novices, "I won't give an instruction today, but take your Gospel and read St. John 15 and make your meditation." They went, each one sitting under the vine, reading, feeling, touching the vine, reading the Gospel again and again, looking up at the vine. It's strange how this had an effect on the sisters. Each one felt differently. One sister came to say, "Mother, there was not even one grape on the vine but all the grapes on the branches. The branches are full with fruits and it is so strange that there is nothing on the tree. See how our life is so connected, we are the branches and we are supposed to bear fruits." So she gave me an instruction. We, being His love, must bear fruits of compassion, love, and concern for our sisters, our people with whom we work. Another novice came to say, "Mother, I saw four knots of branches joining to the vine and they reminded me of the four vows, how they are united in our life too." Each one came to share their own experience and they realized that they have to be a beautiful branch joined to Christ in religious life, bearing fruits. Profession means to profess—to proclaim that I am a consecrated soul. I proclaim that I belong to Jesus, when I make my profession. He gave a call, it is a personal call. He did not call us in a group, not even at the same time but each one of us separately. There are thousands of young girls in the world. Why then you and I are called? There is no answer. It is good for us to examine before the Blessed Sacrament: How did He call me? When did He call me? Why did He call me?

An Everlasting Love

If we think, Sisters, imagine God being so busy with you, so occupied with each one that He gave us a personal call. He did not send anyone to call me but He called me personally. He said, "I have loved you with an everlasting love."[75] To think that He had me in His mind before eternity. Thousands of people are in the world, but He called me personally—I, from this country or town or village.

God Chose Me Personally

God knows us personally. It is said in the Gospel, "Even the hair of your head all have been counted."[76] I don't know how much hair I have, but God knows. He has called me and you, chosen me and you, kept me and you as a person. That is why, when you are rough, unkind, harsh with the sisters, with the people, we are unworthy of our name. The sister with whom you are harsh has also been called personally by Christ.

A Profession to Love

We religious make our profession not as a "professional," but I make a profession to love Jesus only.

Chastity: I belong to Him, therefore, undivided love.
Poverty: Freedom. Riches can come between me and Him. If I am

---

[75] *Cf. Jer 31:3.*
[76] *Cf. Mt 10:30; Lk 12:17.*

rich, I am not clean of heart, I cannot see Him. I cannot belong to Him.

Obedience: That surrender. I belong to Him. He can use me in whatever way He wants.

Wholehearted Free Service to the poor: If something belongs to me, I've got full power to use it as I want. This is belonging to Christ.

This is the one thing that must be clear in your mind—that conviction—two plus two makes four. No matter who says what, nobody can change this for me. I belong to Jesus; He can do to me whatever He wants. The work is not our vocation. . . . The work is not our vocation. Our vocation is that we belong to Him. Our profession is that we belong to Him. Therefore, I am ready to do anything: wash, scrub, and so on; like a mother who gives birth to a child. The child belongs to her. All her washing, staying up at night, and so on, is proving that the child belongs to her. She will not do this for any other child, but she will do anything for her own child—even dirty washing. If I belong to Jesus, then I will do anything for Jesus.

Today, just meditate on all this. What is my attitude to Jesus? Have I a living love for Christ?

Fall in Love with Jesus

God has chosen you, called you—each of you—by name. It is part of His plan, part of His infinite mercy that He has called us all together, each of us with our particular characters and faults. We need each other.

He has chosen us; we have not first chosen Him.[77] But we must

---

[77] Cf. Jn 15:16.

respond by making our Society something beautiful for God—something very beautiful. For this we must give all—our utmost. We must cling to Jesus—grasp Him—have a grip on Him and never let go for anything. We must fall in love with Jesus.

Let us not be like the rich young man in the Gospel. Jesus saw him and loved him and wanted him, but he had given his heart to something else—his riches. He was rich, young and strong.[78] Jesus could not fill him. Instead, be like Zacchaeus. He was a little man—a small man—and he knew his smallness. He recognized his smallness and took a very simple means to see Jesus. He climbed a tree, because he knew he was small. If he hadn't opened his heart and responded to Jesus in that simple way, Jesus could not have shown His love; could not have said, "Come down, Zacchaeus! Come down!"[79] This is the foundation of everything— "Learn of me—that I am meek and humble of heart."[80] Be small. When Sister scolds you, is angry with you, doesn't love you, think just for a minute, "Am I guilty?" If I am, say, "sorry"—it is a beautiful gift to God. If I am not, offer it. There is nothing so beautiful you can give. Share with Him. He was called so many names: Beelzebub,[81] a devil, a liar and He never answered. He never said a word—and He was the Son of God.

Be one with Him, joined to Him, united to Him, so that nothing, absolutely nothing, can separate us from the love of Christ. He belongs to me, I belong to Him. As simple as that. I must accept whatever He gives me and give whatever He takes with a big smile. Yet, we forget. We love the leper; that broken and disfigured face and hands, but when our sister is proud or impatient we forget . . . forget that it is only a distressing disguise—that the person is really Jesus. We do not

---

[78] Cf. *Lk 18:18–23.*
[79] Cf. *Lk 19:1–10.*
[80] Cf. *Mt 11:29.*
[81] Cf. *Mt 12:24; Mk 3:22.*

have that undivided love for Christ but we let the devil trick us with the distressing disguise. We must be holy. We must be able to see Jesus in our sisters and in the poor.

THE RULES ARE MEANT TO UPLIFT US

The rules are not meant to crush us but to uplift us, and help us to make our life beautiful in the eyes of God. For that reason I accept them lovingly. Christ does not force us to serve Him. "If you love Me keep My commandments."[82]

JESUS WANTS US TO BE HOLY

Jesus wants us to be holy. Holiness is *nothing* extraordinary, still less extraordinary for a sister to be holy because she has consecrated herself to God. It is a natural state of life for a religious to be holy, for Jesus my spouse is holy. The Gospel says, "Be thou holy as your Father in heaven is holy."[83] . . . There is nothing special for a professed sister to be holy and pure, to pray, to be all for God, for she has given herself to God. Vow is a worship, therefore holiness is a duty for us. Nothing extraordinary. There is no luxury. Just as a married woman who takes care of her husband and children, it is also for us who are married to Christ. If my whole heart is given completely to Jesus, then we must be holy. If *anyone else* says anything contrary to this, believe me, they are trying to deceive you. . . . Never, never, joke about holiness. Holiness is not a joke. I read in a book, "Jesus' love was not a joke." His dying on the Cross was not a joke. He loved me and delivered Himself

---

[82] Cf. *Jn 14:15.*
[83] Cf. *Mt 5:48.*

for me.[84] I love Him, I deliver myself to Him. So let us never make fun of holiness. It is foolishness for us to say, "I am not meant to be holy." I belong to Him, I have consecrated my life to Him, then I must be holy. Examine yourself whether there is that desire burning in your heart. Do I really want to be holy? . . . Ask Our Lady to help you understand how to receive Jesus and take Him to others as she took Him.

THE RELIGIOUS LIFE

It is a privilege for us to be religious. Why we and not others? Very often I said to myself, I was a Loreto nun for twenty years and I said, why, why there are so many nuns there, why did God choose the most stupid one, the most helpless one, the most nothing one—and He could have chosen somebody—this is a mystery of His love, this is the privilege. And the closer we get to Jesus, the more we will understand what He has done for us. And very often we don't understand His love, and we only keep on saying I love You, I love You, but very often we must allow Him to love us. We must allow Him to enjoy our presence because He loves us and He is as much in love with us, and He wants our total surrender. He wants that loving trust, He wants that joy of belonging to Him. We have not been forced. On the eve of final vows, this year we had forty-four sisters who took final vows; we had eighty-one novices who took first vows and on the eve of the profession, I tell the sisters: Sisters, if you feel like you cannot love Christ with undivided love, if you feel that you cannot surrender yourself totally to obedience, you have come happily, I will help you to go home happily, but don't take vows, don't bluff Christ.

It has been wonderful, each one of us to go before the Blessed Sacrament and examine that point—Do I really want totally to belong to

---

[84] *Cf. Gal 2:20.*

Him? And to use human means to live that religious life of surrender. Unless we surrender totally, we cannot experience that unity. Like husband and wife, I always explain that love between a sister and Christ as married life. Reading the Gospel, the man and woman, they give up everything and they cleave to each other[85] and the cleaving is always the family, the child. The fruit of their love, the fruit of their cleaving is that—that oneness. Same thing for us. When we make those vows, when we make the vow of chastity, the vow of obedience, we cleave to Christ; Jesus and I become one and the fruit of that oneness is the work entrusted to us by the Church and this is why our lives must be completely woven with the Church. We are not just left like that, we belong, and the Church is called the Mother Church, we must see her tender care, we must feel that presence in our lives. We are not just left like that . . . we must not feel lonely because we have always somebody and that Somebody is Jesus, always in His presence. Abide in Me . . . and I will abide with you.[86]

As I have read, No water will drown you—no matter what temptations, no matter what difficulties, water will not drown you; fire will not burn you.[87] Maybe terrible things may happen in the work [but they] will not burn you. You are precious to Him. We are precious to Him, we forget this. We think that we are just a number in the congregation. We are precious to God, He has called us by our name. We really belong to Him body and soul, and He must have rights to use us. That vow of chastity is the greatest gift God could give to a human being; that vow of obedience. We don't have to worry—I never had to obey blindly as I had to obey these few years when I have to go, leave everything, go. I told the Holy Father, I am simply torn to pieces. I love my sisters and I want to be with my sisters; I love the poor, I want

---

[85] Cf. *Gen 2:24; Mt 19:4–6; Mk 10:7–8.*
[86] Cf. *Jn 15:5.*
[87] *Is 43:2.*

to be with the lepers, I want to be with the dying, and having to come like this—it's one real act of blind obedience and I feel this is what is obtaining grace, that surrender, that obedience to the Holy Father, that obedience to the Church. This is something that we have all to pray for, to feel the need as religious and to ask ourselves, am I really, totally, freely belonging to God in such a way that He can use me?

CONSECRATED TO BELONG TO JESUS

And where do the sisters get that joy of loving? The fidelity to the vocation, to the consecration that the Church has given to us, has accepted us to be consecrated, and to put our consecration into a living action for our vocation is not to serve the poor. Your vocation is not to take care of the sick in the hospitals or to teach or . . . our vocation is to belong to Jesus with the conviction that nothing and nobody will separate us from the love of Christ, and that is why we need that complete surrender in obedience. . . . The Church has given us this gift— to belong to God—accepted us, accepted our consecration, accepted our lives. So this is something that we can understand only when we realize what is our vocation, and the work that we have been entrusted, the work of our obedience, of our surrender, is our love for Jesus in a living action, and this is where you and I must be able to face Jesus and to surrender to Him completely.

WOMEN'S ORDINATION

We religious who have consecrated our lives totally to God, let us today pray for our people. Let us grow in the humility of Mary more and more that we may be able to be holy like Jesus and help our people to grow in that holiness. See Our Lady was so, so holy, so full of grace, so full of God and yet the humble maid. She just very, very simply said: "Behold the handmaid of the Lord."[88]

✦

Once some people came to our house and they asked me, regarding women to be priests, and I said nobody could have been a better priest than Our Lady and, yet, she remained only the handmaid of the Lord. Next morning, I believe it was in all the newspapers: "Mother Teresa says that the women can be better priests." Thank God many people took it up and they tried to prove that it was not that, that it was really the joy of proclaiming the humility of Mary, the beauty and purity of Mary. And it is so true, she gave everything to Jesus. That's why you as priests, cling to her, love her, she'll be a real Mother to you. She will help you, she will guide you, she will protect you from so many difficulties, so many temptations that surround us all in the world today. . . .

✦

We, women, we have a wonderful, wonderful part to play in the world, to give Jesus by our presence, by our action, by our love; because God has given something specially in our heart, to love and to be loved. And so, let us live our chastity chaste, let us live our purity pure, let us live our virginity virgin, let us be free of anything that will take us away from God because that's what poverty is meant to be—a freedom. For us to understand the poor, we need to know what is poverty. We need to understand the poor, to understand their suffering, we must know.

---

[88] *Cf. Lk 1:38.*

TWO GREAT GIFTS

On the night before He died, Jesus gave us two great gifts—The gift of Himself in the Eucharist and the gift of the Priesthood to continue His living presence in the Eucharist. Without priests, we have no Jesus. Without priests, we have no absolution. Without priests, we cannot receive Holy Communion. . . . There is no comparison with the vocation of the priest. It is like a replacing of Jesus at the Altar, at the confessional, and in all the other sacraments where he uses his own "I" like Jesus. How completely the priest must be one with Jesus to use him in His place, in His name, to utter His words, do His actions, take away the sins, and make ordinary bread and wine into the Living Bread of His own Body and Blood. Only in the silence of his heart can he hear God's word and from the fullness of his heart he can utter these words: "I absolve you" and "This is My Body." How pure the mouth of the priest must be and how clean the heart of a priest must be to be able to speak, to utter the words: "This is My Body" and to make bread into the living Jesus. How pure must be the hand of the priest, how completely the hand of Jesus must be the hand of the priest if in it, when the priest raises that hand, is the Precious Blood of Jesus. A sinner comes to confession covered with sin, he leaves the confessional, a sinner without sin. O how pure, how sacred a priest must be to lift away sin and to utter the words: "I absolve you."

GIVING PEACE

I have seen it again and again, our people in our home for the dying after they have made their peace with God . . . When I was last time in New York, we have a home for AIDS and there was a phone call, a young man was phoning: "Mother Teresa, I think I have got the disease. I'm going to the doctor and if he says that I have it, I want to come to you, I want to die with you." And I said, "Yes, you'd be most welcome." Next day, he phoned again, he said, "Yes, I have it." I said, "Come immediately, I'll be very happy to have you. Come." And he came. And that joy on that man's face that he was wanted, that he will be able to make his peace with God, that there will be some priest there to forgive him, to help him to make the peace with Jesus. He was not there two weeks and we prepared him to die. And he died a beautiful death, beautiful death. What the priest could give to that man—that joy, that peace that no one can give. He died a holy death because his heart was all so spotlessly pure. We have most wonderful happenings in these homes where people come face to face with God, face to face.

Giving Jesus

Jesus made Himself Bread of Life that we may have life.[89] He made Himself so that you and I can receive Him, can live with Him, can keep Him in our heart. That is why it is very important that during the day very often we say, "Jesus in my heart, I believe in Your tender love for me, I love You," again and again. "In union with all the Masses being offered throughout the world, I offer you my heart." What a wonderful gift of God the priest is, but what a wonderful and great responsibility to bring, to give Jesus. When we went, when we were allowed to come to enter Russia, one doctor in charge of a very big hospital accepted us, and we came there and he gave us three rooms. And we began the work in that place by cleaning the toilets—that was our first apostolic work. And we do all the little humble works all over the place. And then by the evening, the priest came and brought—and in our little chapel, we have a little tabernacle, we had Holy Mass, and he gave us Jesus and he changed the whole attitude—the whole place looked quite different after. We had

---

[89] Cf. Jn 6:53, 56.

Mass once a week in our little chapel and so, after one week, the doctor came to me and said, "Mother Teresa, what's happening in my hospital?" I said, "I don't know, doctor, what, what is happening?" He said, "I don't know, something is happening. I see the nurses and the doctors much more kind, much more loving with the patients. I see the patients are not screaming with pain as before. What's happening? What are the sisters doing?" And I looked at him and I said, "Doctor, you know what is happening? Jesus is in this house now. There in that little chapel, He is living, He is loving, He is there, He's the cause, He's the maker, He's the giver of this joy, of this peace, of this love." And he just shook his head, "Thank you." And it was wonderful to feel that Presence of Jesus in that hospital, after seventy years, that presence was felt. Everybody knew that there was Somebody there thanks to that priest who gave us Jesus. And it brought that tremendous change in that place.

THE PRIESTHOOD

I will pray for you that [the] resolutions you have made here, to grow in a living reality of holiness with Mary, that you may be able to be true to your word. Give your word of honor to God that you will be a priest according to the heart of Jesus. And I will pray for all the people that will come in contact with you, that when they look up, they may see only Jesus in you. And that whatever you do—not so much by words maybe, because you have to speak the Word of God—but by your presence, the way you touch the people, the way you give the sacraments . . . that tenderness and love in confession [maybe] for hours and hours—very difficult, but that is [how] Jesus spent hours in His agony, and that's your turn now. This is why you are another Christ. Let us ask Our Lady in a special way today and let us promise to her that we'll love her Son, that we'll consecrate our life totally to Him to use. Ask her, that Jesus may use you without consulting you, without [asking]—even if you don't know why—but that He can use you because you belong to Him. You are His and only His. And let the prayer of Cardinal Newman live in you and through you among the people that you serve.

Poverty Is Freedom

If you want to become holy, become poor. Jesus became poor to save us, and if we really want to become poor, like Christ, then we have to be really poor, spiritually poor.

SUITCASES AND SHOES

[Sometimes when I travel] I [carry my belongings in] a cardboard box and people will offer to give me suitcases. I said, "I don't feel embarrassed." It is not wrong for me to have a suitcase, but I choose not to have a suitcase. This is the thing. You must have the courage to choose, even with your superior. Another time someone [wanted to replace my worn-out old shoes] said to me, "Mother, I'll give you three hundred dollars, give me the shoes." "Three hundred dollars? Give me the dollars [for the poor], but I'll keep the shoes."

THE FOUNTAIN PENS

I remember my brother before he died, he had never given me anything. I had never given him anything. This time I don't know what happened—he went and bought the most beautiful pen and he wanted me only to use it. Without exaggeration, [at] that moment a lady came with two fountain pens and she gave them to me without any condition. I did not take the pen which my brother gave because he has given for my personal use. But I took the pens which [the] lady had given me for the poor. I cannot tell you the joy that came to his face. He was proud of me, knowing within two weeks time he would die. Our people expect us to be faithful to our vows. We must be free. [If not], you cannot look up and face the poorest of the poor. St. Ignatius has a beautiful expression—"love poverty as a mother."

IMITATION OF CHRIST

It is not enough for us to practice the vow of poverty; we must strive to acquire the true spirit of poverty which manifests itself in a love for the practice of the virtue of poverty in imitation of Christ, in imitation of Him who chose it as the companion of His life on earth when He came to live among us. Christ did not have to lead the life of poverty— He led it in order to work out our redemption—and yet He chose to be poor and to love the poor. Thus He taught us how important it is for us in the work of our sanctification.

JESUS' POVERTY

When [Jesus] was born, He was so helpless, so small. He could have been born in a palace, in [an] ordinary family life, then again He was born in a stable.[90] There were no windows, no air; He was with the animals. Mary's faith must have been so strong to accept. Jesus was the Son of God. Then He had to bring the good news to the poor.[91] What is that good news?—That God loves us and we should love one another

---

[90] *Cf. Lk 2:7.*
[91] *Cf. Is 61:1; Mt 11:5; Lk 4:18, 7:22.*

as He loves us. So poverty has much to do with charity. Before, people were frightened of God. When we read some of the Psalms, we see how terrified people were of God. Then Jesus came, full of gentleness; anybody could have destroyed Him. He was so poor.

THE POVERTY OF CHRIST

In the eyes of God, even the richest man is an object of poverty. Now turn the page. Here is the MC. Maybe we had all that money could buy, but we left all these things. It is our choice to have privations and all the difficulties that come from our poverty. Then why do we resist the graces that come from our poverty? If Christ, the Holy Father, and the people would look at our poverty what would they say? "Oh, is he not the carpenter of Nazareth?"[92] Poverty must be a living reality. I must want it, and each time I do this I choose with Christ, and because I want it, I love [it]. Knowledge leads to love. Do we love poverty in the sense it is given to us? Voluntary poverty does not consist in asking permission to use things, but [in being] truly poor in spirit and choosing the poverty of Christ.

Christ being rich emptied Himself.[93] This is where contradiction lies. If I want to be poor like Christ—who became poor even though rich—He renounced, He gave—I must do the same. People nowadays want to be poor and live with the poor but they want to be free to dispose of things of money value. This is riches. They want both and you cannot have both. This is another kind of contradiction.

✦

---

[92] Cf. *Mt 13:55; Mk 6:9.*
[93] Cf. *2 Cor 8–9, Phil 2:6–7.*

What is the practice of the virtue of poverty? It is that virtue, which makes us love to imitate the life of poverty Christ chose for Himself. For that reason we are spurred on to rejoice when our religious life gives us the opportunity to practice true poverty. The virtue of poverty will make us go out of our way to look after all that is given us for our use, whether personal or common, by the Society. St. Ignatius tells us to love poverty as we love our own mother—as tenderly and as dearly.

THE VOW OF POVERTY

We take a vow of poverty out of love for God, not forced. I give up for the love of God everything that is mine that has a money value. I cannot keep, give or destroy without permission. I must take care of the things given into my hands. It is not *my* sari—only given for my use for some time. The superior has the right to take away everything from me. She does not do it, but she has the right. I give up my freedom to use the things as I like, out of pure love of God. I have to ask the permission. It is madness to grumble when we are not getting nice things. Sometimes the sisters grumble when they do not get nice food or if it is not served properly. We wanted to be poor, so we eat this food—bulgar and so on. We must be happy to be poor. Naturally, we do not like it. We want to like it but it is difficult, but supernaturally we like it.

We must love our poverty. We must be happy to be poor, to be without things, to have the worst things in the house. For the love of God we gave everything up. God made things beautifully—we gave it up. Some sisters in other congregations told me that they are using nice things to give others the opportunity to earn money. But for us it does not fit. For Loreto Sisters, it is all right to have things like that, or for others to have nice hospitals. They cannot work like in Nirmal

Hriday. They need these things. But we have to live in another way. Otherwise we cannot understand the people. Now in the slums, I can tell that we have the same thing in eating and clothing like they, themselves. We have no fans—we could have—we do not want it. Then we can feel how the poor people feel. Why have we so strict a poverty? We cannot serve the poor when we do not love them. I love them and want to give them my love. We deprive ourselves for the love of God. I want it, nobody forced me. Each time I say, "I want it," I say and do it for the love of God. I grow in this love from aspirancy and postulancy, noviciate, junior professed to final vows [until] I die.

Poverty means also to ask permission, taking care of the things, mending the clothes properly. Mother[94] and we, all have the same privilege to live the life of poverty to the full. I want to live the life of Nazareth that I may love poverty for the love of Jesus. Cling to poverty—that is the best way to show the love of God. Jesuits in Rome said in the Chapter: "We must bring the Society [down] to the poorest of the poor." Poverty is a privilege. Our sisters in Venezuela were happy to give away the nice things they had in the beginning. We must love poverty.

THE COURAGE NOT TO HAVE

I can have but I choose not to have, and that choosing of "not to have" needs lots of courage, because we all like to have. The more we are in love with Jesus, the more we will love poverty and the more we love poverty, the more we will know that freedom, that freedom of heart and of all things also. In our Society, poverty asks something more—

---

[94] *It was customary for Mother Teresa to refer to herself in the third person, as is the custom among the Sisters in India.*

the total giving of self to the poorest of the poor: the unwanted, the unloved and uncared—freedom from all material things that would keep us away from the joy of loving Jesus. . . . The more free you are, the more Christlike you will be and the more Christlike you are, the more loving you will be. Poverty is a gift of God. If you look into the life of Our Lady, you will see it, and in the life of Jesus, too, you will see it. He being the Son of God, born in poverty—He could have had a palace, but chose to be born in a poor place. Poverty has a great attraction for heaven, so let us ask Our Lady to make it clear for us.

PRACTICING THE POVERTY OF CHRIST

We practice the virtue of poverty when we mend our clothes in time and as beautifully as we can. To go about in a torn habit and sari is certainly not the sign of the virtue of poverty, for remember, we do not profess the poverty of beggars but the poverty of Christ. Let us also remember that our body is the temple of the Holy Spirit and for that reason we must respect it always with neatly mended clothes. We would never dream of using dirty, torn clothes as a tabernacle veil which covers the door of the dwelling Christ chose for Himself on earth since He ascended into heaven. In the same way, we should never cover the temple of the Holy Spirit—which is our body—with torn, dirty, untidy clothes. . . . Patched clothes are no disgrace. It is said about St. Francis of Assisi that when he died, his habit—the one he wore daily—had forty patches. The original cloth was no longer there.

TEMPTED BY THE SMALL

Money is a danger—it can do such great harm, and be the cause of suffering. It is a dangerous weapon in the hand of the devil. My feeling for poverty goes. Let us free ourselves. Be very strict with yourself. The devil will never come and tell you to do something which you are forbidden to do. . . . Give that example to your sisters—not the strictness of a slave . . . but that I have given my word to God. . . . None of us are so safe that we can play with fire. The devil will never try to tempt you with something big, but with a small thing. If the devil had to get a Nobel Prize, it should be for patience.

A CONSTANT VIGIL

There is another kind of poverty, what they call spiritual poverty—to accept to be where you are, to do what you are told to do, sometimes with people that are very agreeable, sometimes with people that are disagreeable, maybe they have not the same culture, the same thought, and to be able to be all love with that kind of people, I think that is a great practice of poverty. And in our congregations, I think we need that more and more, in all of our congregations—that complete freedom that makes us the whole time say, "May I?"

We are beginning to forget that little word[95] but that little word makes all the difference in our poverty—that we possess nothing and in possessing nothing, actually we possess everything because we possess Christ. And for all of us, for you and for our Society also, we need that constant vigil lest the riches of the world suffocate us. This is what I feel in the States. I mean in India, it's easier for us to practice poverty,

---

[95] *Meaning "Please, may I . . . ," which is the MC's way of asking for permission.*

much easier, but for you—you have so much—I find it very difficult, it must be very difficult for you. For us it is not, because we don't have those things even here, but you, when you are surrounded with so many things, and to have the courage to say, "it is there, but I don't use it."

POVERTY AND CHOICE

Somebody asked me, "When will the poverty of India be lifted?" and I said, "When you and I begin to share with them." It is a joy that I can share with you what I have and I cannot hold it by myself, I must give it to my brother, to my sister who hasn't got and that sharing brings peace, joy, love. Even the abortion is a great poverty because people are afraid of the child, they are afraid of having to feed one more child and to get one more child, the child must die. And so it is fear. Another kind of poverty which we see very much in the West—we have material poverty with our people in India and Africa, they have to go through—but in the West and other and American countries, you have the poverty of heart, poverty of spirit, too caught up—and they are surrounded with things that make them starve. . . . There's a much greater greed for power, for things [in the West]: I must have one more thing and one more thing and one more thing—that kind. And to have those, you have to give up something, so they give up the child.

DO NOT LOSE YOUR FREEDOM

A gentleman, a rich man, came to Shishu Bhavan and said he would give whatever the sisters would ask. He wanted to give a generator. This costs thousands. I told him "No." Today a generator, tomorrow a washing machine. You must have the courage to refuse what is not for us. In the Motherhouse, very often the power goes off and it is very hard for the sisters to study. They go outside onto the terrace, and so on. Then a very rich gentleman offered to give us a generator, so that, even if there is no current, we can have light. I told him, "Thank you. We don't need it." Do not misunderstand me, Sisters. There is nothing wrong in having it, but I must choose not to have. . . . I told him to give it to the Little Sisters of the Poor because they have a very big home and the old people might fall in that sudden darkness. So he gave it to them.

After two weeks that man came back to me and told me, "Mother, because you refused me, my life has completely changed. Before, I was always thinking how to get more and more money but now I want to give." So he gave us some kerosene lamps.

Sisters, we must be convinced and keep to the most humble means. . . . All these things are surrounding the sisters and they have lost the joy and simplicity of poverty. They are tied tight by all these things so that they cannot move any more. I must have everything. Further, further, further, more and more. . . . You will lose the freedom of poverty. If you are seeking affection from everyone, that also is riches. You must be free and convinced that you belong to Jesus.

It is so beautiful to be free, otherwise I feel suffocated.

An Undivided Love

Chastity for me is not only no marriage, but undivided love.

A PURE HEART

If you're all for Jesus, He will do great things. How? Because if your heart is pure, God will come and dwell there, because He has great attraction for a pure heart. I read the other day—God was like "forced"—Jesus was "anxious" to come down to Mary because she was so beautifully pure. So, ask Mary to teach you to be pure so that Jesus will be able to come to your heart and make you holy.

TODAY'S WORLD

In the world of today, chastity is the virtue that is most attacked. It is good to take precautions. Mother told some young couples that the best gift they could give each other on their wedding day is a pure heart, pure body, and virgin body.

TRICKING THE DEVIL

We are created with that power to love as women. We give that power to Jesus—to really be in love with Him. Impure thoughts, bad imaginations, and evil desires—meet them with, "I don't want it." Keep away the will. I have learnt one very easy trick with the devil: "I am very sorry, but I am very busy now."

CONSECRATED WOMEN AND LOVE

To be able to become true consecrated women, we must more and more fall in love with Jesus. Love Him with all the powers of body and soul. Let it not be said that a woman in the world loves her husband better than we do Jesus. This is our right and privilege, for as women we have been created to love and to be loved. The more closely a soul is held captive by love, the more she is identified with all humanity, for love causes her to enter into all suffering wherever souls are to be saved. As missionaries and consecrated women, we must give love the first place in our lives. Our vows, our apostolate, our community life are all the fruit of our love-union with Jesus.

THE VOW

The vow of chastity is not just a list of don'ts, it is love. . . . It is to give and to take—I give myself to God and I receive God. God becomes my own, and I become His own. That is why I become completely dedicated to Him by my vow of chastity.

FIDELITY

In Rome, a woman told me her story. The day she came out of the church, married, she fell in love with another man. For twenty-six years she lived with that love —for that man. "But I gave my word to this man [my husband] and for the sake of my faithfulness to God and to the man to whom I gave my word, I have had to say 'no' to him [the other man]. Each day has been a real crucifixion. Each time he comes to Rome: 'no'—while I have no love for the man whom I married." This woman said, "Death, yes; sin, no." Twenty-five [years] by three hundred and sixty-five [days] by sixty minutes! I am talking now of a Christian. Now she loves her husband with an undivided love. I have given my vows to God, and only death can separate. This is chastity.

DENIAL OF MARRIED LIFE

By the vow of chastity, I deprive myself of the married state, of having a home and founding a family, for the love of God.[96] We Catholics understand it easily, but non-Catholics cannot understand how a woman can live without getting married. For them it is most unnatural and yet they admire it; they do not understand what makes us give up that right.

By the vow of chastity, I not only renounce the married state of life, but I also consecrate to God the free use of my internal and external acts—my affections. I cannot, in conscience, love a creature with the love of a woman for a man. I no longer have the right to give that affection to any other creature but God. . . . For a friendship to be harmful, it has to be something that we take away from God and give to creatures. As long as I do not take away anything from God, it is all right. The minute I break a rule for that friendship, I am taking away from God; it is therefore harmful.

What then? Have we to be stones, human beings without hearts? To just say, "I don't care; to me human beings are all the same." No, not at all. We have to keep ourselves as we are, but keep it all for God, to whom we have consecrated all our external and internal acts. Therein lies the full meaning of all the rules regarding touching, kissing, looking, and so on. Don't say, "I will never love a sister in my life." Our Lord at His dying moment thought of His mother,[97] that is the proof that He was human to the last. Therefore, if you have a loving nature, keep it and use it for God; if you have a smiling temperament, keep it and use it for God.

Listen well: as long as you know your weakness, you are safe. People who are inclined to particular friendship never want to own up to it.

---

[96] *Cf. Mt 19:12.*
[97] *Cf. Jn 19:25–27.*
  Cf. Mt 5:27–30, 18:8–9; Mk 9:43–46.

For peace of mind, learn to measure your affections. Do I break a rule for that sister, that child? No. Perfect. But you must be sincere. Then it does not matter what anybody says to you. But if your conscience says "*yes*" then you must take a knife and cut, for it is leading you to danger. Then you will never grow into a sister who is in love with God, who loves everybody because she loves God in every soul. Don't be afraid to love your sisters with a deep sincere love. Very often Mother wonders who she loves more—Jesus or the sisters? That is a foolish question, for it is Jesus in and through the sisters that Mother loves.

THE FREEDOM TO LOVE ALL

People in the world think that the vow of chastity makes us inhuman, makes us become like a stone, without feelings. Each one of us can tell them it is not true. It is the vow of chastity that gives us the freedom to love everybody, instead of becoming a mother of three or four children. A married woman can love but one man; we can love the whole world in God. The vow of chastity does not diminish us, it makes us live to the full if it is kept properly and we don't just limit ourselves to the don'ts. The vow of chastity is not simply a list of don'ts; it is love. That is why we can look at everybody and say, "I love all." In our Constitutions, we read that we must love each other with intense love. We can do that because we love God. It is to give and take—I give to God myself and I receive God. God becomes my own, and I become His own. That is why I become completely dedicated to Him by the vow of chastity. And when we stoop down to dirty thoughts we throw away precious stones and take up mud. In our spiritual life, we have the immeasurable Almighty God, and yet we stoop to a creature. It is inconceivable how we turn away from the Almighty God to busy ourselves with a creature, however good that creature may be. It is like a little child who turns away from sweets to eat wall plaster or even mud.

We must look straight at ourselves because that craving to stoop to "mud" is in every one of us; but some eat and others turn away from it.

SMALL BUT DANGEROUS

Is it possible for the religious to break her home with Christ? Yes. And how? Through very small infidelities. Just like a tin of oil gets empty through a leakage. Remember we shall never be tempted straight-away on big things. It is small breaches that will tempt us. Two years ago, there was a very big fire which began with a matchstick. Now a very little bit of destructible matter at the end of a matchstick caused immense damage. That little matchstick is the little temptation to break the different points of our rule. These may seem so insignificant and yet, like the matchstick, they can cause immense damage in the soul! To break silence, to give without permission, not to take the trouble to prepare our class, and so on—it is these little breaches that are very dangerous. Unless we really love God and are really and fully dedicated to Him, that little breach will finally turn us away from the intimacy with God.

"I AM NOT WHAT MY FEELINGS MAKE ME"

Don't think it is enough for us to surrender ourselves to God once and for all. If we do not practice daily self-control, daily self-denial, we shall become a bundle of nerves. Jesus grew in age and wisdom before God and man.[98] We too have to grow in the same way. Our superiors are there to help us cut and pull out what is harmful to our spiritual lives. There is no meaning in showing temper when you are corrected. Then there is

---

[98] *Cf. Lk 2:50.*

no sense in joining a religious society if you don't want to be holy. We must watch our moods very closely and check them in the very beginning. When we find out that we are inclined to be moody and hysterical, watch, watch, watch. Women are inclined to that—we live on our feelings, but as religious we can't do that. Because I am very fervent today, don't think I am fervent; I am not what my feelings make me, but I am what I am before God. I beg of you Sisters, watch yourselves well in the beginning. Be harsh with yourselves now rather than later on when it will be so much more difficult. That I am inclined to be dragged down—that is all right, but I must not give in to that inclination.

"Lord, don't allow my feelings to spoil the beautiful handiwork you have begun in my soul." All that moodiness is nothing but a type of selfishness. The truth is nothing but humility, and when we are humble, we are holy. Help yourselves to become steady. Get that conviction that you love God and that it is because you love Him that you are here.

THE WEDDING

At the first World Youth Day when all the English speaking young people were gathered at the Church of Santa Sabina and Mother Teresa was prepared to speak to them, all of a sudden the doors opened into the Basilica and in walks an entire wedding party. The people who scheduled the activities of the Basilica had made a mistake and they had also permitted a wedding to be scheduled for the same time as Mother Teresa was going to be speaking. So after we worked through what the problem was, Mother Teresa says well, let's go ahead and have the wedding. It's alright. And so the young people separated and made an aisle for the wedding party to come down through and the wedding proceeded and Mother Teresa spent the time over praying at one of the alcoves—an altar on the side. It was a phenomenal thing and it showed just how human Mother was. She greeted the bride and groom, she was very kind to them and blessed them and everybody enjoyed it very much and it only took a few minutes for the wedding to be completed and then she spoke to all the young people there and they really brought the house down with applause and affirmation of Mother and what she said.

Nakedness is not only for a piece of cloth, nakedness is the loss of the human dignity, the loss of that beautiful virtue, purity—it is so misused nowadays. You see it in the streets, in those big cities, you see loving and kissing and embracing in the streets. You see our homes filled with unwed mothers—how? Why? . . . Let us, you young people, let us make a strong resolution today before the altar of God, before Our Lady, that we will keep our purity pure, we will keep our chastity chaste, we will keep our virginity virgin. And the greatest gift you can give to each other on the day when you get married or the day when you join priesthood or religious life—a virgin heart, a virgin body. How wonderful it is to see that greatness, that likeness to Mary, so we need her. Let us pray to her that she may obtain for us that great grace of purity, and during these days that you are here with the Holy Father in the heart of the Church, ask and make a resolution that our purity will be pure, our chastity will be chaste, our virginity will be virgin. And that is the grace I will pray for you, for that is the grace that will help you, that will make you holy. Holiness is not the luxury of the few, it is a simple duty for you and for me. And if God calls you, if He calls you by your name, if He has chosen you to be His very own, if He has chosen you to espouse you in tenderness and love, be not afraid. Say "yes" and follow Him as the apostles did. And who will be the one to guide you, protect you, help you, love you? Mother Mary, Mother of Jesus. And we will ask her again. I will pray very specially for you that you grow in that purity of Mary so that you and I and all of us together bring glory to God through our tenderness and love that we offer to Him.

Purity

To love a young girl is beautiful and a young girl to love a young man is beautiful but the greatest gift, the most beautiful gift that you can give each other on your day of marriage is a virgin heart, a virgin body, a pure heart, a pure body. And this Our Lady will obtain for you if you, every day, pray the three Hail Marys to her. She will protect your purity, and your purity will remain pure, your chastity will remain chaste, and your virginity will remain virgin because she will obtain the graces for you from her Son.

We Are Free

Given on behalf of the Kingdom, it [consecrated chastity] frees the heart in a unique way and causes it to burn with love for God and for all mankind.

Obedience

You will not have the readiness to say "yes" to the great things if you do not train yourselves to say "yes" to the thousand and one occasions of obedience that come your way throughout the day.

JESUS' OBEDIENCE

It is that total surrender to God that makes me a religious. Again, we come back to Our Lord and Our Lady: "I am sent by my Father[99]; my Father is greater than I."[100] Jesus need not have done all that He did. He is equal to God, God from God, Light from Light, and yet He submitted—to obey, to be born, to go down to Nazareth. He accepted to be put here and there. When the high priest asked Him, "Tell us whether you be the Christ,"[101] Jesus obeyed and gave the answer. He knew that if He obeyed it would be crucifixion, but He was totally sur-rendered. Have we come here to be equal? We have come here to be totally surrendered, but instead we go on saying that the superior said it nicely or harshly, she is black or white. Yet Jesus obeyed all whether it was Mary, Joseph or Pilate.

In the Gospel we find many proofs of Christ's obedience. If we were to go to Nazareth in spirit, we first hear Our Lady's answer to the angel, "Be it done to me according to thy word."[102] Then we read about Jesus, "He went down and was obedient to them,"[103] to a carpen-ter, Joseph—and to Mary, who according to human calculation was a simple village girl. Then we hear Jesus say, "I have come to do the will of my Father, of Him who sent me."[104] Then throughout His pas-sion, He obeys His executioners blindly. On these examples that Christ gives us in the Gospel, we must build our obedience.

✦

---

[99] *Cf. Jn 5:36, 6:38, 8:16.*
[100] *Cf. Jn 10:29.*
[101] *Cf. Lk 22:67.*
[102] *Cf. Lk 1:38.*
[103] *Cf. Lk 2:51.*
[104] *Cf. Jn 6:38.*

Jesus, how He obeyed! Some time back, I was meditating and it struck me so much—thirty years Jesus lived in that little house in Nazareth, with the cleaning, with the washing, with the cooking, with His mother; just [doing] ordinary things, so ordinary that the people afterwards said, "How is He doing what He is doing?"[105] They were shocked, simply. Thirty years in that little house in Nazareth, a real house of the poor, like some of our families have, simple houses—not three years, not fifteen years; the same house, same work, same place, with His father and mother. It really shocked me that for thirty years He lived in a little house like that. He, the Creator of the world, [the] living God, but He lived a life of total obedience. I want you sisters to understand what I am saying. Love obedience. Don't say, "I have to obey" but "I love to obey." That little bell, "I love to hear it," that little work I have to do, "I love to do it." Always "I love" not "I have to." I always make myself say that, "I love."

THE FIRST SIN

Obedience must be something spiritual, since it is found also in heaven. Disobedience was the first sin; right there in front of God, Lucifer—the most beautiful angel—refused to submit, refused to obey, not in chastity or anything else, but he said, "I will not serve."[106] When he was cast out of heaven,[107] he wanted more companions, so he went to Adam and Eve—God had told them, "You can eat from all the trees, this one, this one and thousands of trees—a garden full of beautiful trees."[108] Then God said such a small thing, "Don't eat from this one tree."[109]

---

[105] Cf. Mt 13:53–55; Mk 6:1–3; Lk 4:20–22; Jn 7:15.
[106] Cf. Is 14:12–15.
[107] Cf. Rev 12:1–8.
[108] Cf. Gen 2:16.
[109] Cf. Gen 2:17.

They say it was an apple tree. There must have been many other apple trees, but that one tree they could not touch. What happened was a continuation of that first sin—they refused to obey and ate that fruit.[110] When we disobey, it is a continuation of that same first sin—that first sin makes us sinners; because of that first one, the inclination [to sin] is there. I must face that in myself. As religious, we seek to cover up, to make reparation for that sin, and so we take the vow of obedience.

OBEDIENCE IN EVERYDAY LIFE

Today we have many broken homes because there is not that obedience—that surrender to each other—between husband and wife, parents and children. There is so much trouble with the young people because they want to be free to do everything as they like. There is so much trouble in our own communities, so much disturbance, because sisters want to do what they like, live the way they like. Nowadays, many religious speak of the need for dialogue, "personal freedom," as if a life of obedience was something where these things are absent. They also speak of the great need for community life—but you cannot have community life without a superior, and the presence of a superior automatically brings obedience. In community life we need someone to take the place of God, and the superior is the means He uses to express His will. So it is not "she" it is "He." The superior is like the pencil in the hand of God. If you were to receive a letter from Mother, you wouldn't look to see what kind of pen I used, or whether the ink came out properly, or what quality the paper was. No, you would be busy to see what is the message that Mother has written, what is Mother saying to me. By reading that letter, you want to enter my mind, to know what Mother wants to say to you. Same thing in obedience, we want to know what God wants, and

---

[110] *Cf. Gen 3:6.*

by obeying the superior's command in everything, except sin, we fulfill it perfectly. Let us not look on the vows as something cruel. Nowadays, there is an attitude that once you have lost the freedom to do what you like, as you like, that there is no point in staying as religious. Actually, religious, who speak like that, they are the ones who have lost that real freedom to live as true religious, and they would be better off outside.

"If You Knew You Were to Die . . ."

One of the saints—John Berchmans or Aloysius—was playing football when one of his companions said to him: "Brother, if you knew you were to die just now, what would you do?" St. Aloysius replied, "I would continue playing because at this moment, it is the will of God for me." Do we have that same conviction, that whatever we do in obedience is blessed as God's will for us?

A Free Heart

We cannot obey when our heart is impure—jealousy, criticism, grumbling, lazy. When these things are there, we are not pure. To be pure in heart, to have a free heart, is the same thing. We have only to say "yes," we have not to break our head. But to have a pure heart we must pray, these two things go together. And we will become holy.

Not the Obedience of a Slave, but of Love

Today youth cannot obey. I was trying to find out why they are so anti-obedient. Nowadays even in communities you have the "group" making the decisions. Families are unable to control even the youngest child of seven years old, and when I was told this I asked, "Why can't you take them by the hand and control?" A book has been written, and every mother has been asked to read that book. There it says let the child do what he wants from the age of one, so from that age he can say, "Oh no, I won't go today, I will go where I want." This is the spirit and we know the reason of this terrible upheaval. It is riches. The man in the Gospel could not give them up and we too.[111] The person given totally to God knows obedience. I am not talking of the obedience of a slave, but of love. My parents—I love them and they love me and so I obey. There must also be some fear: The fear of offending God, of offending our parents, of offending our superiors. What an empty life is ours as religious if we have not understood this: that I belong to Him and He can do with me what He wants.

LOVE FOR LOVE

For our obedience to be cheerful and prompt, we have to be convinced that it is Jesus we obey. And how do we reach that state? By the practice of a heroic virtue of obedience—love for love. If you want to know whether you love God, ask yourselves the question, "Do I obey?" If I obey, everything is all right. Why? Because everything depends on my will. It depends upon me, whether I become a saint or a sinner. So you see how very important obedience is. Our sanctity, after the grace of God, depends upon our will. Don't waste time in waiting for big things to do for God while you let pass by all the little rules of the religious life. You will not have the readiness to say "yes" to the great things if you do not train yourselves to say "yes" to the thousand and one occasions of obedience that come your way throughout the day. For example, it happened to one of the Sisters of Charity. One young

---

[111] *Cf. Mt 19:16–22; Mk 10:17–22.*

sister was sent to study and completed her B.T.[112] The morning of the day the results came out, she died—two hours before their release. When [one young sister] was dying she asked, "Why did Jesus call me for such a short time?" And Mother answered, "Jesus wants you, not your works." She was perfectly happy after that. We have to do our work according to obedience. Hence, obedience must be something very important, since everything must be founded on it.

Knowledge of God, love of God, service of God—that is the end of our life—and obedience gives us the key to it all. . . . Now if I live constantly in the company of Jesus, I too will do the same as He did. Nothing pleases God more than when we obey. Let us love God, not for what He gives but for what He deigns to take from us—our little acts of obedience that give us the occasion of proving our love for Him.

EASIER TO CONQUER A COUNTRY THAN TO CONQUER OURSELVES

We obey *simply* because it is Jesus we obey. It is so simple that it is hard to understand the complications that sometimes arise. We must use the eyes of faith to see Him who has called us and to obey *promptly*, now, not tomorrow. That "tomorrow" easily leads into the tepid way. *Blindly:* Blind obedience puts all the "whys" out of the mind. Once you start using the little word "why?" you will end nowhere. Your life will be an empty life. You obey with your hand, but you disobey with your heart. That is false obedience, says St. Ignatius. It is not easy and we cannot help those "whys" coming into our minds, but we can prevent them from conquering us. As soon as you become aware of them, keep your will away. We waste so much precious time because we are busy

---

[112] Baccalaureus Theologiae *(Bachelor of Theology).*

with ourselves. Superiors are not bound to give us the reasons but we are bound to obey. *Cheerfully:* The sisters that obey thus are like strong pillars in the Society. You don't know how hard it is sometimes for the superiors to make a little change. Your security in the Society comes first and foremost from your vow of obedience. If you obey, you will never make a mistake. From early morning till night I can be certain that my actions are right because I did them under obedience. This sense of security makes us happy. Turn the picture: If you don't obey then you become unhappy, restless. You have to experience that obedience to be able to feel at perfect ease. It is much easier to conquer a country than to conquer ourselves. Every act of disobedience weakens my spiritual life. It is like a wound letting out every drop of one's blood. Nothing can cause this havoc in our spiritual life as quickly as disobedience.

We must be at ease with God, and God must be completely at ease with us.

CLOSER TO GOD

What does perfect obedience mean? It is an unfailing source of peace. When sisters come and tell Mother they are unhappy, dissatisfied, the first thing Mother asks them is, "Do you obey?" and their sincere answer gives Mother the clue to their restlessness. No half measures with God; let us not serve God according to our moods. The price of our love is inward joy—we must be able to smile twenty-four hours a day. Inward joy comes only from perfect obedience. If you are not happy in the Congregation, don't blame the Congregation, blame yourself.

Close union with God is a natural result of obedience, perfect obedience. From a human point of view, we come closer to our superiors when we obey and from a supernatural point of view we come closer to God when we obey.

Eyes of Faith

St. Bernard tells us that if we look at our superior only with our bodily eyes we shall see only the body of our superior with all her defects, but if we look at our superior with eyes of faith then we meet Jesus, the all beautiful, the all holy, and in all orders and corrections we would see the hand of God shaping us in His loving way.

Go back to the angels, to Adam and Eve, the difficulty was always a difficulty of obedience. It is obedience that will control our apostolate[113] of charity. Let us be firm in this one resolution: "I will obey without grumbling or criticizing."

Acts of disobedience are acts of pride, and pride is hateful to God. If a religious chooses to disobey deliberately, she can be in the state of mortal sin for not striving to reach perfection once she has embraced a state of perfection. Let us now think of what my infidelities deprive God [of]—I will not fulfill His plan concerning me. . . .

The holier I become the more souls I can draw to God. Each of us has a certain number of souls dependant upon us for salvation, therefore I must grow holy for the sake of those souls. The holier I become, the closer they will draw to God. Sanctity is doing the will of God with joy, in other words sanctity is obedience. Our superiors convey this will of God to us, they are the channels through which the will of God comes to us. We must for that [reason], love and respect our superiors and thank God that we have superiors. . . . Our Lord never calculated in His obedience, "I have come to do the will of Him who sent me."[114]

---

[113] *The MC's work among the poor.*
[114] *Cf. Jn 6:38.*

OBEYING IS NOT BELOW OUR DIGNITY

How did the angels become devils? They were all in the sight of God. Lucifer, the angel of light, became the devil of darkness. We read that God gave them a test, that when the Son of God will become man, [they should serve Him]; in their pride, they said *"non serviam."* Hell was not in the original plan of God, but God was forced to create it. God who is merciful love, had not created hell until the angels disobeyed and became devils. Remember those little Latin words *"non serviam."* [God] created the angels, He created human beings. He who is the Creator obeyed. Obeying is not below our dignity.

Eating an apple is not sin. In fact, we eat many. Yet God told Adam and Eve not to eat. I don't think that Eve ate the whole apple, she must have eaten only a bite. That was enough for the devil; *"non serviam"* was done in that bite. Each time when we disobey, we say and do the same way. How did disobedience come? Like sanctity [comes] by fidelity in little things, [so disobedience comes by] infidelity in little things. Today one thing does not matter and tomorrow two, and it goes on. No fall ever comes all of a sudden. . . . You are hurting yourself. Who gave the example of obedience? Our Lord Himself— from birth until the last breath, one perfect obedience. [A] constant saying of His: "I came to do the will of My Father."[115] "My food is to do the will of My Father."[116] There was no other concern as if, always "My Father, My Father"—that filial obedience, that child-like obedience.

Our Lady didn't understand, but "Be it done to me . . ."[117] was her reply—a humble obedience. It is frightening, Sisters, if deep down

---

[115] *Cf. Jn 6:38.*
[116] *Cf. Jn 4:34.*
[117] *Cf. Lk 1:38.*

in your heart you say, "*Non serviam.*" "Tomorrow I will obey"; that tomorrow will never come. In obedience there is no question, "I can do better, I have more experience [than my superior]," and so on. Obey and surrender completely, totally. See Jesus with Pilate: "Since you have the power from above,"[118] Jesus said. . . . The power of God, no other power. It has to be used as God wants it to be used.

SACRIFICE

Obedience is very difficult. It is meant to be a sacrifice. Jesus did not come on His own, He was sent. If we are real religious, either we obey or no need to be here. Why so many broken families? Children do not obey. If we do not obey the time of prayer, work, then naturally we will die of starvation. What was wonderful in Mary: "Be it done to me according to your word."[119] Obedience must be something special if she became the Mother of God through obedience. Jesus at Gethsemane [said]: "Your will be done."[120] See the obedience—that father, when he consecrates, Jesus obeys and that bread becomes Jesus. Just see, Sisters, the obedience of Jesus!

We can obey only if we are meek and humble. It is necessary. I won't call it a virtue; it is like blood that is necessary for the body, so is humility for the soul. The fruit of humility is obedience.

---

[118] *Cf. Jn 19:11.*
[119] *Cf. Lk 1:38.*
[120] *Cf. Lk 22:42.*

ABANDONMENT

Charles de Foucauld has a beautiful prayer. It is a prayer that I find closely connected with obedience:

> Father, I abandon myself into Your hands, do with me what You will. Whatever You may do, I thank You. I am ready for all, I accept all. Let only Your will be done in me, and in all Your creatures—I wish no more than this, O Lord. Into Your hands I commend my life: I offer it to You with all the love of my heart for I love You Lord, and so need to give myself, to surrender myself into Your hands without reserve and with boundless confidence, for You are my Father.

I BELONG TO CHRIST

If I really understand that I belong to Christ, that nothing and nobody can separate me from the love of Christ,[121] obedience is natural, completely natural, because if I belong to somebody, then that person has the right to use me. No wonder that Our Lady said, "Be it done to me.[122] . . . She belongs to Him, immediately she went in [haste] to give Him to others, immediately.[123] And you know what she did after that? She was completely at ease because she has said yes, and Mary said yes when she knew that it was the will of God. And, it's very strange, I'm always surprised that God nowhere spoke to Our Lady directly. He spoke through the prophets, He spoke to Moses, He spoke to every-

---

[121] Cf. *Rom 8:35, 38.*
[122] Cf. *Lk 1:38.*
[123] Cf. *Lk 1:39–45.*

body possible in the Bible, but we don't see anywhere [that] God spoke to Our Lady directly. It was through the angel, it was through St. Joseph, and so on. And what did she say to the angel: "Be it done to me according to thy word." She also never mentioned the Word of God. "You, angel, what you are saying,[124] be it done to me . . ."[125] and this is obedience. That surrender. I belong to Him, He can use me, He can do what He wants with me. And to us, Sisters, God is not going to speak to us. He will speak to us through our Constitutions which are the written will of God to us through the Church. And then through our superiors—she may be black, she may be white, she may be clever, she may be stupid, she may be holy, she may not be holy, and yet God is going to use her to tell me how to go, where to go, what to do, how to do. It is so, so beautifully simple—obedience. And we can make it difficult for ourselves because we lose that whole and undivided love for Christ.

THE LIFE OF LOVE IN ACTION

Obedience is the life of love in action through the spirit of sacrifice, so natural for a religious. Even in the family life, the most natural thing in the family life that keeps the family together, that nourishes the life of the family together is that surrender to each other, that obedience, that accepting each other. If there is not that obedience and surrender of the father and mother to each other, there would be very little courage to ask that obedience from their children. And if today we are having all the trouble with family life, I think it begins there. That thing is missing and the same for our young people who want to join us. . . . It is difficult for them to obey, but they want, they want to see, they want to see. Many times the girls have told, the sisters have told

---

[124] Cf. Lk 1:34.
[125] Cf. Lk 1:38.

me, our young aspirants, "Mother, it is so difficult. I don't mind washing a leper, but so difficult to bend." I think that's where love begins in that bending. It is not how much [you are doing, or] what you are doing, but how much love you are putting in the doing, and obedience is that love in action.

This is what young people want to see, and in that action of obedience, they see how we love one another and how we love the one [the superior] who has the power to say come, go, do and so on. And, really, I have learned such a love from our young aspirants, from our young sisters, at the beginning of their religious life. Though I have now finished fifty years of religious life. Still I learn so much—the joy, the humility with which they surrender themselves to God. I mean it is for you and for me to feel that great gift that is in the young people. I do not believe when people say there are no vocations in United States. There are many vocations, many more now than ever before. But, they have much greater demand, they want to be holy, they want to surrender, they want to give up all and have nothing. And this is everywhere not only the United States. I see that in Europe—we have a novitiate in Rome—here in India, I see it in Africa, I see it in Philippines. I see exactly that same demand: I want to give all, I want to be holy, I want to grow in the likeness of Christ, I want to allow Jesus to live His life in me, I want to share in His passion, I want. And then we must come there in the picture to show them how we live that passion of Christ; how we allow Jesus to live His life in us; how we share that joy of loving with others. They want to see.

Our Vocation Is to Belong to Jesus

I never forget, one day one of our brothers . . . he loves the lepers. He takes care of 93,000 lepers, and he came to me and he had said he had a little difficulty with his superior . . . and he said "I love the lepers, I want to be with them, I want to serve them, I . . ." so on and so on. "My vocation is to be with the lepers, to serve the lepers." And I let him speak and after that I said to him: "Brother, you are making a very big mistake. Your vocation is not to work for the lepers, not even to love the lepers, your vocation is to belong to Jesus with the conviction that nothing and nobody, not even the lepers, must separate you from the love of Christ.[126] The work for the lepers is the means to put your undivided love for Christ in a living action."

I can't tell you, Sisters, how the whole attitude of that brother changed and he does the most wonderful work but that conviction that it is his love for Christ in action. It has changed because of his surrender, his surrender to obedience. Because if we really understand, we religious, I belong to Jesus, Jesus must have the right to use me where, when, as He likes. Do you live "without consulting me?" I remember some years back I wrote that for our Cardinal, and I believe he keeps it very carefully—the picture where I wrote, "Allow Jesus to use you without consulting you." And this is so true—that is the very life of our vocation—of belonging and being used. Look when the people get married—doesn't matter who that lady was before marriage, she was Miss and the moment she gets married, she changes her name, she becomes Mrs. And I don't know what she becomes, but she no more is recognized by the name that she was before because now she belongs to that man. That man and she cleave to each other and become one.[127] So the same thing for us—once we have given our word to Christ, once we have made that vow of chastity, that I will love Christ with undivided love in chastity, once He has called me by my name, He and I must also cleave like that, and that oneness is the love that we put to our neighbor, whoever, in whatever form the Church has accepted us.

It is the Church that has accepted us to be Missionaries of Char-

126 *Cf. Rom 8:39.*
127 *Cf. Gen 2:24; Mt 19:5; Mk 20:7; Eph 5:31.*

ity, or this congregation, that congregation, whatever form, and by accepting to belong, to surrender ourselves totally to God through our vows, we make the Church present because our Constitutions have been accepted by the Church to lead us to the perfect love of God and our neighbor. They have that power. So very often, nuns write to me and they want to join our congregation. I refuse and I say to them your Constitutions have the power to fill you with deep desire for greater union, greater love, greater sanctity, only live your Constitutions at least for one full year, really with great love and with great holiness. And then after one year, you write to me. And each time, they write back, "Thank you, I have found what I was looking for." This is, they have the power because the Church has accepted us in that form. We belong to Christ—in whatever congregation we feel that God wants us to be in and then by living the life according to our Constitutions, according to obedience, we proclaim the presence of the Church in whatever place we are, in whatever work we do.

We in the slums, and you maybe in the university level, college level, hospital level, whatever level—kitchen level, I don't know—there are so many ways. But there is no work for a religious that is out of place. Once I was asked what will you do when you will not be Mother General anymore? I said I am first class in cleaning toilets and drains. So, when I go to the home for the dying on Sundays, after taking care of the dying, going round, I go straight to the toilets and clean all the toilets there. And I have learned to clean them beautifully. And so this is something—it is not what we do but how much love we put in the doing.

If I belong to Christ, if that moment He wants me to be cleaning the toilets or take care of the lepers or to talk to the President of the United States, same level. Because I am where God wants me to be, and do what He wants me to do, I belong to Him. And God will never speak to us directly. . . . He speaks through our superiors, through our Constitutions, which are the written will of God and the superior, is the word of God, spoken word of God. She may not be holy, she may be holy. I always tell my sisters—we make our obedience in the hands of our superiors but she may be holy, she may not be holy; she may be clever, she may be stupid; she may be—I don't know what all what she may be. And yet, yet she may be making a mistake. I don't make a mistake in obeying her. And this is something that has to do so much with our religious life.

Total Surrender

We may be saying many prayers but maybe we are not praying fully, in that total surrender, in that loving trust. This is very important for us to live our religious life, to fulfill the reason for our existence as Missionaries of Charity or whatever it be, whatever form God has called us, because He is the one who has chosen us. And to be there. It is wonderful—this morning a young girl came, she said, "I think I must go, I must go and see." As I told you this morning—"come and see." She will go to New York and do "come and see"—there is something talking there inside of her. I said that the only person that knows what is happening inside of you is you. And it is between you and Him and nobody else. Nobody can tell you go here, go there, you must decide, and it is you—you will be able to decide if you pray. For the fruit of prayer is always deepening of faith, and if we have faith, then no difficulty with obedience. Cause that obedience is the only real sacrifice of our life. Not to get married—thousands of people don't get married. It is not that sacrifice but what is very important [is] to love Christ with undivided love in chastity—nothing and nobody.[128] And how? Through that total surrender in obedience. "I belong to You, You can do with me what You like and anytime, anywhere, through anybody but You can

---

[128] *Cf. Rom 8:39.*

decide and You must decide." This is something, Sisters, I think . . . we must experience [it]. And obedience is so closely united, woven with poverty. Very often, obedience becomes very difficult because we have so much. It suffocates the love, the surrender. And to be able to really obey fully, really to make that total surrender, we need the freedom of poverty, and we must experience the joy of poverty, that freedom, that having nothing in possessing. It is extraordinary how God uses [us] when we have nothing and how He penetrates the souls of people when He draws them to Himself when they have nothing.

A LITTLE MISUNDERSTANDING

Some years back, we had a talk from a priest [about obedience]. . . . He was explaining to us how obedience [today] has to be observed, and we have to explain and give reasons to the sister when we have to transfer her and so on. And so—I have never experienced that—so when I went home . . . And I [thought] I better practice what Father said. . . . I called one of the sisters and I said, "Sister, I would like you to go tomorrow to this place but know the reason . . . " I gave her all the possible reasons that I could think of, and then she began to cry. And I said, "But why?" "I didn't come here for you to give me reasons— you say go, I go." So next morning I went again for the instruction, for another instruction on obedience. I told that Father, I said, "Father, I went to practice what you told yesterday, and this is what happened to me." And he said, "Well if it is like that, you continue like that." And, see, the young people want, they want to give all, and if there is difficulty in their obedience, I think we should examine ourselves.

We, superiors, have a very big responsibility for our religious life, for our sisters, very great responsibility. We must not give them permissions that we have no right to give. [We must] treat them with dignity, with respect and with deep love, as somebody special to God

Himself, as somebody very precious to Almighty God. And always with kindness, always with thoughtfulness, always with that touch of compassion, because I am sure none of us would be able to do what we are doing if we didn't have our sisters and that generosity. There are failures, there are many failures in every religious life, in every family. In the best of families, there are difficulties. That is the human nature, that is the cross, and Jesus has asked us to take the cross and follow Him. He didn't tell us to go ahead of Him. . . . I think this is the cross of our community life. That little misunderstanding. I always jokingly say we pray together, we work together, we eat together, and we fight together. We must live our life but with love, with understanding love, with that compassion, with that thoughtfulness.

Wholeheartedness

The work we do for the poor people binds us—the fourth vow of giving free service—so we must take great care to do the work with our whole heart. We must be able to tell Jesus that we are serving Him with our whole heart. As you know, the other vows help us to [live] the fourth vow—up to now no one has taken a vow like that, *wholehearted* [and free service]—[so] you cannot do slapdash work, not going in time or doing [things] anyhow.

HIS GREAT LOVE

Seek wholeheartedly to love God and long to find Him. In this way you satiate the thirst of God who thirsts for us to thirst for Him. Jesus, God made man, has come to reveal God to us. Listen prayerfully in deep faith to His teachings and strive to do what He says. For Jesus tells us: "If you love Me, you will keep My commandments, and My Father will love you and we will come and dwell in you."[129] Jesus also tells us: "Love one another as I have loved you—as the Father has loved Me, so I have loved you."[130] It hurt Jesus to love us, yes, it hurt Him. To make sure we remember His great love, He made Himself the Bread of Life to satisfy our hunger for His love[131]—our hunger for God—because we have been created for that love. Jesus also made Himself the hungry one, the thirsty one, the naked one, the lonely one to enable us to love Him in return, for He says: "Whatever you do to the least of mine, you do it to Me."[132] Jesus is hungry for our love, and this is the hunger of our poor people. This is the hunger that you and I must find. It may be in our own homes.

SERVICE

Our devoted, wholehearted service given to Christ in the poor is a living proof to the Church that we are a living part in the Body of Christ and that Christ is pleased with us and shares His love for His Father with us.

St. Martin

The poor . . . allow us to love and serve Jesus in them. I think you know the story of St. Martin—how, as an ordinary man in the world, he was riding along on his horse, when he saw a beggar shivering with the cold. Without a second thought, he took his sword and cut his

---

[129] Cf. *Jn 14:15.*
[130] Cf. *Jn 15:12, 15:9.*
[131] Cf. *Jn 6:35.*
[132] Cf. *Mt 25:40.*

mantle in half. That night, he had a dream in which he saw Jesus covered with his mantle. Beautiful! The mantle was the means for him to become a Christian, since at the time he was not. We sisters can be with Jesus twenty-four hours—even in this house. This is the living of our fourth vow. Only when we have understood it can we love it, and when we love we can put it into action.

FREE FOR THE KINGDOM OF GOD

"Blessed are the clean of heart—they shall see God."[133] "I was hungry and you fed me."[134] We can do that only if our mind is clean—if our chastity is chaste, purity pure. We cannot give if we haven't got. We cannot give wholehearted free service unless we are free. Chastity frees us, "Seek you first the Kingdom of Heaven and all the rest shall be added unto you."[135] By my vow of chastity I free myself for the Kingdom of God. I become His property and He binds Himself to take care of me. I must then give wholehearted free service. What is this wholehearted free service? It is the outcome of chastity, of my binding to Christ. Therefore, I bind myself to give, not halfhearted, but wholehearted service. When we neglect to do well whatever work we must do, this vow suffers most—our service to the poor—because we become preoccupied with that thing to which we are giving our affection.

---

[133] *Cf. Mt 5:8.*
[134] *Cf. Mt 25:34–36.*
[135] *Cf. Mt 6:33.*

DON'T MISS THE OPPORTUNITIES

Let each sister see Jesus Christ in the person of the poor: the more repugnant the work or the persons, the greater also must be her faith, love and cheerful devotion in ministering to Our Lord in this distressing disguise. The more repugnant the work, the greater the effect of love and cheerful service. Detachment from our likes and dislikes . . . When Mother first picked up that woman who was eaten up by rats—her face, legs, and so on—if I had just passed by when I had seen and smelt her, I could not have been an MC. But I returned, picked her up and took her to Campbell Hospital. If I had not, the Society would have died. Feelings of repugnance are human and if in spite of it we still give all our wholehearted free service, then we are on the right path and will be a holy sister.

St. Francis of Assisi hated lepers but he overcame it and here was the stab of [death to] himself. He died, but Christ lives. Here it is. We must be humble in our gratitude for the great vocation which is ours. God has chosen us to do this special work—to give our wholehearted free service. Let us say to Jesus often, "I will give You wholehearted free service in whatever form You come to me." Maybe to a sister who is in a temper and needs help. Accept her. Don't lose the chances that come your way. Be happy; kiss the hand that hurts. We must train our eyes of faith.

"DO YOU LOVE ME?"

"Lovest thou Me?" Our Lord asked St. Peter after His resurrection. "Lord, thou knowest that I love Thee" was St. Peter's reply. As a reward for this love, Jesus told him, "Feed My lambs." Jesus said this thrice but at the third time Peter was saddened and said "Lord, Thou knowest all things. Thou knowest that I love Thee."[136] Now, Sisters, let us think that Our Lord is asking each one of us in particular the question, "Lovest thou Me?" And according to our reply, we will hear Him answer us, "Feed My lambs." In those words, Our Lord is inviting us to work for His dear ones, the poor; to work and to work constantly. If our answer to God is sincere then we shall have to take the trouble to feed His lambs.

WHAT THE SEED BECOMES

The tree becomes what the seed is. If I put an apple seed, I will not get bananas because whatever seed I put, that kind of fruit I will get. It is the same for you postulants. What seed am I putting up now? Is it the seed of obedience, seed of poverty, seed of chastity, seed of whole-hearted and free service to the poorest of the poor? Then I will get the tree of a spouse of Jesus Christ, a missionary of charity. When Jesus comes to us, He says, "I want to love you tenderly." The reason of my coming to this Society is to know Jesus, to love Him and to put my love into living action by my fourth vow.

THIS IS THE VOW

It is said here, *this call from the heart of Jesus*—clear vocation. One of the bishops wanted the sisters to do something else, and I said: "Bishop you choose: this is the vow. I am ready to take away the sisters if you cannot accept us as we are. No question of hurting them." We are serving the poorest of the poor and we must know what is our vow.

---

[136] *Cf. Jn 21:15–19.*

We are forgetting the poorest of the poor. If there are only ten people, all right only ten, but we must choose the poorest of the poor. The last time when I was travelling, a rich man was sitting next to me and [he] said: "Mother Teresa, why don't you give [to the poor] the rod to fish instead of the fish to eat?" And I said to him: "The people to whom I give the fish to eat cannot stand; they are the lepers, the dying, the mentally ill. When they are strong enough to hold the rod, I'll send them to you, and we will complete the work and together do something beautiful for God."

Love Begins at Home

How do you know, love, and serve [God]? How do you prove that you love Him? In the family, the father proves his love by all that he does for his children, for his wife. We prove our love for Jesus by what we do, by who we are.

⁕

For each one of us, for you and for me, it is necessary first of all to love those in our own family. Maybe we have the suffering and the lonely and the crippled and the mental in our own family, and we have no time—no time even to smile at them. And love begins at home. If you really want to be God's love in the world of today, begin to be God's love in your own home first. And then you will become the sunshine of God's love to everyone you meet.

THE TRINITY AND THE BLESSED FAMILY

Community life is connected with the Blessed Trinity—that oneness of Father, Son, and Holy Spirit. Again we have Jesus, Mary, and Joseph—that oneness and unity of family life in Nazareth. That's why we religious must be united as a family. Our Constitution has it, "We all have to make our community another Nazareth where Our Lord can come and rest awhile." From all the unhappiness of the world, all the hatred of people, all the killing—from all that, Jesus can come and rest in Bethany.[137]

BEHOLD YOUR MOTHER

As we know, the heart of the family is the mother and today, if there is much trouble in the world, it is because the mother is not acting as a mother, as the heart of the family. We read in the Gospel something that looks impossible, "Even if a mother forgets her child, I will not forget you. I have carved you on the palm of my hand."[138] Today the mother is doing that which is impossible—killing her own child. Today, let us look into our own hearts and see if there is anything there that is preventing me from my mother. Even Jesus could not come, even Jesus could not be born, even Jesus could not grow without a mother's love. Who is our mother? When Jesus was dying, His last words were, "Behold, your mother,"[139] and from that time Mary has appeared so many times, in so many places. Why do people go to Lourdes and Fatima and Velankanni?[140] Because we all need a mother's love, a mother's care.

---

[137] *Cf. Jn 12:1–3.*
[138] *Cf. Is 49:15.*
[139] *Cf. Jn 19:27.*
[140] *A Shrine to Our Lady of Good Health located on the Bay of Bengal.*

GOD'S LOVE FOR CHILDREN

We will ask Our Lady to be a mother to us as she was the Mother of Jesus and she taught Jesus how to live the life beautifully in His family at Nazareth. I am very happy to be with you because Jesus had a very, very special love for children. And many children came to see Jesus and the apostles said, "Don't come," but Jesus said, "Let the children come to Me.[141] I love them." You know God loves you so much—that is why Jesus comes amongst us and He again and again said, "love one another as I have loved you."[142] Jesus loved us so much that He died on the Cross for us and to remain with us, He remains in the Blessed Sacrament. And so most of you have received Jesus and you remember that when He comes in our heart, because He loves us so much. We have in India and other places many, many, many children, many poor children. Many of them have no one to love them. That is why you must thank God for giving you such wonderful parents who love you so much.

THE SUNSHINE OF GOD'S LOVE IN YOUR HOME

You must make your home a center of burning love, the sunshine of God's love must be in your home first. You must be that hope of eternal happiness to your husband, to your wife, to your child, to your grandfather, grandmother, to your servants—whoever is connected with you. You are working in a big firm, you are a co-worker, but you don't even know your people. There you have to be the burning flame of God's love to the people that are working with you or working for

---

[141] Cf. Lk 18:16.
[142] Cf. Jn 13:34.

you. Can they look up and see the joy of loving in your face? Can they look up and see the joy of a clean heart? Can they look up and see Jesus in you? This is very important for a co-worker. And how to do we reach to that? By prayer. Love begins at home, prayer begins at home, and the family that prays together, stays together. And if you stay together, you will pray together, you will love one another if you stay together.

CONTINUING THE LOVE IN OUR CHILDREN

If we help our children to be what they should be today, I think tomorrow, when tomorrow comes, when tomorrow becomes today, they will have courage to face it with greater love. And right from the very beginning, as the love begins at home, I think we should teach our children that love for one another at home. And they can learn that only from their father and mother, if they see that love of the father for the mother and mother's love for the father, I think that will be the strength of our children to be able to continue that love in the future.

ARE WE PRESENT?

I never forget an opportunity I had in visiting a home where there were all these old parents of sons and daughters who had just put them in an institution and forgotten, maybe. I went there, and I saw in that home they had everything, beautiful things, but everybody was looking toward the door. I did not see a single one with a smile on their face. I turned to the sister and I asked, "How is that? How is it that these people, who have everything here, why are they all looking toward the door? Why are they not smiling?" I am so used to see the smiles on our people, even the dying ones smile. She said, "This is nearly every day. They are expecting, they are hoping that a son or daughter will come to visit them. They are hurt because they are forgotten." And see—this is where love comes. That poverty comes right there, in our own home [we] even neglect to love. Maybe in our own family we have somebody who is feeling lonely, who is feeling sick, who is feeling worried, and these are difficult days for everybody. Are we there? Are we there to receive them? Is the mother there to receive the child?

No One Unwanted

Love begins at home. See that in your family never [anyone]—no man, no woman, no child, no unborn child—feels unwanted. Do not be afraid to love as God loves you with a tender love, with a concern, with a worry—where is my child, like Mary and Joseph walked back. They looked for Him for three days.[143] They did not rest until they found the Child. Do we feel like that? My husband, my wife, my child—where? How? Worried? Sick? Lonely? Am I the joy to him or to her? What is my concern—maybe just a smile, maybe just a little flower to bring, maybe just a little shake of the hand.

The Greatest Gift of God to the Family

And it is strange to say that it was that unborn child [John the Baptist] that recognized the presence, the reason for Christ's coming, that He has come to proclaim the good news to the poor.[144] What was the good news that Christ had come to give? That God is love,[145] that God

---

[143] Cp. Lk 2:41–52.
[144] Cf. Lk 1:44.
[145] 1 Jn 4:8, 16.

loves you, God loves me. But God has made you and made me for greater things: to love and to be loved. We are not just a number in the world—that's why it is so wonderful to recognize the presence of that unborn child, the gift of God. The greatest gift of God to a family is the child because it is the fruit of love. And [it is] so wonderful today that God has created that child, has created you, has created me, that very poor person in the street, that hungry person, that naked person. He has created in His image to love and to be loved—not just a number. And there is something very beautiful in the Scripture also where God speaks and He says: "Even if a mother could forget her child, I will not forget you. I have carved you in the palm of My hand,[146] you are precious to Me, I have called you by your name."[147] That is why as soon as a child is born, we give it a name, the name God has called from all eternity to love and to be loved . . . the most beautiful creation of God's love, the gift of God.

LOVE OF THE CHILD

Motherhood is the gift of God to women. How grateful we must be to God for this wonderful gift that brings such joy to the whole world, women and men alike! Yet we can destroy this gift of motherhood, especially by the evil of abortion, but also by thinking that other things like jobs or positions are more important than loving, than giving one-self to others. No job, no plans, no possessions, no idea of "freedom" can take the place of love. So anything that destroys God's gift of motherhood destroys His most precious gift to women: the ability to love as a woman. God told us, "Love your neighbor as yourself."[148] So

---

[146] *Is 49:15–16.*

[147] *Is 43:1, 4.*

[148] *Cf. Lev 19:18; Mt 19:19, 22:39; Mk 12:31, 33.*

first I am to love myself rightly, and then to love my neighbor like that. But how can I love myself unless I accept myself as God has made me? Those who deny the beautiful differences between men and women are not accepting themselves as God has made them, and so cannot love the neighbor. They will only bring division, unhappiness, and destruction of peace to the world.

A GIFT FROM GOD

I remember in Calcutta a lady came and she has thirteen children and she has to work, her husband has to work and the first child was completely disabled child, completely. And I told her, "Give me that child, we will take care of the child. You have to do so much." And the mother looked at me and she said, "Mother, what are you saying? That child is a gift of God. All of us, that little one is teaching us how to love, that little one is giving us a beautiful joy, beautiful chance how to love God—by doing little things. Each one of us has a part to play in that child's life and that child plays a very important part in our life." Then this . . . a non-Christian would speak to me like that and so I think this is a wonderful lesson for us, wonderful lesson, that she had the courage not to throw away the child, not to put the child in some institution—the gift of God, our child, my brother, my sister. It's wonderful. And I thought that it was only the mother who spoke like that, so I went to the family and I saw the little children so busy— somebody doing this, somebody doing that for that little one . . . the youngest one trying to make him laugh and pulling the chin and pulling the chin—to make that crippled child respond to his smile. See, this is something so beautiful.

FAMILY AND PRAYER

The coming of Jesus at Christmas completed the Holy Family. We must bring that presence of God into our families. And how do we do that? By praying. The family that prays together stays together, and if you stay together, you will love one another. If you pray, your heart will become clean, and a clean heart can see God.

At that first Christmas, there was no room in the inn for Jesus.[149] He, being God, became so humble, so small, so helpless. He became dependent on a human mother.

Today, Jesus is still humble, small and helpless in the unborn, and in those who are materially or spiritually poor, hungry for love and friendship, ignorant of the riches of the love of God for them, homeless for want of a home made of love in your heart. He is hungry, naked, sick and homeless in your own heart, in your family, in your neighbors. Are we there to welcome Him, to offer a word of comfort, a smile?

When our attention is turned only to the parties and the presents, it becomes too easy to forget Christ at Christmas. Let us not forget the best and the most wonderful gift that God has given to us—Jesus. And let us give Jesus to each other, beginning in our families, by loving each other with a tender and most personal love as God loves each one of us.

✦

From our own actions we can always tell what tomorrow will be. For example, like when we hear the cry of the unborn child . . . we know where we are going, that it cannot bring happiness in the world, can-

---

[149] *Cf. Lk 2:7.*

not bring peace in the world, because if a mother can murder her own child, what is left for us to murder each other. And so, looking at that today, that cannot bring peace, that cannot bring joy, therefore, the future looks very dark from that point. . . . I think we are forgetting that we have been created for greater things. We forget that we have been created to love and to be loved and that we have been created in the image of God. And so forgetting that, we forget all that is beautiful, all that is sacred, all that is . . . and I think that is coming especially from the break in the family life because less and less we are together, less and less we pray together. And if we don't pray together, then it is impossible to live together.

✦

Jesus came to give us the good news how to love one another, and where does this love begin—at home. In our family. How does it begin? By praying together. Because the family that prays together, stays together, and if you stay together, you will love one another as God loves you. And if today we have so much difficulty in the world, it is because in our family we are not praying together. We have so many broken homes, so many separated families. Why? Because the love has died, because we are not praying. If we pray, we have a clean heart and a clean heart can see God,[150] can love as God loves. So let us bring prayer back again in our family. Ask your teachers to teach your children. Ask, I ask you parents teach your children how to pray and pray with them. Let them see you pray and by looking at you, by praying with you, they will learn to pray, and if they learn to pray, they will learn to love. And if they learn to love, they will learn to share that love with each other, first in your own family and then in their own.

---

[150] *Cf. Mt* 5:8.

V

Be a Cause of Joy
to One Another

Of the eight Beatitudes, "the heart of Jesus' preaching,"[1]
Mother Teresa most frequently mentioned the sixth:
"Blessed are the pure of heart, for they shall see God."
Only a clean heart, as she rendered it, can "see God under
the appearance of Bread and in the distressing disguise of
the poor." A pure heart is a heart freed from all attachment,
a heart centered on God and able to perceive His presence
in others. And "if you see God in each other you will love
each other as God loves you," you will "become a cause
of joy to each other."

Purity of heart enables one to perceive God's presence
and His loving action in all the events of life, the most
trivial as well as the most demanding. The natural response,
then, is to return love for love. "Take whatever He gives
and give whatever He takes, with a big smile." This
exhortation that Mother Teresa formulated while in deep

---

[1] *Cathechism of the Catholic Church*, 1716.

spiritual aridity reveals her characteristic response to God in any given circumstance: that of total surrender, loving trust, and cheerfulness.

"Let Him do with me whatever He wants, as He wants, for as long as He wants." These words express the degree of her surrender to God. A conversation she had makes explicit the reason for such a response: "Once a nun told me she was surprised at my surrender to God—because she was afraid to give God her fingers lest He take her hand. I am not afraid of the One who is in love—who loves me in such a way as to die for me."

She abandoned herself to His good pleasure, not out of fear but because she knew she was loved and was drawn by the force and tenderness of that love. Determined to "give Jesus a free hand and let Him use [her] without consulting [her]," she held nothing back, endeavoring to give always more, to give all, surrendering to Him unconditionally and without reserve.

"God in the New Testament is the God of love, compassion, and mercy. That is why we can trust Him fully, there is no more fear." Believing that God's love was without limit she in turn placed no limit on her trust in God. No obstacle or failure could lessen her trust in God's infinite wisdom and unfailing love; she knew that He could work out His designs in spite of the inadequacies of the instruments.

The confidence by which Our Lady lived inspired her own: "Mary too showed her complete trust in God by accepting to be used for His plan of salvation in spite of her nothingness, for she knew that He who is mighty can do great things in her and through her." Hence Mother Teresa put her own "nothingness" at God's disposal, trusting that

He would do marvels through her while she fulfilled the mission He entrusted to her. And her trust was not disappointed.

Joy, expressed by her radiant smile, was one of Mother Teresa's distinctive traits. Hers was "the joy of loving," "the joy of sharing," "the joy of giving," and it is this joy that made God's presence tangible to those she met. It required faith, and was an expression of faith.

It was a challenge at times not to give into discouragement in the face of her interior darkness and the daily encounter with the terrible sufferings of her poor; she deliberately chose not to act not on her feelings but on her convictions, taking the firm resolution to offer "a hearty 'Yes' to God and a big smile for all." From her own lived experience, she could tell her sisters: "An MC must be an MC of joy. By this sign the world will know you are MCs."

"I prefer you to make mistakes in kindness than to work a miracle in unkindness," Mother Teresa wrote to her sisters. This was a principle she herself followed. It was precisely this attitude of being kindly disposed that led her to look at others' actions in a favorable light, to give them the benefit of the doubt or to overlook a mistake. This kindness made her approachable and sought after even by people whose opinions were opposed to hers. Such kindness that communicates love was what she demanded of her sisters: "Be the living expression of God's kindness: kindness in your face, kindness in your eyes, kindness in your smile, kindness in your warm greeting. In the slums we are the light of God's kindness to the poor."

Compassion—not just sympathy for the sufferer, but a suffering with the person—had become "second nature" to her. She never grew accustomed to other's suffering; nor could she ignore it or resign herself to being a helpless spectator. Rather, she consistently challenged herself and others to do something for those whose distress she witnessed, even when it involved sacrifice on her part or on the part of those who could help.

Mother Teresa was spontaneous and natural in what she did and in the way she attended to her work. No matter how simple or seemingly insignificant the task at hand, she performed it with deliberateness and with care for the least detail. This was how she expressed her love. She often repeated, "it is not how much we do but how much love we put into our doing." Attracted by the "little way" of St. Thérèse of Lisieux, Mother Teresa's well known exhortation to do "small things with great love, ordinary things with extraordinary love," was an expansion of her patroness' teaching. She further added, "The smaller the thing the greater the love."

"Love begins at home"; this is where the practice of doing small things with great love begins. It was "at home"—in one's family or in one's community, with those closest—that the genuineness of love is easily tested and proved. "How can you love other people if you do not have love in your own family?" she would ask. She herself was noted for her thoughtfulness, and expressed her love through small gestures, often hidden, that caused the recipient to "light up" with joy and gratitude.

Mother Teresa held that loving those closest to us is the way to begin transforming the world: "Love begins at home and so from here—from our own home—love will spread to my neighbor, in the street [where] I live, in the town [where] I live, in the whole world." She reminded

those desiring to share in her service to the poor that loving the members of one's family could be more challenging
than doing occasional service to the distant needy but just
as valuable.

Mother Teresa focused on bringing comfort to those
on the fringes of human society, showing to those who
felt unwanted, unloved, and uncared for, that God wants
them, God loves them, God cares for them. This was her
lifework. Her accomplishments were extraordinary, but
in reality they were made up of simple, ordinary actions,
"humble deeds of love," which anyone could perform.
Daily life, by and large, is made up of precisely these "small
things," while opportunities to do great things are relatively
few and far between. Mother Teresa therefore availed
herself of the thousand and one opportunities of "doing
ordinary things with extraordinary love" that allowed
others to recognize that they are loved and cared for.

She was wholly convinced that her mission to the poor
was God's work because she had embarked on it in answer
to His call. She was afraid of her weakness and limitations,
yet God had shown her numerous times that He was "in
charge." Answering her complaint that she was inadequate
for the mission He was entrusting to her, Jesus had told
her, "You are, I know, the most incapable person, weak &
sinful, but just because you are that I want to use you, for
my Glory! Wilt thou refuse?" These words, not all that
flattering, had a sobering effect on her. Her weakness and
sinfulness were not sufficient reason for rejecting His call
or an excuse for not doing what Jesus asked. How could she
refuse? And God kept using her as a channel of His love to
the poor for years to come. This awareness made her assert:
"God is using nothingness to show His greatness."

Conscious that her work among the world's poor was not her own, Mother Teresa stated: "I am only a pencil in God's hand." She knew her gifts as well as her weaknesses. Her gifts did not make her proud or fill her with self-complacency nor did her weaknesses cause her to despise herself or wallow in self-pity. She accepted the reality of who she was and welcomed all she received with gratitude. Desiring always and only to do God's will, she feared losing her role of being a simple instrument.

"I want the work to remain 'God's work' in every detail. It is true, I do it with my whole heart and soul but I do it for Him—letting Him use me as He pleases—to the full of His will—I claim nothing in the work as I know by myself I have nothing in me which could do this work." Great respect for the sacredness of her mission kept her on guard against pride in the face of her visible accomplishments and the subsequent praise it brought. She warned her followers as well against this danger and often concluded her speeches asking, "Pray for us that we may not spoil God's work."

Mother Teresa traversed the world numerous times to bring help and solace to the poor. Despite all the good she did, however, changes were not particularly notable. Many challenged her efforts by citing lack of results: There were still so many poor, and the causes of their poverty for the most part remained unchanged. But she had never promised or pretended that she could change social structures and erad-icate poverty. God had not called her to deal with the social or political problems of the world but to touch the individual sufferer in his or her immediate need. She was aware that her work was but "a drop in the ocean," yet as she said, "without that drop the ocean would be one drop less." She contributed what she could and encouraged others to do the same.

"Many people say that we should work with social programs and with development programs; we are not here for that. Those are some other peoples' work. Let everyone do what each can. I beg you sisters, never get mixed up. Love is for today, programs are for the future." Though she sincerely appreciated the efforts of those working to improve the lives of the vulnerable members of society, she insisted that she and her followers were not social workers. Her mission, while similar in its attempt to bring help to those in need, was of a different scope. It had its origin in a precise call from God and its aim in a mandate received from Him. By her concrete service, she was to bring "souls to God, and God to souls." She remained dedicated to this call with utmost fidelity, proving to those she served that—even if they felt abandoned and rejected—they were truly loved and cared for.

Mother Teresa brought hope to those who felt helpless in their suffering, often by simply reminding them of God's love. When people came to her with any difficulty, she always found a way to console and encourage them. Her support in suffering, advice in doubt, or practical aid in a time of need were a sign of God's love to many. At other times, all she could give was a smile, a kind word, a holy card, or a medal with a promise of prayer, yet these small tokens of love also helped to restore hope, enthusiasm, a reason to live, or a desire to love.

Even during her lifetime, people recognized Mother Teresa's exceptional holiness and called her "a living saint." To indiscreet remarks made about her sanctity, she would respond with utter simplicity: "Holiness is not a luxury of the few, but a simple duty for you and for me." Since sanctity should be our normal state, there was no reason for self-glorification.

In stating that holiness was a simple duty for everyone, Mother Teresa was not implying that it was easily achieved. Fully aware that holiness is a fruit of the action of the Holy Spirit in the soul, she also stressed that it required effort and a strong resolution on our part. "I will, I want, with God's blessing, be holy," was a recurring refrain on her lips in the last years of her life. Though her physical strength failed over time, her determination to strive for holiness never diminished.

Mother Teresa touched what is most fundamental in every person: the need to love and to be loved. Directing her life's work to those in whom this need was least met, she revealed to them something of God's love and compassion. Thus she became a sign that God IS, that He is present and that He still loves the world. She used to repeat often, "God still loves the world through you and through me." For this reason, she insisted that her followers live conscientiously their calling of being a Missionary of Charity—a carrier of God's love.

The situations of extreme material or spiritual poverty that she identified and confronted in the developing as well as in the developed world were often a challenge to society's structures and to the individual conscience. Inspired by her example, many desired to participate in her mission of love, but not everyone was called to work directly with the poor. All, however, are called to carry out his or her particular mission and contribute to building up a "civilization of love," as John Paul II called it. Mother Teresa knew how to respect, appreciate, and encourage the distinctive talents and efforts of others: "All God's gifts are good, but they are not all the same." To those who wanted in some way to imitate her example, she replied: "What I can do, you cannot. What you can do, I cannot. But together we can do something beautiful for God." Doing something beautiful for God in every instant of her life was precisely her way of making the world a better and more loving place to live in.

Pure Heart Can See God

To be able to see God in the silence of your heart—you need a pure heart. A pure heart only can see God, can understand what He speaks to us.

IF OUR HEART IS PURE

When I was in Delhi, I was traveling by car along one of the big streets. There was a man lying on the road, half on the pavement and half on the road. Cars were passing by, but no one stopped to see if he was all right. When I stopped the car and we picked up the man, the sisters were surprised. They asked me, "But Mother, how did you see him?" No one had seen him, not even our own sisters. If our heart is pure, we will see God . . . if our heart is free from sin, we will see God.

A Humble Heart

This is why Jesus and Mary and Joseph keep on teaching us humility for a humble heart is a pure heart and a pure heart can see God,[2] and we will for sure grow in holiness like Jesus through Mary.

Be the One to Comfort

For the pure can see and share the terrible suffering of Christ. Be the one to comfort Him when He needs someone to comfort Him, especially where there is so much sin.

A Humble Heart Can Hear

Grow in the likeness of Christ through humility and purity of heart—a humble heart can hear God speak in the silence of her heart, and a pure heart can see and speak to God in the fullness of her heart, and serve Him in the distressing disguise of the poorest of the poor.

We Need a Clean Heart

We serve Jesus without seeing Him face to face. We must learn to see and serve. For that we need a clean heart, for only a clean heart can see God,[3] can touch God, can serve God. A clean heart is a free heart, free of sin. What is the difference between us and a social worker? That

---

[2] Cf. Mt 5:8.
[3] Ibid.

minister in New Delhi gave the answer: "We do it for something. You do it to Someone." And he knew who that Someone was, that it was Jesus. We need a heart free of sin to be able to see.

Total Surrender

Be a cause of joy to each other. You are precious to Him. He loves you, me, her. He has that delicate love for you. Jesus loves me because I love you. Where is our home? Right in our community. How does love begin? By prayer, prayer gives a clean heart. Remember three things that Mother is telling you: total surrender to God, loving trust with each other, joy with all. Then we will be really holy like Jesus. Be holy like Jesus, be only all for Jesus through Mary.

TOTAL SURRENDER

Total surrender consists in giving ourselves completely to God. Why must we give ourselves fully to God? Because God has given Himself to us. If God, who owes nothing to us, is ready to impart to us no less than Himself, shall we answer with just a fraction of ourselves? To give ourselves fully to God is a means of receiving God Himself. I for God and God for me. I live for God and give up my own self and in this way induce God to live for me. Therefore, to possess God we must allow Him to possess our soul. How poor we would be if God had not given us the power of giving ourselves to Him. How rich we are now! And how easy it is to conquer God! We give ourselves to God; then God is ours and there can be nothing more ours than God. The money with which God repays our surrender is Himself.

We become worthy of possessing Him when we abandon ourselves completely to Him.

To surrender means to offer Him my free will and my reason, i.e., my own light to be guided by God's word, in pure faith. My soul may be in darkness, but I know that darkness, trial, and suffering are the surest test of my blind surrender.

Surrender is also true love. The more we surrender the more we love God and souls. If we really love souls, we must be ready to take their place, to take their sins upon us and expiate them in us by penance and continual mortification. We must be living holocausts, for the souls need us as such. There is no limit to the love that prompts us to give. To give ourselves to God is to be His victim—the victim of His unwanted love—i.e., of the love of God which has not been accepted by men. The spirit of our Society is one of complete surrender. We cannot be pleased with the common. What is good for others is not sufficient for us. We have to satiate the thirst of an Infinite God, dying of love. Only total surrender can satisfy the burning desire of a true Missionary of Charity.

CHRIST SURRENDERED TO HIS FATHER

Christ was entirely at the disposal of His Father for the ransom of many. Though He was God, He did not count equality with God, a thing to be grasped; but emptied Himself, taking the form of a servant being born in the likeness of men.[4] And Our Lady —"Behold the handmaid of the Lord, be it done to me according to your word."[5] Mary was completely empty of self, so God filled her with grace so that she was full of God. She allowed Him to use her according to His wish with full trust and joy, belonging to Him without reserve. And

---

[4] Cf. *Phil 2:5–7.*
[5] Cf. *Lk 1:38.*

our total surrender: in giving ourselves completely to God because God has given Himself to us, we are entirely at His disposal to be possessed by Him so that we may possess Him, to take whatever He gives and give whatever He takes with a big smile, to be used by Him as it pleases Him, to offer Him our free will and our reason, our own life in pure faith so that He may think His thoughts in our mind, do His work through our hands and love with our hearts. Our total surrender consists also in being totally available to God and His Church through our availability to our superiors, our sisters and the people we serve.

SURRENDER LIKE JESUS

"Total Surrender"—this is the spirit of Christ in the Gospels from the beginning to the end: "I have come to do Thy will."[6] "My Father and I are one."[7] "My Father, not Mine, but Your will be done."[8] "My meat is to do the will of Him who sent Me."[9] "Father, into Your hands I commend My spirit."[10] This is how Christ lived and this is how we MCs live. There is no other question "Why?" or no addition to it. This is also how Our Lady lived. This is why she became the Mother of Sorrows because she had to say "Yes" continually, with full trust and joy, belonging to Him without reserve.

We must be able to give ourselves so completely to God that He must be able to possess us. We must give whatever He takes and take whatever He gives, not what she—the superior or the sister—gives, but what He gives through her. If you understand this, you will have no difficulty in community life.

---

[6] *Cf. Jn 6:38.*
[7] *Cf. Jn 10:30.*
[8] *Cf. Mt 26:42; Mk 14:36; Lk 22:42.*
[9] *Cf. Jn 4:34.*
[10] *Cf. Lk 24:36.*

This Will Change You

"Our total surrender to God means to be entirely at the disposal of the Father as Jesus and Mary were." The Constitution doesn't ask anything extraordinary. Just be like Mary and Jesus. "In giving ourselves completely to God, because God has given himself to us, we are entirely at his disposal." No explanation. We know how we have given ourselves and how God is in our lives. What is our surrender to God? Don't say, "I don't know." You are telling a lie. Because God has given Himself to us, we are at His disposal.

When the changes come: "That climate doesn't suit me." How can it be like that? All right, go there and die. Die. There was war in Jordan. A sister phoned from Amman in the time of shooting. It came straight from my mouth, "Sister, let me know when you die." I did not prepare that. They did not phone again. If you have to die, die. Wonderful, Sisters. And another thing, I sent a sister to a difficult place. Sister was not happy to go there. When she arrived she wrote, "When I arrived, my Husband was waiting for me." She found Jesus waiting for her. She found peace, joy, because she said "Yes." You must get into that habit. That is the spirit of the Missionaries of Charity. "Go," go. "Come," come. I have changed a sister from one place. When she was in Motherhouse, again I had to change her. The cold in Darjeeling had frozen her nose. It became completely black. After I had to change her again. I forgot about her nose. She didn't say anything. That time I was taking the sisters to the station. At the station on the train I remembered about her nose, and I said, "Sister, please come down, bring all your things." She was happy. . . . Are we ready to be like that?

There was a Jesuit, I know him very well. In thirty-nine years he had been changed thirty-seven times. And this morning the provincial came again and said, "I would like you to go to that place." And what did this father say? He did not say, "This is my thirty-eighth time." He said, "What train do you want me to catch?" I wonder what would have happened to you and to me? No crying, no inviting this one and that one [to say goodbye]. Was it a real sacrifice? Obedience is a·real sacrifice if I want to belong to Jesus.

Another Jesuit told me a worse story. He got a change. He got into a train. He was on the train going very happily to the place. And then after one day the train came into that station and there was a telegram for him, "Change train, go to another place." "How did you feel?" "All right, he has a right to do this. That telegram is the will of God for me." He did not question. Our obedience is that total surrender. . . . If I have understood that I belong to Jesus, He has a right to use me. Total surrender and obedience are the same thing. I don't have to explain to you obedience if you understand total surrender today.

One cardinal asked me to write something for him. I wrote in my big letters—especially big I have for cardinals, so big! I wrote, "Let Jesus use you without consulting you." He said it has brought peace and joy from the time I have sent this to him. And how do we make that total surrender? Constitution 17: *"To be possessed by Him so that we may possess Him. To take whatever He gives and give whatever He takes with a big smile."* Learn this by heart. The superior corrects you. Take, accept. Today He gives you that, He takes your health, the work you like, the companion you find it easy to work with, the house, today is so cold. Accept. I'm sending you to a place where it is so hot. Accept. I don't say that you must be immune, you don't feel anything. That's not a right spirit. It is a sacrifice. But I accept. I offer it. This will change you.

ACCEPTING THE WILL OF GOD

I always connect the Passion of Christ with obedience. Just to accept and to accept in such a way without doubting, without grumbling, without complaining, without explanation. It is good . . . to face ourselves with this one question: have you really experienced the difficulty of obedience and the surrender? . . . . Maybe there were times in your life when it was difficult to obey. Ask 1) Did you pray? Jesus prayed the longer when it was difficult to accept the will of God.[11] What did you do? 2) Did you grumble? 3) Did you criticize? Examine yourselves so that the devil cannot overcome you. 4) Did you experience the joy of total surrender? God didn't speak to Jesus directly nor to Mary—it was through an angel,[12] or through Joseph,[13] or through Caesar,[14] but never directly. See the total surrender of Mary. She is the living example of total obedience, not only in a book, but in her heart. 5) How many times have you obeyed with determination? . . . These are details, but think, Caesar wrote that everyone must come and register his name in his own country.[15] He was proud, he just wanted to know how many people he had. Joseph and Mary didn't judge him, they didn't criticize, they just went. They could have said: "It's already nine months, the baby could be born at any time." But no. Caesar said go, so they went. Again, somebody wants to kill the child [and they decided to] run away.[16] They could have just hidden somewhere, but they went.

---

[11] Cf. Lk 22:44.

[12] Cf. Lk 1:26–38.

[13] Cf. Mt 1:18–25; 2:13–15; 19–23.

[14] Cf. Lk 2:1–7.

[15] Ibid.

[16] Cf. Mt 2:13–15.

TO REACH THAT PERFECT LOVE OF GOD

If we really keep to that total surrender, we are sure to reach that perfect love of God. Let us not waste our time. God knows us best of all. He knows our capacities—His knowledge of each one is complete. Something of His beauty is in each person. We are made to the image of God. His lovableness is in each one, so let us see what there is of God in each person. For this we need pure eyes and a pure heart to be able to see that beauty.

Loving Trust in the Good God, Who Loves Us

One thing Jesus asks of me: that I lean upon Him; that in Him and in Him alone I put complete trust; that I surrender myself to Him unreservedly. I need to give up my own desires in the work of my perfection. Even when all goes wrong, and I feel as if I was a ship without a compass, I must give myself completely to Him. I must not attempt to control God's action, I must not count the stages in the journey He would have me make. I must not desire a clear perception of my advance upon the road, not know precisely where I am upon the way of holiness. I ask Him to make a saint of me, yet I must leave to Him the choice of that saintliness itself, and still more the choice of the means which lead to it.

SHE COULD SURRENDER UNCONDITIONALLY

"Mary, too, put her complete trust in God."

Because she knew Him, she loved Him, so she could surrender to Him totally, *unconditionally*. If you know, in the history of Israel all women married with the intention of becoming the mother of the Messiah, but Mary and Joseph had agreed to remain pure. They made the vow together. As a rule, the Jewish boy and girl could live as husband and wife after engagement, but Mary and Joseph agreed to live as brother and sister always; that is why Mary questioned, "[How can this be since] I know not man," to the angel's salutation.[17] When the angel explained everything, see her total surrender and trust, "Behold the handmaid of the Lord."[18] She accepted the message of the angel to become the Mother of God, Queen of heaven and earth. She trusted fully that God [could] do all things in her and through her. Then she did not run and tell everyone, "See, Joseph, an angel came and told me so and so." No, Mary kept silent. Even when Joseph [came] to know about her pregnancy by the external signs, she did not say anything. She trusted God to intervene. Joseph trusted Our Lady. He could not [think] that she could go and sin, yet he did not understand. So, he decided to put her away quietly. God intervened and settled everything.[19] See the trust of Our Lady and St. Joseph.

WE DON'T HAVE TO BELIEVE THAT

"Our loving trust in God implies our trust in . . . the reality of Jesus, Son of God made man in the truth of His teaching in the Gospel." Trust what He has said. "I have chosen you. . . . Whatever you do to the least of my brethren you do to Me."[20] We don't have to believe that. We don't have to believe that two and two make four. We know. It is like that, the teaching of the Gospel. Today there are so many difficulties because they don't trust the teaching of the Church.

---

[17] *Cf. Lk 1:34.*
[18] *Cf. Lk 1:38.*
[19] *Cf. Mt 1:18–21.*
[20] *Cf. Mt 25:40.*

UNCONDITIONAL TRUST

"Jesus trusted His Father so completely that He entrusted His whole life and the mission for which He was sent [into the hands of His Father]." He knew the Father would bring salvation in spite of the utter failure. To all human wisdom the Cross is utter failure. Jesus' trust is *unconditional.* He accepted to become man like us in all things except sin. We do not realize what this means, "He being rich became poor."[21] He who is "God from God, Light from Light, begotten not made, one in substance with the Father, through whom all things were made . . . born of the Virgin Mary." The Creator chose to become a creature, one with us, like us, to be dependent on others, to need food to eat, clothes to wear, drink to quench His thirst, to need rest, to be tired like us . . . One with us in all things: Why? For love of us, with unconditional trust in the Father. He chose to be born of a woman, the Virgin Mary, to take human flesh and blood. "To live in Nazareth."[22] "Can anything good come out of Nazareth?" asked Nathanael.[23] Christ accepted to belong to that utter lowly place that had no good name, to work as a carpenter. "Is He not the Son of Mary and Joseph?"[24] You know Christ was not accepted in Nazareth because He accepted to have Mary and Joseph as His parents.[25] His preaching was not accepted there and they wanted to stone Him because he claimed to be the Son of God.[26] He was totally rejected. "He came among His own and His own knew Him not."[27]

---

[21] Cf. 2 Cor 8:9.
[22] Cf. Mt 2:23.
[23] Cf. Jn 1:46.
[24] Cf. Jn 6:42; Mt 14:55.
[25] Cf. Jn 6:42.
[26] Cf. Lk 4:28–29.
[27] Cf. Jn 1:11.

WHEN THE CROSS IS HEAVY

"*. . . full trust in His Divine Providence for all our necessities . . .* " You are more important to me than the grass, than the birds.[28] Remember those words. I am more important. Even the sun and the moon cannot receive Holy Communion—as beautiful as they are, [I can.] He created for me the sun and the moon, trees, birds, all for me. If He can give us His own Body, His Flesh, what are all these things in comparison with Holy Communion? In Manila, at the twelfth Station of the Cross, after the prayer for the twelfth Station, they sing "No Greater Love."[29] I would like you to sing that. Learn that by heart. When the Cross is heavy, sing it for yourself. It is time for me to show greater love.

✦

To depend solely on Divine Providence—and I can tell you—all these years that we are dealing with thousands and thousands of people, we have never yet had to send anybody away because we didn't have. It has always been there. There has always been one more plate of rice, one more bed there. We have never had to say to the people, "I'm sorry, I cannot take you in or I cannot give you anything." The good God has always been there. That Divine Providence has been a most wonderful living reality of that freedom, of that belonging to Him, of that loving Him with undivided love.

---

[28] *Cf. Lk 12:7, 24, 27, 28.*

[29] *"No greater love, there is no greater love nor could there be than God's great love, infinite love, He revealed through Christ on Calvary."*

Two Truckloads

God will never, never, never let us down if we have faith and trust Him. One week, on the Friday and Saturday, for the very first time we had no rice to give the people. The Sisters feed, I believe, four thousand people each day and these people are the ones who simply won't eat unless the Sisters feed them—but we had nothing. Then, about 9:00 on Friday morning one, two truckloads full—full of bread [more] than they had ever seen in their lives. So, you see Sisters, God is thoughtful. He will never let us down if we trust Him even if He has had to play a trick on the people and close down the schools. He will always look after us. So we must cleave to Jesus.

✦

I remember when we went for the first time to Venezuela. The Sisters knew not a word of Spanish. We rang the bell on the street to call the people for Mass, talking with the people. . . . First one or two people came slowly, slowly. Now they have more than they can do, the Churches are full. What the novices do in Calcutta is beyond understanding. The other day in one house, newly opened, the Sisters have prepared children eighteen and twenty years old, boys, for First Communion. The bishop himself came to give them First Communion. He came from far away. That small shy sister prepared them. She went around and found them. See Sisters, when we have complete trust in God what God will not do through us.

We Have to Grow

Don't think it is enough for us to surrender ourselves to God once and for all. If we do not practice daily self-control, daily self-denial we shall become a bundle of nerves. Jesus grew in age and wisdom before God and man.[30] We too have to grow in the same way.

Joy

I want to be a saint according to His Heart, meek and humble[31]— therefore at these two virtues of Jesus I will try my best. My second resolution is to become an apostle of joy—to console the Sacred Heart of Jesus through joy. Please ask Our Lady to give me her heart so that I may with greater ease fulfill His desire in me. I want to smile even at Jesus and so hide if possible the pain and the darkness of my soul even from Him.

Let Me Go . . .

Let me go, and give myself for them, let me offer myself and those who will join me for those unwanted poor, the little street children, the sick, the dying, the beggars, let me go into their very holes and bring in their broken homes the joy and peace of Christ.

---

[30] *Cf. Lk 2:52.*
[31] *Cf. Mt 11:29.*

THE FIRST CHRISTIANS

In Bethlehem, joy filled everyone: the shepherds, the angels,[32] the kings,[33] Joseph, Mary[34].... Joy was the characteristic mark of the first Christians.[35] During the persecution, people used to watch those who had this joy radiating on their faces. By that joy they knew who the Christians were and thus they persecuted the Christians. St. Paul, whom we are trying to imitate in our zeal, was an apostle of joy. He always urged the early Christians to rejoice in the Lord always.[36] His whole life can be summed up in one sentence, "I belong to Christ."[37] "Nothing can separate me from the love of Christ, neither sufferings nor persecutions, nor anything."[38] "I live now, no longer I who live but it is Christ who lives in me."[39] That is why he was so full of joy.

LOVE ONE ANOTHER

Jesus has said very clearly "by this love for one another, they will know you are My disciples,"[40] and this is the only way for us to proclaim Christianity, Christ's message. Why people are taken so much by the work? What we are doing is nothing extraordinary, nothing special— the sisters, not only what they are doing but they are happy to do it and that happiness that comes from that union with Christ. And peo-

---

[32] Cf. Lk 2:1–20.
[33] Cf. Mt 2:1–12.
[34] Cf. Lk 1:46–47; 2:10–16.
[35] Cf. Acts 2:43–47; 13:52; 16:34.
[36] Cf. Phil 4:4.
[37] Cf. 2 Cor 10:7; Gal 13:29, 5:24.
[38] Cf. Rom 8:35–39.
[39] Cf. Gal 2:20.
[40] Cf. Jn 13:35.

ple see that and then they want to share that happiness—people are hungry for happiness, they want happiness. And so many come, we get many young people as volunteers coming and working—there's many, many, many from all over the world.

⋆

A joyful sister is like the sunshine of God's love, the hope of eternal happiness, the flame of burning love.

THE VIRTUE TO SMILE

Joy is one of the most essential things in our Society. An MC must be an MC of joy. She must radiate that joy to everyone. By this sign, the world will know you are MCs. Everyone in the world sees you and remarks and speaks out about the MCs, not because of what they do but because they are happy to do the work they do and live the life they live. By this joy I do not mean boisterous laughter and screaming. No, that is deceitful, it can be there to hide something. By this joy I mean that inner depth of joy in you, in your eyes, look, face, movements, actions, swiftness, and so on. "That My joy may be in you,"[41] says Jesus. What is this joy of Jesus? It is the result of His continual union with God, doing the will of the Father. "I have come that My joy may be in you, and that your joy may be full."[42] This joy is the fruit of union with God, of being in the presence of God. Living in the presence of God fills us with joy. God is joy. To bring joy to us Jesus became man. Mary is the first one to receive Jesus, "My spirit rejoices

---

[41] Cf. Jn 15:11.
[42] Ibid.

in God my Savior."[43] The child in Elizabeth's womb leapt with joy because Mary carried Jesus to him.[44] This same Jesus we receive in Holy Communion—there is no difference. Did we go in haste today to give Him to the poor? Did the poor rejoice at seeing us today? Were they happier because of us? Are they better people because they came in contact with us? Are we giving them a living God?

JOY IS . . .

"Joy is prayer—the sign of our generosity, selflessness and close and continual union with God." Everything, in eyes, face, action, that joy must be seen.

☀

When you are full of joy, you move faster and you want to go about doing good to everyone. "Joy is the sign of union with God"—of God's presence.

☀

"Joy is love—a joyful heart is a normal result of a heart burning with love, for she gives most who gives with joy, and God loves a cheerful giver."[45] . . . A man came from Kalighat and went straight to women's [ward]. There was a sister attending a patient who just came. She must have had joy on her face. This man said, "I came here empty. I go away

---

[43] *Cf. Lk 1:47.*
[44] *Cf. Lk 1:44.*
[45] *Cf. 2 Cor 9:7.*

full of God. I saw the love of God in this sister." She was maybe never realizing that the man was looking at her.

※

Our lamp will be burning with sacrifices made out of love if we have joy. Then the Bridegroom will come and say, "Come and possess the kingdom prepared for you."[46] It is a joyful sister who gives most and everyone loves the one who gives with joy and so does God also. Don't we always turn to someone who will give happily and not with grumbling?

A Net of Love

Because we are full of joy, everyone likes us and wants to be in our company to receive the light of Christ we possess. A sister filled with joy preaches without preaching. Daily we pray, "Help me to spread Thy fragrance; Yours Lord, not mine." Do we realize its meaning? Do we realize our mission of spreading this joy, of radiating this joy daily as we go about our daily lives, first in the community and then to the poor?

We Need Joy

Even in our works we need joy—great joy—to do the works we do. Without joy we just cannot do them. Today so many hands came to Kalighat for scrubbing and rubbing because you are so many here. In the mission houses, there is the same amount of work to be done

---

[46] Cf. Mt 25:34.

and there may be only one or two sisters to do it all. Even if you pay money, people do not want to do the dirty works we do. It is then you need joy to do all the works cheerfully and wholeheartedly.

THE BEST WAY TO THANK GOD

The best way to thank God and the Society is to take whatever He gives and to give whatever He takes with a big smile. A joyful sister is like sunshine in the community. She brings God's light, peace, and joy. Do my sisters miss me in the community? Do I bring them Christ's light and happiness? Are the poor better because they come in contact with me? Are they happier? A joyful sister is the hope of eternal happiness. She brings hope because she believes she will go to heaven, because she lives in the presence of God. She is the flame of burning love. Like the virgins,[47] her lamp is always full of love and sacrifices. When the Bridegroom will come, He will say, "Come ye blessed of my Father, inherit the kingdom prepared for you from all eternity."[48]

⁂

A joyful sister—sunshine. . . . Are people better in your company? Better face [yourself]. Never use words that will hurt. . . . The poor people . . . teach us such love. Some of you have been to Kalighat. You never hear a complaint, never screaming, never curs[ing]. . . . They brought a man from the street. After we washed and cleaned him and gave the ticket for St. Peter, he said, "Sister, I'm going home to God!" That's joy!

---

[47] Cf. Mt 25:1–13.
[48] Cf. Mt 25:34.

JOY IN THE EYES, IN THE WALK

Christo Prem Prachanta, preach [to] us of Christ's love. Even though today is a day of passion, I want to speak today of joy. Not that joy— ha, ha, laughing loudly—but that conviction "I belong to Jesus," should produce joy—joy in the eyes, in the walk, in meeting each other. Joy is the fruit of the Holy Spirit.[49] Nobody has seen God, except Jesus.[50] So nobody can make a picture of God. To bring joy, Jesus has come. The Father loved the world so much that He gave His only Son.[51] Jesus loved us so much that He gave Himself.[52] We love each other so much that we give joy.[53] Our Lady went in haste to give joy. "Christianity is giving," said a Hindu gentleman. Jesus could not separate Himself from us and so He dwells with us. His very Body becomes my Body. Tremendous joy! His joy was to love you, to love me. Many, many became martyrs because they were caught by that love. The joy of being together. St. Paul, the great lover of Christ, loved with a human love also, with a heart so tender, so constant. Serve the Church joyfully, let there be no sadness in our life. The only sorrow is sin.

A BEAUTIFUL SMILE

Once they brought a man dying, brought him from the street dead. The Hindus have the custom where they pray around the body, then they put fire in the mouth and the man starts to burn. They put fire

---

[49] Cf. Gal 5:22.
[50] Cf. Jn 1:18; 6–46.
[51] Cf. Jn 3:16.
[52] Cf. Jn 1:14–18; 15:13.
[53] Cf. Lk 1:39–45.

in the mouth of that man and he got up! He said, "Give me water!" They brought him to Kalighat. I was there. I didn't know the story. So I went to see him and he was barely moving. So I said, "This one is already one step up!" So I washed his face. . . . He opened his eyes wide, he gave me a beautiful smile and he died. I phoned, and they told me the story and asked, "Are you really sure that he is dead?" I said, "Jesus, he really found You! I am struggling for so many years to go to heaven! He went like that." I will never forget that radiating joy on his face. Why? Connection with God.

One day, a lady was giving us a ride. She was driving for us and in the conversation, she said "Oh, I have a great love for that congregation." I said, "Why do you have that special love for that congregation?" "Because whenever the nuns meet each other, it is as if they have never seen each other; they meet each other with so much love, so much joy. I see that presence of Christ in them, I see they are really in love with each other." See she was a lay person living a well-to-do life outside and all, and yet what struck her—there the sisters were in love with each other because they showed the joy of each other's presence. And see, this is what the young people want to see. And it is good for us—if we don't get vocations, if the vocations don't persevere with us, instead of examining everything possible, let us examine what we are to them, what do we give them, what do they see in us, what connections do we make with them; what connection do they see in each other, in the work, in the people. Most of you are dealing with young people in colleges, in the schools. What are you to them?

WHY NOT WITH A HAPPY HEART?

Very often it has happened in the lives of the Saints, that an heroic overcoming of a repugnance has been the lift to a high sanctity. Such was the case of St. Francis Assisi, who when meeting a leper completely disfigured, drew back but then overcoming himself, kissed the terribly disfigured face. The result was that Francis was filled with an untold joy. He became the complete master of himself—and the leper walked away praising God for his cure. St. Peter Claver licked the wounds of his negro slaves. St. Margaret Mary sucked the pus from a boil. Why all this if it was not because these Saints believed—and because they wanted to draw nearer to the heart of God. It is very strange that the four vows demand so much cheerfulness. In our case this cheerfulness is very necessary—for without it we shall seldom have the courage to grasp the real meaning of total surrender. Since we do it, why not do it with a happy heart.

A SMILE IS THE BEGINNING OF LOVE

Maybe our people here have material things, everything, but I think that if we all look into our own homes, how difficult we find it sometimes to smile at each other, and that smile is the beginning of love.

And so let us always meet each other with a smile, for the smile is the beginning of love and once we begin to love each other, naturally we want to do something.

WE CAN STILL BE HAPPY

In spite of everything still we can be happy, smile, share with others. Take the trouble to radiate that joy. Constitution 19: "Joy is indeed the fruit of the Holy Spirit and a characteristic mark of the Kingdom of God, for God is joy." We have no reason to be unhappy.

BEING ALL FOR GOD

There is no truer happiness than that of being all for God. If you want to be happy, then strive to let God live in you.

Love Is Kind

Thoughtfulness is the beginning of great sanctity. If you learn this art of being thoughtful, you will become more and more Christ-like, for His heart was meek and He always thought of others—our vocation to be beautiful must be full of thought for others. Jesus went about doing good.[54] Our Lady did nothing else in Cana but thought of the needs of the others and made their need known to Jesus.[55] The thoughtfulness of Jesus and Mary and Joseph was so great that it made Nazareth the abode of God most High. If we also have that kind of thoughtfulness for each other, our communities would really become the abode of God most High. How beautiful our convents will become—where there is this total thoughtfulness of each other's needs.

UNDERSTANDING LOVE

Our poor people don't need our pity; they don't need our sympathy. This morning I went to Nirmal Hriday. I saw a man just struggling for life. Sister told me when they brought him in he was so hurt. You could see the bitterness and the attitude that he just waited to die. Then, I

---

[54] *Cf. Act 10:38.*
[55] *Cf. Jn 2:1–10.*

happened to be there, and I spoke to him, and he brightened up and wanted to live.

KINDNESS TO GOD

We should practice *kindness* to God, to our superiors, to our sisters, to our people and to ourselves. Beginning with the last one, Jesus says, "Love your neighbour as you love yourself."[56] The greatest kindness that we can show ourselves is to help ourselves not to lose our balance; to become holy, good and fervent. We all know that whenever we lose balance with ourselves, the difficulty is much greater. We should strive to keep back an angry word. We should smile when we are inclined to be moody. It is very important to be kind to ourselves in this sense. We must control ourselves as if everything depended on us and leave the rest to God. Be kind to yourselves by keeping your balance.

ARE WE THOUGHTFUL FOR ONE ANOTHER?

Let us be more tender, more compassionate, more loving and concerned with each other—like Jesus on the Cross, bleeding and dying and yet thinking to take care of His mother[57]—that thoughtfulness. That thoughtfulness of Jesus on the Cross for His mother; and even when Judas kissed Him, that terrible pain it caused Jesus,[58] and He said, "Don't let the people hurt the apostles."[59] Are we thoughtful for each other . . . ?

---

[56] *Cf. Lev 19:18; Mt 19:19, 22:39; Mk 12:31, 12:33; Lk 10:27.*
[57] *Cf. Jn 19:26–27.*
[58] *Cf. Lk 22:48.*
[59] *Cf. Jn 18:7–9.*

A REAL LOVE OF GOD

See what a great man he is, so important and so powerful and yet he has a very deep and living faith, a real love of God, which shows itself in the way he works. He has a beautiful family, so united and loving. What really struck me was the way he deals with his workers. Once I went with him to the big factory in Bombay where over three thousand people are working. He started a scheme among them, where they all give something to help feed the people in Asha Dan. I had gone there to thank them and to my surprise I found that many of his employees were disabled. I was also really struck that he knew nearly all of the workers by name and as we went through the factory he had some greeting or word to say to everyone. At one point we passed a table that was empty and he asked where so–and–so was. When he learnt that she had died recently, he was very distressed that no one informed him. She had been a disabled girl and he seemed to have known her quite well. See, Sisters, such a big man, yet these little things were not below him—that taking the trouble to learn everyone's name, that delicate love to notice who was absent. This is what I call love. Such a big man of the world, but not too big not to know and not to find out. He didn't use many words but he knew his work, and the more he spoke and addressed the various workers the more I was surprised. Thoughtfulness comes when there is true love. Never be so busy as not to think of others. Sometimes we are so preoccupied with ourselves that we have not the time to smile at others.

Compassion

God still loves the world and He sends you and me to be His love and His compassion to the poor. Through us, Missionaries of Charity, God shows His love particularly for the poorest of the poor, and He sends us to the poor in particular. The cup of water you give to the poor, the sick, the way you lift a dying man, or give medicine to the leper, the way you feed a baby or teach an ignorant child—all that is God's love in the world today. . . . I want these words to be imprinted in your minds: God still loves through you and through me today. Let me see this love of God in your eyes, in your actions, in the way of your movements.

✦

Today God loves the world through you and through me. Are we there? Are we that love and that compassion? God proves that Christ loves us—that He has come to be His Father's compassion. Today God is loving the world through you and through me and through all those who are His love and compassion in the world.

HAVE DEEP COMPASSION FOR THE PEOPLE

This is a very small thing the sisters do, they do very little. We can do very little for these people but at least they know that we love them and that we care for them and we are at their disposal. This is what I think we will try to do now more and more with the co-workers. That is why this year I said I would go mostly with the co-workers, to try, all of us, to come closer to that unity of spreading Christ's love everywhere we go. Love and compassion, have deep compassion for the people. People are suffering much, very, very much, mentally, physically, in every possible way; and so I think you are there to bring that hope, that love, that kindness.

LOVING THROUGH YOUR JOY

Radiate the presence of Jesus through your joy. Your apostolate is to smile and to pray. Put love in whatever you do; the smaller the thing, the greater the love. It is not how much you do, but how much love you are putting in what you do. And remember you do it to Jesus. Jesus said, "I was hungry and you gave Me to eat, I was sick and you visited Me, I was lonely and you took care of Me . . . You did it to Me."[60]

THE JOY WITH WHICH YOU SMILE

The joy with which you smile at your sisters in the community, the eagerness with which you look at the time to be with your sisters, your attitudes and manners towards them—all that also is God's love in the world today. God still loves the world!

WARMTH OF HUMAN HANDS

One day I was walking down the streets in London and there was a man sitting, simply doubled up, looking so lonely, so like a throw away. And I went near him, and I took his hand and I shook his hand and I asked him how he was. And he sat up and he said, "Oh, after a long, long time, I feel the warmth of a human hand. Long, long time."

---

[60] *Cf. Mt 25:35–40.*

There he sat up, the eyes are full of joy. He was a different being just because there was a human hand that made him feel yes, you are somebody, somebody that I love. This is something that we have in these terrible days of suffering, let us be that—the joy of loving.

MEETING WITH A SMILE

Let us keep that joy of loving Jesus in our hearts and share that joy with all that we come in touch with. That radiating joy is real, for we have no reason not to be happy because we have Christ with us, Christ in our hearts, Christ in the poor that we meet, Christ in the smile that we give and the smile that we receive. Let us make that one point— that no child will be unwanted and also that we meet each other always with a smile, especially when it is difficult to smile.

FULL OF ZEAL

Let us be full of joy, full of zeal, full of that desire to do much for Jesus. Don't let yourself get discouraged, it is pure devilish pride. If we fail, start again. St. Bernard used to start again every morning. If you don't talk at meals and recreation, if you are sad, you become a plaything for the devil.

SMILE AT ONE ANOTHER

Sometime ago, about forty professors came from the United States, and I think our house has become a tourist house or I don't know if it's one of the things to be seen. Anyway, they all came there and we talked, and at the end one of the professors asked me, "Mother, please tell us something that will help us to change our lives—to make our lives more happy." And I said to them "Smile at each other, make time for each other, enjoy each other." One of them asked me, "Are you married?" "Of course," I said, "You don't know what you are talking about." And I said, "Yes I find it sometimes very difficult to smile at Jesus. He can be very demanding." And so this is something, a living reality. We must help each other—we need that.

SERVING WITH JOY

Serve Jesus with joy and gladness of spirit, casting aside and forgetting all that troubles and worries you. To be able to do all this, pray lovingly like children, with an earnest desire to love much and make loved the Love that is not loved.

JOY IS LOVE

Joy is prayer. Joy is a sign of generosity. When you are full of joy you move faster and you want to go about doing good to everyone. Joy is the sign of union with God, of God's presence. Joy is love, the normal result of a heart burning with love.

JOY OF LOVING

Works of love, even maybe a smile, maybe just help a blind person to cross the road, small things with great love. A beggar came up to me and he said, "Mother Teresa, everybody's giving you, I also want to give to you. But today, I just got (what do you call that—ten pennies?) ten pennies, and the whole day I want to give it to you. Then I said to myself, if I take it, he may have to go to bed without eating; if I don't take it, I will hurt him, so I took. And I've never seen the joy on anybody's face who has given his money or food or thing as I saw on that man's face; that he, too, could give something for somebody. This is the joy of loving, and I will pray for you that you will experience that joy of loving and that you share that joy of loving first in your own family and with all you meet.

JOY OF LOVING JESUS

May you keep the joy of loving Jesus in your hearts and share that joy with all you come in contact with. That radiating joy is something real, for you have no reason not to be happy because you have Christ with you—Christ in your hearts, Christ in the Eucharist, Christ in the poor that you meet, Christ in the smile that you give and in the smile that you receive. Yes, you must live life beautifully and not allow the spirit of the world that makes gods out of power, riches, and pleasure make you forget that you have been created for greater things—to love and to be loved.

Small Things with Great Love

These are small things, but deliberately I am choosing small things. They are so small and yet for God nothing is small. Once it is offered to Almighty God it becomes infinite.

HOW MUCH LOVE WE PUT INTO THE GIVING

To Almighty God the smallest action given to Him is great . . . but for us, we always measure how much we did, for how long . . . for God there is no time. What should be important for us is how much love we put into the giving. How much do we love? How close have we come to Jesus?

TAKE THE TROUBLE

Take the trouble to be holy—it is not enough to say, "I want," you must take the trouble. That fidelity to small things with great love— the smaller the thing, the greater the love—and you will see the change. That little fidelity; don't look for big things. Don't look for big things. Big things may come, they may never come. What is really important is that we really become holy—that tender love, that fidelity to small things with great love. Little Flower was canonized because she did small things with extraordinary love.

SMALL THINGS

See the Little Flower, she became such a big saint. In every church— no matter where you go—all over the world, you will find a picture or a statue somewhere, of her. Why? Because she did ordinary things with extraordinary love. She was so simple that even her own sisters— when she was ill in bed—in the community, they were talking about her, "What will Mother prioress write about her? She had done nothing." She heard what they said. What would we have said? We would have complained and grumbled and become moody—but what did she do? She said, "Yes, how true it is. I am coming to Jesus with empty hands." They spoke, she heard, and yet she was the first to be canonized, the first except for the martyrs. The Holy Father is canonizing many now, so better you die soon. When the saints are canonized, they have to find out so many things, but the Holy Father had only one sentence to say about the Little Flower: "She did many things with extraordinary love." I make it more simple: "small things with great love." In our lives, we do nothing big. The way we say the Our Father, get up, genuflect, close the window, sweep or write, say these words of prayer.

BRINGING GOD

I thought this was such a small thing, and yet we bypass those small things very often. And sometime back, the sisters found a very, very miserable person, a man in one of those shut-ins close by in Rome where the sisters are working and they have never seen, I believe, anything like that. So, anyway, they washed his clothes, they cleaned his room, they made some hot water for him and so on, they cleaned up everything. And they made a little bit of food for him also and he never said one word. After two days, sisters kept on going to him twice a day and after two days, he said to the sisters—"Sisters you have brought God in my life, bring Father also." And the sisters went and brought the priest, and the priest heard his confession after sixty years. Next morning he died. This is something so beautiful—that compassion of those young sisters brought God in the life of this man who had for so many years forgotten what is God's love, what it is to love one another, what it is to be loved. He had forgotten, for his heart was closed to everything and this delicate, compassionate, simple, humble work of these young sisters—your children—touched, brought God in his life and what struck me most, the dignity, the greatness of the priestly vocation. That he needed the priest to make the connection with God. I think this is what we all learn from Our Lady—that compassion of Our Lady. And if you and I would only use what God has given to us, for what He has created us, He has created us for greater things: to love and to give love, to have that deep compassion for the world as she had for the world and to give Jesus to others. People are not hungry for us, they are hungry for God, they are hungry for Jesus, for the Eucharist.

EACH OF YOU IS IMPORTANT

The other day we went to Jamshedpur.[61] We went to a big factory where they make all the parts for the airplanes. In one corner, one man was sitting and making little screws. I went near him and asked him, "What are you making?" He looked at me and said, "I am making an airplane." I said, "Airplane?" "Yes," he said, "without these little screws, the plane will not move." See, Sisters, the connection. Each of you is important to the Society. Ask Jesus again and again to make you understand this.

WRITE ONLY A POSTCARD

Do you know that in the hospital, there are many people who have nobody to visit them? Nobody goes to see them. Maybe if you . . . go and visit. Maybe you have to write only a postcard for somebody, maybe you read a newspaper for a blind person, maybe you bring a bucket of water for the mother who is sick in the house. Small things, don't look for big things. Small things with great love.

---

[61] *An industrial city in East India, often cited as one of India's cleanest cities.*

A Small Thing with Great Love

When the children heard that I was going to Ethiopia . . . those little ones came. Everyone brought something, something and again the little ones gave whatever they had. And this little one for the first time had a piece of chocolate in his hand. And he came up to me and said, "Mother, please give this piece of chocolate to a child in Ethiopia." Such a small thing with such a great love. First time chocolate was in his hand, first time he has tasted, and yet he had the love and the joy of sharing. This is love in action.

True Love

To Almighty God, it's not how much we give, but how much love we put in the giving. And so, I would like—if you are truly a co-worker, do that. Maybe just a little flower you bring to your old father or mother, maybe just you arrange the bed a little better, maybe—maybe you are just present to receive the husband when he comes back from work with a big smile. Small things, small things. Maybe when the child comes from school, you are there to receive the child, to encourage the child: "How have you done? What have you done? Have you been good?" There's no more that connection. We are so busy, we have no time to smile even. We have no time to give love and to receive love. . . . If you are a true co-worker, then you understand what I am saying. Love is not measured by how much we do; love is measured by how much love we put in, how much it is hurting us in loving.

TWENTY ACTS OF LOVE

Once I was so tired of signing, signing, signing, I got so tired of signing so then I counted how many letters are in my signature—twenty letters: "God bless you, M. Teresa, MC." "From now on," I said to Jesus, "every time I sign, please take twenty acts of love"—cheating a little bit. And from that time I look forward to signing because of those twenty acts of love.

Works of Love Are Works of Peace

To be able to pray for peace we must be able first of all to listen, for God speaks in the silence of the heart, and that is the beginning of prayer, that is the beginning of peace. He speaks, and we must have the courage to listen, we must have time to listen to the word of God. And then only, from the fullness of our hearts, we can speak, we can speak the prayer of peace. The fruit of prayer is deepening of love, deepening of faith. If we believe, we will be able to pray, and the fruit of faith is wrought of love, and the fruit of love is service. Therefore works of love are always works of peace, and to be able to put our hearts and our hands into loving service we must know, we must know God, that God is love, that He loves us and that He has created us—each one of us—for greater things. He has created us to love and to be loved, and this is the beginning of prayer—to know that He loves me, that I have been created for greater things. Therefore who is my brother, who is my sister, where is the face of God that I can see, to whom I can pray? My brother, my sister is that hungry one, that naked one, that homeless one, that lonely one, that unwanted one—they are my brothers and my sisters because Christ himself has told us so.

But to be able to see the face of God you need a clean heart,[62] a heart full of love, and you can only have a heart full of love if it is completely pure, clean and free; and as long as we in our own hearts are not able to hear that voice, the voice of God when He speaks in the silence of our hearts, we will not be able to pray. We will not be able to express our love in action—for every act of love is our prayer that brings peace. All works of love are works of peace. And therefore today if we have no peace it is because we have forgotten that we belong to each other—that that man, that woman, that child is my brother or my sister.

Religion Must Unite Us

Religion is a gift of God and is meant to help us to be one heart full of love. God is our Father—and we are all His children—we are all brothers and sisters. Let there be no distinction of race or color or creed. Let us not use religion to divide us. In all the holy books, we see how God calls us to love. Whatever we do to each other we do to Him because God is our Father. Religion is a work of love—it must unite us and not destroy the peace and unity. Works of love are works of peace—to love we must know one another. Today, if we have no peace, it is because we have forgotten that we belong to each other—that man, that woman, that child is my brother, my sister. The poor must know that we love them, that they are wanted. They themselves have nothing to give but love. We are concerned with how to get this message of love and compassion across. We are trying to bring peace to the world through our work. But the work is the gift of God. And works of love are works of

---

[62] Cf. Mt 5:8.

peace. If everyone could see the image of God in his neighbor, do you think we would still need guns and bombs? Religion is meant to be a work of love. Therefore, it should not divide us and destroy the peace and unity. Let us use religion to help us become one heart full of love in the heart of God. By loving one another, we will fulfill the reason for our creation—to love and be loved. My brothers and sisters, let us ask God to fill us with the peace that only He can give. Peace to men of goodwill—who want peace and are ready to sacrifice themselves to do good, to perform works of peace and love.

A YEAR OF PEACE

We shall make this year a year of peace in a particular way—to be able to do this we shall try to talk more to God and with God and less with men and to men. Let us preach the peace of Christ like He did. He went about doing good: He did not stop His works of charity because the Pharisees and others hated Him or tried to spoil His Father's work. He just went about doing good.[63] Cardinal Newman wrote: "Help me to spread thy fragrance everywhere I go—let me preach Thee without preaching, not by words but by my example—by the catching force, the sympathetic influence of what I do, the evident fullness of the love my heart bears to Thee." Our works of love are nothing but works of peace. Let us do them with greater love and efficiency—each one in her or his own work in daily life, in your home, in your neighbor.

GOD USES NOTHINGNESS TO SHOW HIS GREATNESS

What God does with nothingness—for me this is the greatest miracle.

---

[63] Cf. *Acts 10:38*.

REALIZING OUR NOTHINGNESS

If we face God in prayer and silence, God speaks to us. Then only, we know that we are nothing. It is only when we realize our nothingness, our emptiness, that God can fill us with Himself. When we become full of God, then we can give God. "From the fullness of the heart, the mouth speaks."[64] And when we are full of God, we will do all our work well—we do our work wholeheartedly.

CARRIERS OF GOD'S LOVE

And it happened, the same thing, when we went to Yemen. In all this completely Moslem country, not a sign of Christ in that land. Many people told me, "Don't wear the cross, don't pray the rosary in the street, hide everything." Then I went straight to that governor, and I said "This is the sign, it's an external sign, but it is a sign that I belong to Him. This is the rosary that we pray, and if you can't accept us as we are, then we need not be here." Then that man said, "You come to bring love into our country. You are the carriers of God's love, you come as you are, and what is your sign, you keep your sign, don't destroy anything." . . . I'm asking you, are we that? Are we really a carrier, a branch on the vine of Jesus? You are leading the people to Christ like this, through works of love, through works of peace, as every work of love is a work of peace; it doesn't matter how small it is, it's a work of peace. You are guiding the people. Is your presence amongst them that fruitful branch? Can they look up and see Jesus in you? That's why I want you, right from the very beginning—I think I will repeat myself a thousand times, but I don't mind because I feel

---

[64] *Cf. Mt 12:84.*

that you are part of my very life. Like our sisters, we are so close to each other, and I don't mind repeating—unless we love one another in our own homes, unless we are somebody very special to each other in our own homes, in our own communities, we are a bluff before God, we are a bluff before the angels. Love begins at home.

LOVE BEGINS AT HOME

Do we really know that in our own family, maybe there is my brother, my sister, my wife, my husband, who feels unwanted, unloved, exhausted, looking for little compassion, little sympathy and I have no time. Love begins at home. This is the great poverty and I think unless and until we begin to love at home, we begin to love in our communities [with] that love for one another, as Jesus has loved us, as He was loved by His Father, we cannot hope for peace.

THE PRAYER OF THE WHOLE WORLD FOR PEACE

What was necessary a hundred years ago may not be necessary today. But I am surprised, the prayer of St. Francis, made five hundred years ago, today we find so necessary. It has become the prayer of the whole world for peace.

> Lord, make me a channel of your peace,
> that where there is hatred,
> I may bring love;
> where there is wrong,
> I may bring the spirit of forgiveness;
> where there is discord,
> I may bring harmony;

where there is error,
I may bring truth;
where there is doubt,
I may bring faith;
where there is despair,
I may bring hope;
where there are shadows
I may bring light;
where there is sadness,
I may bring joy;
Lord, grant that I may seek rather
to comfort than to be comforted;
to understand than to be understood;
to love than to be loved;
for it is by forgetting self that one finds,
it is by forgiving that one is forgiven,
it is by dying that one awakens to
eternal life.
Amen.

A Pencil in God's Hands

It has been just a simple surrender, a simple "yes" to Christ in allowing Him to do what He wants. That is why the work is His work. I'm just a little pencil in His hand. Tomorrow, if He finds somebody more helpless, more stupid, more hopeless, I think He will do still greater things with her and through her.

✦

If I want to write I use a pencil. It doesn't tell me, it obeys me. It has only to obey me. If my writing is good, the pencil is happy, I suppose. Be a little pencil. Will you remember that, Sisters? Maybe that hand has so many defects, so many maybe, but the pencil never makes a noise—"Don't write like that!" "I don't want to write to Mother." Be a pencil in the hand of your superior, obey whoever it is who has been put in the hand of Jesus.

Hope Giver

As we love God we must love the poor in their sufferings. The love of the poor is an overflow of our love for God. We must find the poor, serve them. And when you have found them, you must take them to your heart. We owe our people the greatest gratitude, because they allow us to touch Christ. We must love the poor like Him. A Hindu told Mother, "I know what you do in Nirmal Hriday, you take them from the streets and bring them to heaven." A priest from Ireland said, "Nirmal Hriday is the treasure house of the archdiocese." God has chosen us and given us the privilege to work for the poor. The difference to social work is that we give wholehearted free service to them for the love of God. In the beginning, when Mother started the work, she got fever and had a dream about St. Peter. He said to her, "No, no place for you here. No slums in heaven." "All right," Mother answered him, "then I shall go on working. I'll bring the people from the slums to heaven."

OBTAIN PEACE FOR THE WORLD

I remember at Christmastime, I gave a talk to our lepers—we take care of 158,000 lepers—and I was giving a talk to them, and I said, "Your disease, your suffering is not a punishment, it is a gift of God, you are a chosen one to share in the passion of Christ, you are a chosen one to be able to offer [it] for peace in the world, in thanksgiving for what God has done for all the others and for you." and I went on repeating that they are chosen ones, that they are specially loved and there was one man sitting near my feet I think—it was so crowded—and was pulling my habit. "Say that again, say that again," and I had to repeat it three, four times "You are chosen one, you have peace because God loves you and you can make use of it, offer it to God, accept it and offer it to God and you can obtain peace for the world."

HE DIDN'T COMPARE HIS LOVE

[Jesus] loved the world so much[65] and . . . He made Himself the leper, that miserable mental person of the street He made Himself, so that you and I can love Him, that you and I can satisfy His hunger for our love, and that's why He says at the hour of death, you and I are going to be judged—not from what big things we have done, but what we have been to the poor: that hungry man, that man that came to our gate, that lonely person, that blind person passing through the street, that person so lonely, so unwanted, so unloved in my family right here. Maybe I have an old father, old mother, maybe I have a sick child and I have no time. I'm so busy, I've no time. I've no time to smile at others. My crippled daughter, my crippled wife, my sick husband, I have no time and

---

[65] Cf. *Jn 3:16.*

that is Jesus in the distressing disguise. That is the hungry Jesus right in my family, right in my community, my sister, and we have no time. We have no time today to even smile at each other and yet Jesus loves us with an everlasting love. And Jesus said, "Love as I have loved you."[66] No, He didn't compare His love with any other love.

BRINGING RICE

Sometime ago a man came to our house and he said, "Mother, there is a family, a Hindu family, that has eight children. They have not eaten for a long time. Do something for them." So I took some rice and I went. When I arrived at their house I could see the hunger in the children's eyes. Their eyes were shining with hunger. I gave the rice to the mother, and she took the rice. She divided it into two, and then she went out. When she came back, I asked her, "Where did you go?" She said, "They are hungry also." Next door neighbor, they were also hungry. What struck me most, not that she gave the rice but she knew they were hungry. And because she knew, she shared. And this is what we have to come to know. I did not bring more rice that night. Next morning I brought, but that night I allowed them to enjoy the joy of sharing, loving.

Love, to be true, has to hurt and this woman who was hungry—she knew that her neighbor was also hungry, and that family happened to be a Muslim family. So it was so touching, so real.

✦

That woman loved like Christ, she loved Christ in that Muslim family. The Hindu and Muslim are so different and yet she loved until it

---

[66] *Cf. Jn 13:34.*

hurt. It hurt her to take away from her children but her love for the neighbor was much greater than her love for her child. This is what we must know, do we really know that in our own family, maybe there is my brother, my sister, my wife, my husband, who feels unwanted, unloved, exhausted, looking for a little compassion, a little sympathy and I have no time. Love begins at home. This is the great poverty and I think unless and until we begin to love at home, we begin to love in our communities, that love for one another as Jesus has loved us, as He was loved by His Father, we cannot hope for peace. That's why the poor are the hope of salvation. The poor are the hope of mankind, the poor are the hope for you and me to go to heaven for at the last judgment, we are going to be judged on that. "I was hungry and you gave Me to eat, and I was naked and you clothed Me."[67] Not only hungry for bread and rice but hungry for love, to be wanted, to be known, that I'm somebody to you, to be called to it, to be called by name, to know my name, to have that deep compassion—hunger. Today in the world there is a tremendous hunger for that love. Thirsting for understanding. Very often we pass by our own brothers and sisters; we don't understand their difficulty.

Bring Christ's Presence Where You Are

Some time ago, in Calcutta, many principals of different schools and colleges came to our house and they were saying, "Mother, we would like to give up the schools and colleges and come and share the work with you." Then I said to them, "This is the most devilish temptation for you, most devilish, because if the devil can remove you, he will be able to destroy all the young people. You are the only ones who are Christ's presence to them. You are the only ones who can give the light

---

[67] *Cf. Mt 25:31–40.*

of Christ to them. You are the only ones who can live the joy of loving for them. You are the only ones who can teach them what is purity, what is obedience, what is life of love for each other. Therefore, stay where you are—but open your schools to our poor people, and the slums will not be slums anymore. Open your hospitals to our poor people, and no need for you to come and work with us. We'll bring people to you." And I think we came to a wonderful understanding, and so I was very happy because many schools were open to our children. Many hospitals offered to take care of our sick, and I told them, "I will close down every home for the dying if you take our dying destitute to your hospital. I will close every single school that we have for slum children if you take our children." And so now many priests and nuns are taking our children and to make sure that our children don't feel cut out, because these are all paying schools, these are schools of better off people. . . . So what I do, we give them a little money, 50 cents in your money, in our money one rupee, and they go and they pay fees so in the school they sit side by side, the child who is paying 100 and this little one [who] is paying one only, but that one also is not free, that one is also paying something. So this is so beautiful, and it has created a wonderful feeling between the children. The children don't know and gradually they come to know clearly this is a poor child, my brother, my sister. And there is a wonderful sharing between the children—wonderful. And how? Because the sisters understood that they are going to be the light of Christ and to share the joy of loving by bringing these children together. This is where many vocations, now, are slowly coming up because of this contact of girls and boys with each other.

HOPE FOR ETERNAL HAPPINESS

You have been chosen, you have been called by your name. To be a co-worker is not just to join an organization, it's not just to belong to an association, it's not just to be a name in a group of people. A co-worker is a person who has to be the love and compassion of God today. God loves the world so much that He gave His Son[68] and today, He gives you to the world. First, to your own family, to your family, to your parents and then He gives you as a proof that He loves the world, He loves today the world through the co-worker. That's why you are not just going to be a number. We don't need numbers. God doesn't need numbers. But He says, "Give Me your heart." That heart has to be the sunshine of God's love in the world, the hope of eternal happiness, the burning flame of God's love in the world today. . . . Actually you are the co-workers of Christ Himself, and He wants you to be so totally His wherever you are, whatever work you are doing, there to be that sunshine of God's love. There is so much darkness in the world today and you, a co-worker, have to be that sunshine there. There is so much less hope, there is so much despair, so much distress in the world, and a co-worker has to be the hope of eternal happiness. There is so much hatred, there's so much killing, so much destruction in the world and a co-worker has to be the burning flame of God's love and compassion. And that's why we need to pray.

---

[68] *Cf. Jn 3:16.*

Jesus in the Eucharist, Jesus in the Poor

Like her [Mary], let us be full of zeal to go in haste to give Jesus to others.[69] She was full of grace when, at the Annunciation,[70] she received Jesus. Like her, we too become full of grace every time we receive Holy Communion. It is the same Jesus whom she received and whom we receive at Mass. As soon as she received Him, she went with haste to give Him to John. For us also, as soon as we receive Jesus in Holy Communion, let us go in haste to give Him to our sisters, to our poor, to the sick, to the dying, to the lepers, to the unwanted, the unloved, etc. By this we make Jesus present in the world of today.

Going Home to God

How Much Have We Loved?

At the hour of death when we all come face to face with God we are going to be judged on love: how much we have loved, not how much we have done but how much love we have put in our action. And for love to be true, it must be first for my neighbor. Love for my neighbor will lead me to the true love of God. And what our sisters and brothers and our co-workers throughout the world are trying to do is to put that love for God into a living action.

[69] Cf. Lk 1:39–45.
[70] Cf. Lk 1:26–38.

IN YOUR HEART

Just now a man came downstairs. His wife died some time back, and he was telling me how much he is missing her, they loved each other so much. "Your wife was such a beautiful person, she was close to God and God is in your heart. Now she has gone to God, so she must be there also in your heart." He asked me to repeat that again and he was happy.

TO GO HOME WITH JOY

A simple duty for you, for me, for Bishop and for the Holy Father and even everybody else, for that man dying in the street, dying of hunger or nakedness or whatever—it's a simple duty, and we have been created for that: to be in love with God. We have come from Him and we have to go back to Him. I have a very beautiful simple story. The other day we picked up a man from the street, dying of hunger and we brought him to our home. And after we spoke to him about God and we gave him a ticket for St. Peter. And then this man looked at me and said, "Sister, I am going home to God." And he died with such a beautiful smile on his face. "I'm going home to God," and he died. How wonderful it is that we can help people to go home to God with joy with a big smile. That is real holiness, so let us help each other to grow in holiness, and if we are holy, we will be one with the Church.

Holiness

True holiness consists in doing God's will with a smile.

HOLINESS IS NOT THE LUXURY OF THE FEW

I will pray for you that you may grow in the love of God through this love for one another. Spread this peace through love because works of love are works of peace. Spread it at home first in your own family and then to all. And through this love of God growing in you, you will become holy. Holiness is not the luxury of the few, it is a simple duty for each one of us. So when we look at the Cross, we understand how much God has loved us, and we, too, must learn from Him how to love one another so that we, too, are ready to give our all to save life, especially the little unborn child, which is a gift of God to the society.

BRINGING THIS INTO YOUR LIFE

Bring this love, this holiness, into your very life, your home, your neighbors, your country and the whole world. For this we need to pray—we must feel the need to pray. We must want to pray. Let every co-worker begin the family prayer—for the family that prays together stays together. Help your neighbor to do the same. Through this prayer and sacrifice, we will overcome the world. My prayer is with each one of you—and I pray that each one of you be holy. And so spread His love everywhere you go, light His Light of truth in every person's life, so that God can continue loving the world through you and me.

NOTHING EXTRAORDINARY

Jesus wants us to be holy. Holiness is nothing extraordinary, still less extraordinary for a sister to be holy because she has consecrated herself to God. It is a natural state of life for a religious to be holy, for Jesus my Spouse is holy. The Gospel says, "Be thou holy as your Father in heaven is holy."[71] Sisters, pay attention to what Mother is saying. There is nothing special for a professed sister to be holy . . . to be all for God, for she has given herself to God. Holiness is a duty for us. Nothing extraordinary. There is no luxury. . . . If my whole heart is given completely to Jesus, then we must be holy. If anyone else says anything contrary to this, believe me, they are trying to deceive you. I wish you all could understand what Mother is saying. Never, never joke about holiness. Holiness is not a joke. . . . It is foolishness for us to say, "I am not meant to be holy." I belong to Him, I have consecrated my life to Him, then I must be holy. Examine yourself whether there is that desire burning in my heart. Do I really want to be holy?

PRIDE CANNOT ENTER HOLINESS

Holiness is to do the will of God with a big smile. That total surrender "Cut me into pieces . . . every single piece is only for You." Holiness is joy, love, and compassion, especially humility. A sister who is humble, sure she is on the way to great holiness. Pride cannot enter holiness. Pride is a devilish thing. How do we become humble? By accepting humiliations. Whenever you are scolded, called names, adjectives are given to you, grab with both hands. That humiliation will make you holy, accept it. So let us ask. Let us be holy like Jesus, only all for Jesus

---

[71] *Cf. Mt 5:48.*

through Mary. I really want you to make your communities another Nazareth, full of radiating joy, peace, compassion: holy communities, holy Society.

I Will—I Want

We have our ten fingers to remind us "I will, I want, with God's blessing, to be holy" and "You did it to Me."[72] We are so lucky to have Jesus in the Blessed Sacrament and Jesus in the poor.

✦

Let us make this one strong resolution: I will—I want, with God's blessing—be holy, and so satiate the thirst of Jesus on the Cross for love, for souls, by laboring at the salvation and sanctification of poorest of the poor. "I will, I want with God's blessing be holy."

DETERMINATION

Let us have a competition in holiness, to be only all for Jesus. Make a sign of the Cross on the lips when you know your temper is rising—beautiful if we can get into this habit. "Jesus in my mouth, let me not say that ugly word," and you remember "I looked for one."[73]

---

[72] Mother's *"five-finger gospel."*
[73] Cf. Ps 69:20.

ABLE TO LOVE

One priest was made bishop. He said, "Mother Teresa, console me." I asked, "Who died?" He said "I've been made archbishop." Really, he was afraid. So I told him, "If you don't love, if you are not in love with this duty, you will never be able to give Jesus to your people." He was just listening. Next day he told the people: "Unless I am happy to be a bishop, I will not be able to love you. I am very happy to be a bishop!"

Love One Another

I have asked but one grace for you—that you may understand the words of Jesus: "Love one another as I have loved you."[74] Can you tell me how He loved you? Ask yourself and then see, do you really love your sisters as He loves you? More and more I understand [that] unless and until this love is among us, we can kill ourselves with work, it will be only work, but not love. Work without love is slavery. We have so much to thank God for.

EMPTY OURSELVES OF SELFISHNESS AND INSINCERITY

Once a Father from Katmandu,[75] was giving a talk on the love God has for the world and how great it must be for Him to have sent His Son. So I asked him, "Jesus said, 'Love one another as I have loved you,'[76]

---

[74] Cf. *Jn 13:34.*
[75] *The capital of neighboring Nepal.*
[76] Cf. *Jn 13:34.*

and He also said, 'As the Father has loved me so I love you.'⁷⁷ Therefore for us to know how we must love each other, we must know how
the Father loved the Son, so I ask you, 'How did the Father love the
Son?'" He looked at me and said, "Mother, your question is very beautiful and logical but I would not be able to answer you." The great
responsibility we have—to love as the Father loves the Son—nothing
less than that. If I do not have that love, then it is a bluff, a deceit. We
cannot truly love and serve the poor unless we have that love of God
in our hearts. We will only have that if we are empty of all selfishness
and insincerity. This love must start here at home. Ask Jesus to give
you His heart to love with.

WHATEVER IT TAKES

Jesus gave His life to love us and tells us that we also have to give
whatever it takes to do good to one another. . . . Jesus died on the
Cross because that is what it took for Him to do good to us; to save us
from our selfishness and sin. He gave up everything to do the Father's
will, to show us that we, too, must be willing to give up everything to
do God's ways, to love one another as He loves each one of us. That is
why we, too, must give to each other until it hurts. It is not enough for
us to say I love God, but I also have to love my neighbor.

THE LOVE OF GOD AND NEIGHBOR

We are commanded to love God and our neighbor⁷⁸—both on the
same level—no difference. Love for our neighbor must be equal to

---

⁷⁷ *Cf. Jn 15:9.*
⁷⁸ *Cf. Mt 22:38–40; Mk 12:30–32; Lk 10:26–28.*

our love for God. Here we don't have to look for the chance to fulfill this commandment. We have the opportunities twenty-four hours [a day], right here.

CAN YOU BE RECOGNIZED AS A CHRISTIAN?

In our community we live the life of the Trinity, loving each other as Christ loved us. This is absolutely important to remember: Loving each other as Christ loved us. Sometimes we can be all sweetness, all kindness, all joy to everyone outside, but in the community just the opposite; as someone said, "She is all honey outside, but inside she is a tiger." Why? It was said of the first Christian community that people were able to know them by their love for each other.[79] That was the sign that they were—are—Christ's disciples. Is that true of you today? That was the sign by which the soldier caught St. Lawrence in the early Church. They saw him doing a kind action to a poor man and they realized, "He must be a Christian." So they caught him and burned him and he became a martyr. Can they say the same of you as MCs? Say if you did not have the blue-par saris, can people, by seeing you and what you do to the poor, say straight away, "She must be a Missionary of Charity. See how she takes care of that leper, that dying person, that crippled child, orphaned child, and so on." Can people in the world today recognize you as a Missionary of Charity by what you do and by what you are? By your love for each other? What is your attitude to the poor? How do you treat them? The poor are right in your own community. . . . How do I prove my love for the poor in my community?

---

[79] *Cf. Jn 13:35.*

U.A.T.

Let us love each other. Let us love each other as we love Jesus. In Nazareth, there was love, unity, prayer, sacrifice and hard work and there was especially a deep understanding and appreciation of each other and thoughtfulness for each other.

U—Understanding
A—Appreciation
T—Thoughtfulness

Everyone Is Called to Spread Love

"A Missionary of Charity *must be* a missionary of love." A missionary is one who is sent. God sent His Son. Today, God sends us. Each one of us is sent by God. Sent for what? Sent to be His love among men. Sent to bring His love and compassion to the poorest of the poor. Every MC is also the poorest of the poor, so sent to bring His love and compassion first to my sisters in the community. We must not be afraid to love. An MC *must* be a missionary of love. Notice the words *must be*. It is not that she can try to be, no, she *must be* a missionary of love. She is sent to be God's love. Again notice in the second line,[80] "*She must be full of charity.*" Study these words by heart and remember them and ask yourselves, "How have I lived this rule?" Examine and see in what have you succeeded and what have you failed and write it down somewhere. Pray during adoration today and ask Jesus, ask Our Lady, to fill you with love. We are sent to be His love. We cannot give what we have not got. So we must be full of love in our own soul through

---

[80] *Of this section of the Constitutions of the Missionaries of Charity.*

our prayer and union with God. Then we must spread that same love
to all nations, "Go and preach to all nations."[81]

SPEND OURSELVES WITHOUT CEASING

Today some protestant ministers came to see me and they said something very beautiful. They said, "You people (MCs), because of your
vow of chastity you can belong to Jesus so fully, so completely, but for
us, because we are married, we have our love for our wives and we cannot give ourselves so fully to Jesus as you do." Then I asked myself, "Is
it true for each one of us? Is our love truly undivided for Jesus? Are
we all for Jesus alone?" When our sisters were in Ceylon, a minister
of state once told me something very surprising. He said, "You know,
Mother, I love Christ but I hate Christians." So I asked him how could
that be because it is such a contradiction, since Christ and Christians are
one. Then he answered me, "Because Christians do not give us Christ,
they do not live their Christian lives to the full." Ghandhiji[82] said something very similar, "If Christians were to live their Christian lives to
the full, there would not be one Hindu left in India." Isn't it very true?
This *love of Christ* should urge us to spend ourselves without ceasing.

OPEN OUR EYES TO SEE

Maybe if you go to the station and maybe if you visit some of the very
poor areas, you will find people who are sleeping just in the park or
you will see them sleep in the street. I have seen people in London,
I have seen people in New York, I have seen people in Rome sleep-

---

[81] *Cf. Mt 28:19.*
[82] *Mohandas Ghandi.*

ing out in the street, in the park—and this is not only that kind of homelessness that is terrible—terrible to see in the cold night, a man, a woman sleeping on a piece of newspaper in the street. But, there is much greater homelessness, being rejected, being unwanted, being unloved. . . . And these are the hunger and the thirst and the nakedness and the homelessness of which God is speaking to us. To open our eyes to see that it is not enough to see, we must look and see no brother, no sister is hungry, is naked, is homeless and do something for him—giving the food, giving the love, giving the cloth, raise him up, show respect for him, show him tenderness and love because no human hand is there to love him, to protect him, to guide him.

Something Beautiful for God

This love that we have for our people is a gift, for Jesus said, "Whatever you do to the least of my brothers, you did it to Me."[83] We are with the least all the time. When you give a glass of water, you give it to Jesus.[84] He claims it. . . . I remember last time we picked up one man from the street; he was full of worms. I asked one sister, "How can he go to heaven like that?" We started pulling the worms [out] one by one. I told sister, "Better hold it by the mouth for it can bite you." We removed everything. I asked, "Do you want to get God's blessing by which your sins are forgiven?" Something came out, sunshine, perfect joy. Something spiritual happened to him and after fifteen minutes he died, without worms—I hope that nothing remained inside. So many we picked up like that from the street. But one beautiful thing: no complaint, no words, he accepted. You could see his pain, but not a sound

---

[83] Cf. *Mt 25:40.*
[84] Cf. *Mt 18:5; Mk 9:37; Lk 9:48.*

of complaint. He must have gone straight to heaven. St. Peter said, "How is it, for you had so many worms?" He must have got the best place for he never complained. Something beautiful for God. Pray that we may not spoil God's work—to help people to remove their worms.

WHAT YOU ARE DOING, I CANNOT DO

What you are doing I cannot do, what I'm doing you cannot do, but together we are doing something beautiful for God, and this is the greatness of God's love for us —to give us the opportunity to become holy through the works of love that we do because holiness is not the luxury of the few. It is a very simple duty for you, for me, you in your position, in your work and I and others, each one of us in the work, in the life that we have given our word of honor to God. . . . You must put your love for God in a living action. It is not just I have to do it but I love to do it. And you are sharing through you, through your hands what God is proving to the world: That he loves the world and through you he keeps on giving Jesus to the world. Through you, . . . through the work that we are doing for the lepers, for the dying. I will never forget this beautiful opportunity.

Look up and see only Jesus and there will be peace, joy, love, otherwise we will be burdened. Have that deep respect for each other, we cannot pass by the mistakes of each other—that is why we must allow God to complete each other. What you have I do not have, [what] I can do, you cannot do, but together we do something beautiful for God. If we want a holy Society we must need each other. . . . We need a clean heart to see God in each other—revealing to each other what? That God loves me.

Mother Teresa's
Maxims for the Spiritual Life

PRAYER

The fruit of our prayer is that love for Jesus—
proved by accepting little humiliations with joy.

✦

Prayer gives a clean heart and a clean heart can see God,
can talk to God and peace comes.

✦

The more we pray, the better we pray.

✦

If your prayer is all right, your charity will be perfectly all right.

✦

Souls of prayer are souls of great silence.

✦

Prayer is the means by which we are fed, and
we need a pure heart to pray.

✦

Very often we cannot say much in prayer but that prayer
is like a look, which is everything.

✦

HOLINESS

I want you to take the trouble to be really holy, not in big things,
for we do not have big things to do, but the smaller the thing
the greater the love.

✦

Obedience is the most perfect act of love for God. I obey
not because I am afraid but because I love Jesus.

✦

Instead of saying ten words, say one.

✦

Poverty is your freedom.

✦

We fear the future because we are wasting the today.

✦

LOVE

Don't be afraid to love each other.

✦

What should be important for us is how much love
we put into the giving. How much do we love?

✦

Smile generates smile just as love generates love.

✦

Love only can become our light and joy in cheerful service
of each other.

✦

Growth in the likeness of Christ means growing in holiness.

✦

I would rather have you make mistakes in kindness than
[to work] miracles in unkindness.

✦

Our Lady

Mary, she taught Jesus how to walk, how to talk, gave Him bath
every day, how to take a spoon, held His hands, how to walk.
We forget that. Let us be that little child in her hands.

✦

Do I go with eagerness to the slums? Our Lady went in haste
to Elizabeth because she loved her. We must also go
in haste to the poor like Our Lady.

✦

No one learned humility more than Mary His Mother.

✦

We need Our Lady to obtain the grace of humility.
Cling to her: "Be a mother to me now."

✦

JESUS

Let Jesus speak to you in the silence of your heart.

✦

Say often to Jesus—"Jesus I love You for all those
who do not love You."

✦

Be brave—be generous—accept Our Lord as He comes in
your life now—through suffering.

✦

In spite of all our weakness, God is in love with us and keeps using
each one to light His light of love and compassion in the world.

✦

The only reason of our existence is to: "Live in Him, for Him,
by Him, and with Him," four words—so important.

✦

How do we love Christ? In giving wholehearted free service.

✦

Keep the joy of loving Jesus in the Poor and in the Eucharist and share this joy with all you meet.

✦

Never separate Jesus in the Eucharist and Jesus in the poor.

Mother Teresa's Prayers

My own Jesus do with me as You wish—as long as You wish without a single glance at my feelings and pain. I am Your own. Imprint on my soul and life the sufferings of Your Heart.

✦

Of free choice, My God, and out of love for you—I desire to remain and do whatever be your Holy Will in my regard.—I do not let a single tear come—Even if I suffer more than now—I still want to do your Holy Will. This is the dark night of the birth of the Society— My God give me the courage now—this moment to persevere in following your call.

✦

When you are washing, sweeping—anything—tell Jesus, "I love You, Jesus. Whatever I do today I do for You, every thought, every word, every action."

✦

Keep the joy of loving Jesus in your heart and say often during the day and night. "Jesus in my heart I believe in your tender love for me. I love you."

✦

Dear Jesus,
Help me to spread Your fragrance everywhere I go.
Flood my soul with Your Spirit and Life.
Penetrate and possess my whole being so utterly that my life may only be a radiance of Yours.
Shine through me and be so in me that every soul I come in contact with may feel Your presence in my soul.
Let them look up, and see no longer me, but only Jesus!
Stay with me and then I will begin to shine as You shine, so to shine as to be a light to others.
The light, O Jesus, will be all from You; none of it will be mine. It will be You, shining on others through me.
Let me thus praise You in the way You love best, by shining on those around me. Let me preach You without preaching, not by words but by example, by the catching force, the sympathetic influence of what I do, the evident fullness of the love my heart bears for You. Amen.

✦

Eternal Father, I offer Thee Jesus, Thy Beloved Son, and I offer Thee myself with Him for the greater glory of Your Name and the good of souls.

✦

1) Joy of the Heart of Jesus fill my heart.
2) Compassion of the Heart of Jesus, touch my heart.
3) Love of the Heart of Jesus, inflame my heart.
4) Peace of the Heart of Jesus, strengthen my heart.
5) Humility of the Heart of Jesus, humble my heart.
6) Holiness of the Heart of Jesus, sanctify my heart.
7) Purity of the Heart of Jesus, purify my heart.

✴

Jesus in my heart increase my Faith,
strengthen my Faith. Let me live this Faith
through living, humble obedience.

✴

Mary, Mother of Jesus, be a Mother to us now, guide, protect and keep
us close to Jesus.

✴

Mary, Mother of Jesus, you were the first one to hear Jesus cry, "I
Thirst." You know how real, how deep is His longing for me and for
the poor. I am yours—the whole Society is yours—Sisters, Brothers,
Fathers—Active and Contemplative. Teach me, bring me face to face
with the love in the Heart of Jesus Crucified. With your help, Mother
Mary, I will listen to Jesus' Thirst and it will be for me a Word of Life.
Standing near you, I will give Him my love, and I will give Him the
chance to love me, and so be the cause of your joy. Amen.

✴

Silence of the Heart of Jesus speak to me, strengthen me,
Mary my Mother, give me your heart so beautiful, so pure,
so Immaculate, so full of love and humility that I may be able
to receive Jesus in the Bread of life and serve Him in the distressing
disguise of the poor. Amen.

✦

Lord, keep them faithful to each other—in your love. Let nothing, nor
nobody separate them from your love and the love for each other—
Let the child—the gift of Yourself to every family—be the bond of
love unity, joy and peace. Amen.

✦

Jesus silent in my heart I adore Thee.

Who is Jesus to me?
Jesus is—God
The Son of God
The 2nd Person of the Blessed Trinity
The Son of Mary
The Word made Flesh
Jesus is—The Word I speak
The Light I lit
The Life I live
The Love I love
The Joy I share
The Peace I give
The Strength I use
The hungry I feed
The naked I clothe

The homeless I take in
The sick I nurse
The child I teach
The lonely I console
The unwanted I want
The mentally ill I befriend
Jesus is—The helpless—I help
The beggar—I welcome
The leper—I wash
The drunkard—I guide
The Bread of Life—I eat
The Sacrifice—I offer
The Cross—I carry
The pain—I bear
The prayer—I pray
The loneliness—I share
The sickness—I accept
Jesus is—my God
my Lord
my Spouse
my Everything
my All in All
my Precious One
my Only One
Jesus is the One I am in love with—to whom I belong and from whom
nothing will separate me—He is mine—I am His.

✦

Glory be to God the Father who created me—because He loved me.
Glory be to Jesus Christ who died for me—because He loved me.
Glory be to Holy Spirit who lives in me—because He loves me.

Index